Reversing

Attainment

Developmental Curriculum Strategies
for Overcoming Disaffection
and Underachievement

Diane Montgomery

David Fulton Publishers
London

David Fulton Publishers Ltd
Ormond House, 26–27 Boswell Street, London WC1N 3JD

First published in Great Britain by David Fulton Publishers 1998

Note: The right of Diane Montgomery to be identified as the author of this work has been
asserted by her in accordance with the Copyright, Designs and Patents Act 1988.

Copyright © Diane Montgomery 1998

British Library Cataloguing in Publication Data
A catalogue record for this book is available from the British Library

ISBN 1–85346–561–5

Typeset by FSH Print & Production Ltd
Printed in Great Britain by The Cromwell Press Ltd, Trowbridge, Wilts.

Contents

My thanks to all the teachers on my inservice programmes who helped me develop this theory and practice of teaching and who tested the methods and materials in research projects with their pupils.

Introduction

In recent years there has been increasing concern about the number of exclusions from schools and the low attainments of the excluded pupils. Two thirds of them appear to have learning difficulties of some kind and they represent the tip of a very large iceberg formed of those who have equally low attainments and who are often generally disaffected and alienated from school. Many of these pupils are underachieving in a major way and this seems independent of their ability.

The purpose of this book is to examine the nature and origins of such lower attainment in schools and to identify practical ways in which it might be overcome. The suggestions for intervention are intended to be those which every classroom teacher might adopt and they can be applied across curriculum areas in core skills. The general strategy is a developmental one in which the re-engagement of pupils with the mainstream curriculum and schooling is the over-riding purpose.

Attainment Our attainments are the successes, the knowledge, the accomplishments, the skills and performances which are the tangible products of our learning. They are our achievements. They are the behavioural sum of our concepts, schemas and cognitive structures and they may or may not be recognised by some external validation and they may or may not equate with what has been taught.

Low achievement may be defined as the extent to which we fall short of the goals we set, or are set for us, which we might reasonably be expected to achieve given our age and ability. It is a relative concept since it is impossible to determine what an individual's potential might have been. Even if all external and internal factors were propitious and definable it would still be difficult to define failures to achieve in absolute terms.

Low attainment is the extent to which pupils' achievements fall short of those of peers. It may result not only from lower ability but also from low levels of motivation and interest particularly in school work. Capacity to learn well and manipulate the non-curricular, the extra-curricular and the hidden curriculum may be the only indication of an unfulfilled potential. Better performance in different curriculum subjects, with different teachers and in different teaching and learning environments may also give useful clues. Uneven patterns of attainments can thus be significant indicators of untapped, suppressed or blocked potential.

League tables for schools' academic performance have encouraged not only comparisons between schools but also within them to identify poorly performing children, classes and teachers. When conditions for these comparisons are controlled, which is rarely the case, then lower attainment may be revealed. As yet the appropriate mechanisms are not in place nor the means of recovering such situations except in high profiled cases and special projects.

Standards

Standards have been much discussed since the introduction of the National Curriculum but there are none of the absolutes which seem to be presented. There seems also to be a determination to show that schools generally and teachers in particular are failing – failing in comparison with the past, for which there are no comparable records, and in comparison with pupils in other countries such as Germany, Korea and Japan. These comparisons, however, are not from the same base. For example, Japanese children are found to be two years ahead in subject knowledge by the secondary stage. As their children spend on average 1500 hours per year in school in comparison with our pupils' 900 hours and an additional two to three hours per night in cramming classes it is surprising that they are not four years ahead. Their methods are very different, still mainly geared to rote memorising. Our pupils learn not only content but also a whole variety of other skills and applications in a broader curriculum. This is also important for the technological revolution.

Apart from there being something wrong with the comparisons which have been made, our notions of 'standards' are also somewhat suspect. For example, subject knowledge at each level is a matter of opinion of so-called 'expert' groups, and basic skills levels are based upon research which assesses what pupils of a particular age group can normally read, spell and calculate. Neither method is entirely satisfactory. Each group worked on its subject without regard to child development or the learners' needs or the integration of the subjects to form a coherent and manageable curriculum. The nature and needs of primary pupils were mainly ignored as what they were to learn was forced into a structure to underpin the secondary curriculum. The subject dominated and the teachers' role was entirely misconstrued as the 'experts' reached back thirty years to their grammar school models of learning and teaching. It was assumed without question that teachers taught subjects. In fact the role of the teacher is to teach pupils to learn subjects, a far more complex activity and extremely difficult to do effectively.

Standardised tests are constructed by researchers based upon what a large sample of the population in a particular year group can do at a particular time. It is expensive to collect the data and construct the final test making it reliable and valid, a true test of what it is purporting to measure. There are always inbuilt test errors and the tests are always out of date by the time they are widely used. It could be argued that most of the tests in use, constructed 10 or more than 20 years ago, are bound to show lower attainment for since they were constructed changes have occurred in vocabulary use and the curriculum at all levels has broadened to include science, computing and design technology. Depth has often to be sacrificed for breadth in an already overfilled curriculum and perhaps basic skills practice has been given up for subject learning. This may finally retard development and lead to slower development in the subject areas as well. Finding out what a cohort of pupils could once do may not be the best way of deciding what current pupils should be able to do.

Standards of attainment are relative. Publishing school results on the basis of them is misleading especially when input data is not available. Publishing results before tests have bedded in is deliberately misleading for when any new test or exam is introduced the results in the first two years tend to be significantly poorer as teachers get used to the new format, language and the core themes. By the third year teachers have learned from an analysis of the previous test items how to focus their teaching so that pupils at least learn the main points, in other words they learn to teach to the tests. By publishing the results before bedding in it can be shown 'how poor' they were in the first year – how bad the old methods were – and then how much the results have improved since the introduction of the new methods or system! Claims to have improved standards are not infrequently made on this inadequate basis and when they are they can only be regarded as a confidence trick practised upon a public which is largely naive, in education terms. In effect little may have changed except a narrowing of the curriculum for the learner.

Standardised tests are constructed on the basis that 50 per cent will fall below the mean and 50 per cent above. It is therefore unfair to say that therefore 50 per cent are below standard, when they are simply below the mean for their age.

What is important is that their literacy skills should meet and match the increasing curriculum demands, not conform to arbitrary statistically led standards. It could be envisaged that all children in mainstream school become fluent readers and spellers at the age of eight but the statistics would still make 50 per cent of them below the mean. Most children are expected to be able to be fluent in literacy skills at the age of eight, but a significant proportion will only achieve this by the time they are ten and some not even then. These are standards recognised by teachers on the basis of experience and have been consistent over time. What needs to be questioned is whether or not we have allowed the education system to lapse into a state of underfunctioning on a massive scale. Is it not possible for most children to become functionally literate by the end of year one (age six)? Significant advances in the teaching of literacy skills do suggest this is possible.

It has long been the aim of teachers to help pupils develop to their full potential. Discovering what a person's potential might be is, however, rather difficult, and there are seldom any clear indications of when it has been reached. What does seem to be a common feature is that the potential in all of us is capacious and seldom if ever fulfilled. It is also common frailty and a result of structural stereotyping to underestimate the capacity for learning of babies, young children, the very old, the learning disabled, the average, the gifted, particular ethnic groups, females in some areas, males in others and so on. It is not surprising therefore that teachers, faced with 30 or more individuals can, despite their training, underestimate the potential of many of them and even overestimate the capacity of some. Secondary teachers may be even more prone to this since they may meet 200 different pupils in a week so that getting to know any of them is a problem.

In order to begin to analyse the forms of lower attainment and then to propose what may be done about them the book is organised in two sections. Section one outlines the nature and origins of lower attainment in relation to learning difficulties; learning disorders; specific learning difficulties; social and personality difficulties; high ability and poor motivation. The perspectives on this are not solely 'within child' but within school and in interaction with multiple environmental factors, an ecological approach. The chapter on the curriculum which concludes this section is pivotal for it summarises the curriculum needs of the groups identified as lower attainers and links these with types of curriculum provision which are appropriate to meet their needs in whole-class teaching settings. Differentiation models and strategies are reviewed and a theory and practice for helping lower attainers is developed in relation to relevant theory and research.

Section two shows how the curriculum models and strategies defined in section one can be applied. It gives cross-curricular strategies and examples of differentiation at individual levels and within formal class activities; examples of school-wide policy issues. In the concluding pages a summary of the main ways to improve the learning opportunities for all pupils is given.

SECTION ONE

The nature, origins and indentification of lower attainment

There are known to be a number of pupils in schools whose attainments are lower than teachers and parents expect them to be and the reasons for such lower attainment are not always discovered, or discovered so late that help can only be of the temporary emergency kind. Anyone who has sat quietly in a classroom observing and recording will be able to identify many more pupils who spend large amounts of time off-task but quietly so that their activities in a busy classroom go unobserved. The expert educator will identify many more who are underfunctioning such that as a general rule we can regard at least 50 per cent of pupils to be underfunctioning in most classrooms and many more than this in a few. This is not necessarily the fault of the teacher and the situation is better than in past decades for in every school there are a few teachers at least who are determined to change this and who are highly trained and highly skilled.

Although it is recognised that pupils and teachers are complex individuals who have constellations of individual needs and abilities, starting from the complex does not always clarify thinking about problems and so this first section looks separately at different types of difficulties starting from the pupil but moving on to look at how schooling has often constructed a problem where none need exist. Wider issues are also examined to indicate how the politicisation of educational issues can lead to lower attainments when the claims and the evidence presented might appear to suggest the reverse.

The general outline of the section is as follows:

- Chapter 1 discusses those who have *general learning difficulties* and others who have *learning disorders* which come between them and curriculum learning. Some of these children may be working hard and functioning well but their attainments remain low. For others there may be a failure to progress which may cause them to lose motivation and this can compound the problem and lead to further underfunctioning. This group includes pupils who are for a variety of reasons slower learners than peers of the same age and it will be suggested that an emphasis on expository methods of teaching, backed by current political pundits can seriously damage their learning capabilities causing them to underfunction.

- Chapter 2 deals with those who have *specific learning difficulties* which can impede their curriculum progress. Failure to acquire the rudiments of reading and writing are particularly potent sources of lower attainment in the presence of satisfactory or even high intellectual ability. Dominance of the writing response in the curriculum can become a handicap as well as the failure to identify such pupils in Reception class and begin appropriate intervention.

- Chapter 3 considers *disaffection and alienation*. It discusses the needs of pupils who have missed crucial elements of schooling, or who come from a context in which schoolwork is not valued. It includes those who are difficult to manage, and those who are unwell or going through distressing circumstances and who may have personal concerns which override concentration on learning. These social and personal difficulties cause them to become less involved with school work leading to a pattern of disaffection from school often with compelling counter motivations. The school's role in creating unmotivated and disaffected pupils is also examined. The chapter also examines the characteristics of a range of pupils who are *generally unmotivated* by much of the school curriculum. Although they are perfectly able to cope with it and some of them may be highly able they remain unchallenged and underfunction, never seeming to give of their best. It also looks at ways of identifying and helping those who are never of any concern and pass through the educational system without it having any significant effect on them or giving them anything of real value much less added value.

Whatever the reasons for their lower attainment all these pupils are expected to conform to school rules and to the general standards set by the school and the National Curriculum. Unless we can identify the patterns of lower attainment and the potential reasons for it and develop general strategies which every teacher can easily implement in the everyday classroom then we cannot improve this situation. Having every child on an individual learning programme and drawing up hundreds of *Individual Education Plans (IEPs)* is not, in my view, the answer. Focusing upon teacherly qualities and pupil learning in cross-curricular skills can be shown to make a significant and value added difference to pupil attainment.

- Chapter 4 discusses the curriculum needs of each of the groups defined in Chapters 1 to 3 and then outlines curriculum models and strategies which are available and discusses whether or not these can meet particular needs. *Developmental differentiation* is the strategy identified as the classroom teacher's main method for meeting the pupils' needs and this can be realised through cognitive process strategies in whole-class teaching. The model and methods are then exemplified in the second section of the book within each of the core skills areas.

Over all it is suggested that lower attainment is endemic in many school-wide systems and in the UK is a much larger problem than would at first appear. The problem is one which a return to basics and a return to the methods of the 1970s will not uncover and certainly will not address.

Chapter 1

Lower attainment, learning difficulties and learning disorders

Introduction

There has been a growing concern in recent years that there are a number of ordinary pupils in a large number of schools who are underfunctioning. In the competitive context in which schools now find themselves, they may target pupils at the borderlines to improve their grades leaving others above and below with poorer provision.

Some schools' first responses have traditionally been to locate the problems as lying within the pupils and to judge that their underachievement is a result either of learning difficulties or of laziness. Schools may then seek increased resources to deal with 'learning difficulties' and increase rules and sanctions to produce the 'stick' which will make the rest work harder. Producing IEPs (Individual Education Plans) locates the problems once again with the pupils even though some schools have relabelled these SLPs – Student Learning Plans, a term with which the pupils are happier at least.

Other schools in difficult areas may attribute the school's low placement in the league tables as a function of the impoverished social and economic backgrounds from which their pupils come. They may conclude that there is nothing a school can do in such circumstances and that it is a wider societal and political problem. Their response may be to exclude large numbers of pupils. Even so some schools in the same area successfully do intervene and work with parents and the local community and make a difference (Galloway and Goodwin 1987, Mongon and Hart 1989).

Lower attainment and learning difficulties

Lower attainment will be identified in slower learners as soon as any assessment results are recorded in a systematic fashion or as soon as classwork is handed in to the experienced teacher. A significant proportion of pupils' work may fail to achieve the standard set by the teacher. This may be due to a general learning difficulty and then a pattern of low achievement will be noted across all curriculum areas, but there can be other origins.

Many of these lower attainers make up the 40 per cent who leave school without any formal qualifications. Once free of the formal constraints of school, however, some may at last begin to develop their latent abilities in real world situations and become highly successful people. Many, sad to say, accept the label placed upon them at school and can live out a lower attaining life-style unless this is reversed by some chance success.

What has become clear is that some schools produce a higher proportion of lower attainers than others with similar mixes of ability (Rutter *et al.* 1979; Mortimore *et al.* 1988). Private schools, however, with their small classes and therefore opportunities for the development of broader and better relationships between pupils and staff, high quality facilities and supportive parents, can create high attainers out of those with the most modest of abilities. They develop in their pupils confidence, communication skills and the self-esteem to become successful people. This is something which all schools could learn to do.

At school pupils develop a sense of self-worth through the regard of peers and teachers and their success at something in the school curriculum. Lower attainers, especially those with learning difficulties, are denied this success and often seek regard only of peers through their misbehaviour. For all pupils, but especially lower attainers, it is essential that schools become places where it is possible for them to establish reasonable relationships with those who teach them. In order for this to happen class sizes may need to be halved in the crucial transfer years when pupils enter reception class and then again when they enter secondary school. This is also particularly important for the development and facilitation of literacy skills. As the number of dysfunctional families and environments increases so the need for such stabilising periods in school become more important. The short-term costs would be returned by a long-term increase in the quality of the work force and a more cohesive society with all the advantages that this would bring.

In summary, this chapter sets out to examine the needs of lower attainers with general learning difficulties and to discover general ways in which these needs might be addressed in the ordinary curriculum.

Learning difficulties

'Learning difficulties' is sometimes used as an umbrella term to cover pupils' literacy difficulties, behaviour problems which interfere with learning, and also the sensory or physical difficulties which cut down some pupils' input or possibilities for output. This is not a helpful approach. It lumps pupils together for undiscriminating 'provision' which does not match their needs.

Sometimes learning difficulties are regarded as separate from special needs. In this book, pupils with learning difficulties are regarded as having special needs. These needs may or may not be severe enough for them to be the subject of a Statement for special support.

Learning difficulties may have their origins within the pupil in that they are said to be constitutional. Despite this in some classrooms these never become a handicap. Learning difficulties may also be created by the way in which the curriculum is selected and taught. The Scottish Education Department (SED 1978) survey by HMI found that 50 per cent of pupils in primary and secondary schools had learning difficulties, and 48.5 per cent of the problems were *caused* by an inappropriate curriculum and pedagogy. In 1.5 per cent the pupils' basic literacy skills were inadequate. The position is not likely to be much different in England and Wales and may in fact be somewhat worse, for the Scots are frequently praised for their better standards of education. Rutter *et al's* (1970) survey had indeed shown that 4 pert cent had dyslexic problems and in recent years the British Dyslexia Association have said that the problem might be found in 5 to 10 per cent of the population.

For the purposes of intervention, learning difficulties are considered under three main headings, and each is on a continuum. Specific learning difficulties are discussed in the next chapter.

- *General learning difficulties.* Here the intellectual dimension is the primary area of difficulty and there is a continuum from mild through moderate to severe and profound. A significant number of pupils will have secondary difficulties associated with their primary difficulties for example, motor coordination and speech problems. As general learning difficulties move into the severe to profound range there may be signs of overt organic brain damage accompanying the intellectual difficulties presenting barriers to movement, communication, perception and sensation.

- *Developmental disorders.* The origin of these difficulties is in neurological dysfunction of a mild through to a profound nature. They may give rise to disorders in learning which pervade fundamental areas such as communication and social interaction. The disordered system may block normal development or cause uneven and idiosyncratic development.

  Developmental disorders can occur in the presence of the full range of intellectual ability but tend to depress it and so are included here. Examples of developmental disorders are dysphasia – a language problem, autism and Asperger's syndrome.

- *Genetic syndromes.* The most common genetic syndrome is Down's syndrome (DS) in which the physical characteristics are well known and easily identified but patterns of psychological abilities and difficulties vary considerably as well as the capacity to benefit from mainstream education.

A number of primary and nursery schools specialise in making provision for children with Down's syndrome although with some specialist advice and support there is no reason why most schools cannot accommodate several such pupils or a single pupil with Klinefelter's syndrome (in boys), Turner's syndrome (in girls), or Fragile X syndrome, all of which are very rare. Most genetic syndromes are associated with a mild to severe or profound depression of intellectual functioning and result in a range of learning difficulties in memory, language and thinking. There may also be distinct patterns of additional difficulties and disorders.

The majority of Down's children, about 90 per cent, suffer from a genetic disorder in which there is an extra chromosome, trisomy of chromosome 21. The rest have other trisomies but the general effect is the recognisable syndrome.

The nature of general learning difficulties

To have general learning difficulties means that a pupil has lower intellectual abilities in comparison with age peers. In some ways the functioning is typical of a pupil of a younger age group and may plateau at that level if underfunctioning is permitted. The level of functioning on standardised tests may be a few months to several years below chronological age. For administrative purposes it is sometimes necessary to determine the degree of discrepancy in order to make a case for special support. A discrepancy of 20 per cent is usually used by administrators based on a DES (1979) guideline to consider support for learning in the case, for example, of a ten year old who has the test IQ of an eight year old, or a decrement of 20 per cent in aptitude (IQ) and attainment (RQ–Reading Quotient). A 20 per cent decrement at age 5 is only one years' progress; at age 15 it is three years. In practice the 15 year old's attainments may have plateaued at around the 8–9 year old level and after leaving formal education may well decline so that sheltered placement may be required.

Within any large population it would be expected that there will be some people with lower intellectual abilities while most will be in the average range and a few will be of higher ability. IQ scores in the average band between 85 and 100 are often referred to as 'low average' and those in the band 100–115 'high average'; 68 per cent of the population have IQs in this average range. Pupils with scores between 70 and 85 are regarded as the group with *mild learning difficulties* and make up about 14 percent of the population. Those scoring between 55 and 70 are said to have *moderate learning difficulties*. They, together with pupils of lower IQ, make up 2 to 3 per cent. There tend to be a few more in the very lowest band than the statistical function would predict and this is thought to be due to additional factors such as birth trauma and genetic anomalies.

Pupils with mild to moderate learning difficulties are likely to be found in mainstream schools, particularly primary schools, unless they have additional learning problems. By secondary school many of the pupils with moderate learning difficulties will be receiving some form of special provision such as in-class support or education partly in mainstream and partly in a special group or unit attached to a school. Pupils with moderate to severe learning difficulties may begin education in a special unit and then may be integrated into some mainstream classes with the support of their specialist teachers. Since the implementation of the 1981 Education Act in April 1983 it has become possible for locational and social integration of these pupils to take place. There can also be functional integration for subjects such as art, music and movement.

The extent to which pupils with severe learning difficulties can be integrated remains much a matter for discussion of individual cases between the teachers concerned. In some countries such as Sweden integration is a matter of course. This form of provision could become more feasible if our education system can be made more flexible. More can always be achieved by the pupils working together than may at first be perceived by the adults around them. Integration initiatives should therefore always be given a chance. It would perhaps be best if schools included all local children and then were funded to meet their needs. What could be learned from the cross fertilization of ideas and methods could be beneficial to all pupils and teachers. Sadly league tables take no account of such initiatives and are driving schools to exclude difficult pupils and refuse entry to slower learners in order to improve their rankings.

In terms of numbers, if some pupils in the low average band are included, with IQs up to around 94, then it can be predicted that some 40 per cent of a class may be regarded as slower learners and may not achieve the general standard set for that age group although they may be working hard with their teachers. By the same token there will be 40 per cent who are above average and it may be this group to whom the teacher directs the teaching and learning strategies. This can leave many of the rest to founder in varying degrees. Different catchment areas will bring in different distributions of ability to the school. But we should not be too ready to infer that in a catchment area where there is a low socioeconomic status this status must be matched by low ability in almost all the pupils. Whatever the local context, high or low socioeconomic status, it is better to assume a normal distribution of ability has to be catered for. Even where there is a class selected on the basis of ability, the nature of their different strengths and weaknesses will be such that a variety of teaching and learning strategies will still be needed which include them in learning rather than causing a significant number eventually to underfunction.

The observable nature of general learning difficulties

Children with general learning difficulties usually show a slower pattern of progress in infancy in achieving the developmental milestones of walking and talking. This pattern continues in relation to the developmental milestones of school such as social skills and learning to read and write.

There will of course be some exceptions, children who learn to read easily and write fluently and neatly. What may be noted on careful observation is that they fail to understand at the same level, the content of the writing is immature, and they need extra support with more challenging tasks. In a large, busy classroom their special needs may go unobserved and as they move through the school system they can fall further and further behind, achieving far less than they are capable of doing. Here screening tests can be useful to back identification. For example an IQ test may show mental functioning at the 8 year old level when the chronological age is 10 years but attainment in reading and spelling show performance around the 10 year old level. This pupil's facility in reading and writing can easily obscure the general learning problem and when more challenging tasks are given, the pupil has few learning strategies and resources to fall back upon and unaccountably begins to experience failure for the first time. This can lead to early exit from education without any externally recognised qualifications and feelings of failure, rejection and frustration. Early intervention developing particular learning strategies can help such pupils and support their higher order learning and protect them from low attainment.

General learning difficulties centre upon three main areas – *memory, language* and *thinking.* The problems created by depressed functions in these areas permeate all their school and out of school activities. A general below average performance will be noted across all curriculum areas in the majority of cases.

Just as a few may have a facility with literacy skills so some may perform well in performance arts and psychomotor skills in sports. Where this is the case it is most important to encourage them in these special areas of ability and to offer them better support strategies in the intellectual areas so that they can make the best of their skills and life chances. General learning difficulties are characterised by:

- MEMORY
  – difficulty in getting material into storage;
  – span of 3 or 4 items instead of 6 at 10 years;
  – poor attention span;
  – poor retention of ideas;
  – confused by lengthy sentences;
  – confused by a sequence of instructions;
  – loss of comprehension during reading;
  – loss of main ideas during writing.

- LANGUAGE
  – limited vocabulary;
  – imited grasp of syntax for age;
  – limited powers of understanding language;
  – limited powers of oral expression;
  – limited powers of written expression;
  – tends to be monosyllabic.

- THINKING
  – lacking in spontaneous curiosity;
  – impulsive motor responses to questions;
  – lack of coherence and sequence in explanations;
  – confusion in problem solving tasks;
  – trial and error – shotgun type responses;
  – limited thinking skills and strategies;
  – limited knowledge of cognitive schemas;
  – limited repertoire of concepts;
  – inability to learn easily from experience;

– inability to generalise from experience;
– lack of incidental learning.

It is thus typical of pupils with general learning difficulties that they are usually behind their peers in reading and writing skills, social skills, language skills and thinking abilities. They seem to be immature, may tend to seek the company of younger children and are often picked on and teased by their peers. They may have mild speech difficulties in addition to poor vocabulary and language use so that they may lisp slightly and immediately become the subject of taunting and bullying by others so that they become increasingly reluctant to speak. This further hampers their language development and can make them anxious and depressed or angry and frustrated. In the former case the pupils withdraw and avoid schoolwork whenever they can. It often becomes possible for them to do the minimum or to copy others' work systematically and covertly and so avoid notice. If they can copy very neatly this is very helpful to them in concealing their other difficulties. If not their frustrations may lead to misbehaviour in class as soon as work is set and these pupils can finally become cases for exclusion.

Developmental disorders

Although autism and developmental dysphasia can be considered as severe forms of the broad spectrum of specific learning difficulties they are clinically regarded as disorders. Both autism and dysphasia are included under the heading of *central communicative disorders*. A disorder in language means that pupils have problems in understanding or using basic language processes and their language skills are very slow to develop. The development may not follow the normal pattern and there may be isolated areas of ability and deficit. For example a child may only know two or three items of vocabulary at five years, but in some cases even if 50 words are known they cannot be linked into grammatical utterances. The children have to learn stereotyped phrases to aid communication, and language development needs to be specifically and directly taught whereas in the normal situation children's language develops by them being immersed in an environment of words. In autism, social functions may also be disordered or impaired as well as language. In both, normal levels of functioning are rarely achieved despite specialist teaching although this is essential to give some chance of independence and competence in adult life.

Severe language difficulties, developmental dysphasia

The causes of the developmental dysphasias are not known but they lead not only to very slow development of speech and language but also to difficulties in sentence structuring, making sense of meaning in vocabulary and discourse and therefore in using language as a primary means of learning. If pupils arrive at school unable to make themselves understood this can prove very problematic for them. If in addition they cannot understand what is said to them this is an indication of a severe and more pervasive difficulty. Such difficulties will normally have been identified in the preschool period and special teaching and learning provision in the home and nursery school should have been made.

A number of national surveys have been undertaken which suggest that there are slightly fewer than one case in 1000 births with severe language difficulties. The incidence is higher in boys than girls in the ratio of 2:1. It is also found to be more common in lower socioeconomic groups.

The Quirk Report (1972) was regarded as a definitive national survey and found that 3 per cent of preschool children needed speech therapy; 2 per cent of school age children needed it; and 40 per cent of pupils in special school needed it. The National Child

Development study of all children born in one week in March 1958 (Davie, *et al.* 1972) found that at 7 years of age 11 per cent of pupils were rated by their teachers as having speech and language difficulties. Although estimates vary there is little doubt that there is a large number of pupils in ordinary schools who are handicapped in their educational progress by having language and speech difficulties. These difficulties may arise from a disorder of language in a small minority, from a developmental delay in a substantial number of others, from global developmental difficulties in about 50 per cent of slower learners and from an impoverished linguistic environment in many others.

Language processing deficits or *developmental dysphasia* may affect language understanding and/or expression. In *receptive difficulties* the children may have problems in understanding what is said to them although hearing is unimpaired. In severe cases human speech remains unintelligible and no expressive speech is developed either. Wishes and intentions may be communicated by gesture and mime and special noises may be understood by those close to them. They may undertake nonverbal tasks as well as peers such as riding a bicycle, drawing and painting, playing a musical instrument and so on. Mild cases however, are not easy to identify and there may be many in schools going undetected especially in situations where only one word answers are required, and written work may be copied or stereotyped responses are accepted. The mildest of difficulties in this area can create a significant degree of handicap.

Language production difficulties, *expressive dysphasia* accompany receptive problems but may also occur independently of them. In such cases the pupil may be able to understand what is said as well as others in the class but may not be able to formulate answers in spoken words with the normal necessary speed, or may only be able to use limited 'telegraphic' speech often in ungrammatical forms as two or three word utterances – 'me want', 'no come go'. These utterances sound typical of a very much younger child. Again those with mild expressive difficulties without disordered utterances are very hard to detect. They may often be classed as slow learners when they may very well be much more capable than their language use would suggest. Their primary language difficulties may also depress their ability to learn secondary language functions such as reading and writing. Language production can be hampered in a number of ways in expressive difficulties:

- there may be deficits in articulation;
- programming deficit – inability to order speech sounds or morphemes correctly into words, or words into grammatically correct sentences;
- recall and retrieval problems – word finding difficulties, e.g. 'the er-um-thingummyjig' when referring to some everyday object such as a table, door, comb etc. There may be a variety of retrieval problems evident, for instance in long pauses in running speech, use of association strategies to find words – 'Yesterday we had big – bee – bees – beans'; roundabout descriptions – 'Yesterday we had that sticky wobbly stuff (jelly)'; and phonetic substitutions – 'My mister' for sister – spoonerisms.

Most of us make the odd spoonerism and have occasional word retrieval problems but in these pupils the problem is persistent and pervades all their ordinary communications. Some may become adept at concealing their difficulties and substitute other words with almost imperceptible pauses. Any pupil with even a mild language problem is likely to become the victim of bullying in English schools and so most learn very quickly to avoid any form of verbal interaction with peers and the teacher. This isolation can make them sad, lonely and depressed. Finding friends with similar problems can help them learn to cope with the world much more easily especially where parents and relatives are supportive but not overprotective. Such friends however are rarely found in mainstream.

Secondary language difficulties

Language learning and speech difficulties may also be found in pupils who suffer from any form of hearing impairment, the difficulty usually being most severe in those with severe to profound hearing impairment. Delayed development of language skills will also carry over into literacy skills.

A total communication teaching system with speech-supported signing is recommended by the deaf world to meet their needs. Units attached to mainstream schools seem to be the best organisation in which to offer early years education so that integration can progressively be developed and the school can be equipped with the appropriate aids and facilities and teachers trained in their use (Webster and McConnell 1987).

In some cases of severe emotional and personality disturbance, language may also be affected. Isolation from human contact and communication can also prevent, or more frequently delay, language learning.

Peripheral speech difficulties

Examples of peripheral as opposed to central communication difficulties are the various forms of articulation difficulties, stuttering and cluttering (very rapid and sometimes jumbled speech). Speech therapy is usually beneficial in each of these cases, in the former to aid and improve correct pronunciation and in the latter cases to slow the speech down to give time for clear, smooth and consistent articulation. All such pupils need to be given time to express themselves and this is often at a premium in classrooms. The chapter on speaking and listening will help give some guidelines.

Autism

The origin of autism is as yet unknown but over the years since 1943 when Kanner first described it as a range of autistic behaviours, understanding has increased. It is a central communicative disorder affecting receptive and expressive language. It is also associated with other severe difficulties in perception and social skills. The condition ranges from mild to severe and profound. According to Thomas (1985) chair of the Association of Head Teachers of Autistic Children and Adults (AHTACA), 'autism' is an umbrella term covering a range of ability from children who could be scored within the normal range of intelligence to those whose intellectual development is severely impaired. However the difficulties which all autistic children have in common should determine a unique education. Some autistic children have secondary handicaps and one of the most common of these is epilepsy. Five AHTACA working parties considered the five main areas of difficulty which impacted upon curriculum learning of autistic children. They identified these as follows:

• impaired relationships and self image;
• adaptive behaviour problems;
• language and communication disorders;
• deficits in cognitive skills;
• deficits in perceptuomotor skills.

(AHTACA 1985)

In early literature autistic individuals were sometimes known as 'idiots savants' because in the midst of their low abilities in communication and thinking, isolated areas of talent might be observed in some of them. Nadia (Selfe 1977) was, at the ages of four and five years old, a gifted impressionist painter of horses and riders; others might be able to play the piano by ear extraordinarily well, copy a photograph or picture meticulously, or multiply sets of 20 digit numbers in seconds.

It is estimated that 4.5 in 10,000 live births will be autistic and that there are 3,000 autistics in the childhood population. By comparison there are 30,000 children with severe learning difficulties so autism is comparatively rare in its extreme form. The ratio of boys to girls with the problem is 4:1. In this autistic population the 4.5 cases are made up of 2.1 with 'true' autism, the core cases, while 2.4 are regarded as borderline cases. The EEG record of the brain rhythms tends to show over arousal and so tranquillizers are often prescribed. There is no family history of the problem and sibling incidence is very low. As yet no neurological disorder has been found which accounts for the condition in all cases.

Rutter at the Maudsley hospital in the 1970s did a long term follow up study of 1,000 autistics. He found that 40 per cent were untestable on IQ tests, 30 per cent had IQs in the 50–70 range and 30 per cent had IQs in the 70–100 range. It is rare to find autistics with IQs above 110. Very few of Rutter's group were in employment, half were in a 'mental hospital' and 70 per cent were doing badly at adolescence. There was a 5–10 per cent spontaneous recovery in speaking autistics but they retained a very flat delivery and a formal use of language.

In severe learning difficulties it is possible for some useful speech to be developed when IQs are below 30, however it is rare to find it in autistics at 50 IQ or well above. There is a better chance for autistic children to develop language if they have a high IQ. At the age of five years autistic children will have no speech and signing systems such as Makaton must be used to help them begin to communicate.

The characteristics of their speech and language are: echolalia, repetition of what is said using the same voice and intonation parrot fashion; confusion of you and I, they say 'You want ice' instead of 'I want ice'; there is difficulty associating correct words with objects and persons especially mother/father, brush/comb etc. They make semantic and grammatical errors – 'take park to doggy'; they have very little speech output and it is concrete and they cannot understand synonyms and fables; they use odd voices or may always talk in whispers.

In the social setting they find it very difficult to function. In the early years they treat other children as objects. As they grow older their language disability handicaps any social interaction in which they may be involved. They tend to be solitary and do not seek interaction or necessarily understand it when it occurs. They are generally unable to read the social signs of pleasure and anger or cooperate with others and may behave inappropriately in social settings. Social skills like language have to be laboriously learned for they do not develop automatically. Any complex stimulation may overarouse them and cause them to panic.

Autistic spectrum disorders

Children with these difficulties show the same basic impairments as in autism but not the full autistic picture. It is estimated that 21 children in 10,000 have this form of the problem.

It is also considered to be a disorder of development (Wing 1995) and she describes a triad of impairments affecting social abilities, communication and imagination. The triad is always accompanied by a limited, narrow, repetitive pattern of behaviours. These children need the same kind of behaviour management and teaching strategies as autistic children.

Asperger's syndrome

Interest in this area was recently kindled by Frith's (1991) translation of Asperger's original paper from the German which was first published in 1944. It appears to be more common than autism affecting, according to Wing, as many as 36 children in 10,000 all of whom were of average or high ability (Ehlers and Gillbery 1993). It is also more common in boys than girls and is not usually identified before the age of three. The clinical picture in this condition is as follows:

- Speech usually occurs at the normal age but walking may be delayed. Grammar is usually acquired but there may be difficulties in using pronouns correctly, speech is often in a monotone and the content is abnormal. It may be extraordinarily pedantic, lengthy discourses on favourite subjects may be given sometimes with words and phrases repeated over and over again in stereotyped fashion. Words may be invented and there is a failure to understand subtle verbal jokes.
- Social interaction is impaired. This seems to arise from a lack of ability to understand and use rules governing social behaviour such as speech, posture, gesture, eye contact, clothing, proximity etc. Their social behaviour is naive and peculiar. They may be aware of this and try hard to overcome it. A small minority have a history of bizarre social acts. There is a failure in relations with the opposite sex and a general ineptitude. They may even ask for a set of rules for attracting a partner or try to make an approach to a stranger which leads to trouble involving the police. They may deal with this by becoming solitary and withdrawn but may not be able entirely to control their needs.
- Repetitive activities and resistance to change. They may spin objects and watch them until they stop, over and over again to an extreme. They may become intensely attached to particular possessions and become very unhappy when away from familiar places. This is not uncommon in other children but is part of the Asperger's profile.
- Motor coordination is poor. Posture and gait appear odd. 90 per cent are poor at games and the problems may affect handwriting and drawing too. Stereotypic movements may also be noted.
- Skills and interests in the most typical Asperger form may also show areas of skill and proficiency such as: excellent rote memory, intense interest in one or two subjects such as astronomy, genealogy, football teams, cars, soap opera characters. This interest is to the exclusion of all else and they may talk about it endlessly even when the listener is not interested. Some have specific learning difficulties in reading, writing and number.
- They appear eccentric at school and may be badly bullied and then become anxious and afraid. They are unsatisfactory pupils because they may simply follow their own interests despite anything the teacher or the rest of the class might be doing.
- At adolescence many do become aware of their difficulties and then may become over-sensitive to criticism. They may appear very vulnerable and pathetic or very childish.

In addition to this constellation of symptoms found by Asperger, Wing (1981) found other characteristics in her 34 cases. She found a lack of interest and pleasure in human company in the first year of life. There tended to be a lack of babble or it was limited in quality, lack of attention to things going on around. On beginning to walk they may not have brought toys to show people. There was a lack of gesture, movement, smiles and laughter, lack of real imaginative play apart from stereotyped rituals in some.

The themes seen in their pseudo-play may continue as preoccupations into adult life. Half of Wing's group walked at the usual age but were slow to talk. Only one walked and talked at the normal time. In all of them the content of speech was impoverished, seeming to have been learned by rote. They scored well on memory in IQ tests but low on comprehension and were lacking in common sense. Good self care, a special ability that can be used in some form of paid employment, and a placid nature are required if the person with Asperger's syndrome is to become socially independent. Although there is no known treatment that has any effect Wing reported that the basic handicaps could be diminished by appropriate education and management.

Down's Syndrome

In DS, IQs range from untestable to about 70, putting some of them into the region of mild learning difficulties comparable with many other children with developmental difficulties in ordinary schools. Thus it is that many Down's children can benefit from mainstream education. However their language development does not follow the same pattern as that of other children. For example Carr (1970) in a longitudinal study of 60 Down's children found that there were no social class differences in language development when it would be expected that children from 'white collar' backgrounds would do better on all language measures. Swann & Mitter (1976) found similar effects with 1,400 children with severe learning difficulties and they concluded that this was in part due to an inability in this population to learn incidentally and that a task analytic approach would be more directive and helpful. They went on to demonstrate the power of this technique in the EDY (Education of the Developmentally Young) project.

In the survey it was also found that whilst younger DS pupils in the 3–6 age range made encouraging progress in language development their subsequent rate of progress gave great cause for concern. Between the ages of 6 and 16 they found little progress in the production of single word and two word utterances or more complex sentences. The importance of early language development cannot be overestimated because of the empowerment it can bring and its contribution to intellectual development. Now they are in mainstream education this may facilitate language development after age six.

As a group their ability to learn to read irrespective of IQ (Gillham 1989) is remarkable. Systematic teaching of reading by parents and teachers and using paired reading approaches can put their attainments in line with others in the lower range of the ordinary school. Some are now studying for the more practically based GCSEs.

DS has been far less well-researched than the very large number of affected children would indicate (Wishart 1995). It is much more common than autism, for example, on which there is a far larger body of knowledge. The researches of Wishart have suggested that the characteristic decline seen in the developmental rate with increasing age in children with DS may not be primarily determined by biological factors and neurological deficits but may be being contributed to by the children themselves. They appear to become increasingly reluctant learners as they grow older. She found that they actively avoided opportunities for learning and made inefficient use of the skills they did have. The result was that their learning was unstable and there was a continual problem with its consolidation. An education sensitive to these abilities and differences might counteract the learning decline. It might also have to address the attitude of the child with DS which could be to use the label as a means to manipulate their environment to avoid learning challenge and the attitudes of others which might be making them underfunction.

Summary

This chapter has considered the nature of general or global learning difficulties and developmental disorders. The largest group is those with general learning difficulties and most of them will be found in mainstream schools making up about a third to one half of any class.

The primary area of concern in general learning difficulties was identified as in the intellectual dimension where there are problems of memory, language and thinking. These can depress school achievement unless an appropriate curriculum provision is offered.

The developmental disorders such as dysphasia, autism and Asperger's syndrome were outlined, for pupils with mild forms of these problems are likely to be in mainstream schools. Early specialist and structured teaching in small groups was advocated to try to overcome their learning barriers. If their condition and needs are understood it will also be possible to offer them a more structured and supportive learning environment in mainstream, helping them to achieve a measure of success and independence. In each case they need developmental differentiation methods for whole-class teaching plus specialist language and social support.

Chapter 2

Lower attainment and specific learning difficulties

Introduction

The term Specific Learning Difficulties (SpLD) is generally used by teachers to refer to severe problems in reading but this is not the only group included in this term. Reading difficulties do however predominate and of course are a major concern. The characteristic profile is of a pupil who has low or very low attainments in the presence of apparent higher ability or potential. There is usually an uneven profile of success and failure in school attainments.

SpLD is a broad group which includes dysgraphia, dyspraxia, dyslexia, ADD and ADHD (Attention Deficit Hyperactivity Disorders). These are all to be found on a continuum from mild to severe and profound. In preliterate societies where children are not required to sit quietly for hours on end in large groups reading and writing, those with these difficulties suffer no disadvantage and can function perfectly well. In literate societies they are disadvantaged and the education system is likely to handicap them further as it uses text as the main medium for conveying, reinforcing and responding to information and retrieval. The literacy difficulties do not normally become apparent until schooling begins and may go unrecognised, undiagnosed and unremediated even up to the secondary phase. Recognition of difficulties on its own can be enough to save the pupil from severe underfunctioning and alienation.

Families usually manage to cope with offspring with ADD and ADHD unless the problems are very severe and it is only when the children enter school that problems really compound. The pattern of difficulties is less common than recent interest in the subject might suggest.

The notion behind the term SpLD is that normal development takes place in all other spheres and when the difficulties in the problem area are alleviated then normal development can take place. Some researchers, however, regard dyslexia as a disorder and there are some who do indeed have a form of neurological dysfunction or different neurological structure (Geschwind 1979, Galaburda 1985, 1995) but then their dyslexia could be regarded as a secondary problem to this and could be more intractable as a result with complex patterns of difficulties. This might be the case where there are the large discrepancies between verbal and performance IQ scores (Nelson and Warrington 1974, Mellanby *et al.* 1996)). In the majority of dyslexics there is still no known neurological problem although it does tend to run in families suggesting an hereditary component.

Pupils with mild to severe specific learning difficulties may well be found in ordinary classrooms if they are reasonably quiet and well-behaved. They may, however, be learning little and pursuing idiosyncratic pathways through schooling. It is only recently that the notion that boys are more vulnerable to dyslexia (ratio of 4:1) has been challenged (Shaywitz 1995). It may well be that because girls suffer more in silence that their problems are going unobserved. Stereotypic expectations may also play a part in the apparent differences identified in that teachers expect boys to have more problems and be more of a problem. In a group of 300 dyslexics attending a remedial centre, girls were referred in a ratio of 1 to 5 boys and at least a year later than them (Montgomery 1994a).

SpLD may be found across the full range of ability so that it is equally possible to find a slower learner with dyslexia or ADHD as it is to find a highly able pupil with an IQ of 155 with it. The slower learner thus has a double disability and therefore tends to be left out of research studies on dyslexia giving the wrong impression that it only occurs in the able. The double disadvantage can be extremely handicapping and may lead to referral for special education when this may not need to be the solution. Such pupils in mainstream do, however, require specialist provision which addresses their needs developmentally.

Checking whether there is a disparity, even a small one, between ability and attainment and different aspects of potential can be helpful background information in order to develop appropriate provision. The Cognitive Abilities Tests (Thorndike *et al.* 1986) results can be used by teachers to assess spatial reasoning (PQ) and then these can be compared with scores on the verbal reasoning items (VQ). The PQ test is also useful for testing pupils with hearing difficulties and language difficulties and those with a different mother tongue from English as the instructions do not have to be verbal.

Learning disabilities. In the USA this whole group with SpLD is called 'learning disabled' and may also include pupils with learning disorders as well as those with visual and hearing difficulties.

Brief descriptions of the major types of specific learning difficulties follow which teachers in mainstream are likely to meet.

Dyslexia and associated conditions

Developmental dyslexia, commonly referred to as 'dyslexia' 'dys-', difficulty, 'lexis', with words, particularly in their written form, has for many decades been regarded as consisting of severe difficulties in learning to read and most research and intervention has focused upon this aspect. However in over 500 cases referred to a specialist dyslexia centre all but one of the pupils had an equally severe, if not more severe spelling difficulty (Montgomery 1994a). This had been recorded by other researchers (Naidoo 1972, Vellutino 1979, Frith 1980) but has been given insignificant attention in education except in specialist teaching centres. In terms of school attainments dyslexia is a *reading and spelling problem.*

In the same study 30 per cent of the dyslexics were also referred because of handwriting difficulties. On the WISC-R dyslexics frequently show the 'ACID' profile in which they show performance decrements on the tests of Arithmetic, Coding, Information and Digit Span, but this does not necessarily mean that they have maths or memory problems *per se*. This is because dyslexia, in the large majority of cases, is now regarded as due to a verbal processing problem in particular a *phonological* difficulty (Vellutino 1979, 1987) which also underpins mental arithmetic, memory span and coding. Vellutino found that the majority of dyslexics have a particular problem in establishing and using verbal codes, in other words, learning the names and sounds of alphabet letters even when these are taught in a direct way. Unless they have very good visual memories and can learn words as wholes and have not become confused in their early reading sessions they will begin to fail to learn to read and spell within the first few weeks in school. Highly able pupils with very good memories may have concealed their difficulties up until about the age of eight years when suddenly the subject knowledge is extended and they have to 'read to learn' in a more substantial way.

Other functions also depend on verbal coding and the effect of putting something into words or trying to name it may be affected in dyslexics. For example, a significant number may have difficulties with arithmetic, particularly the more difficult tables such as 6,7, and 8x. They may know 7,14,21,28,35,42,49, etc. are the end products but as soon as they start to say '7x1 is 7, 7x2 is 14' they begin to stumble and give wrong answers (Miles 1993). They may in addition have word-finding difficulties, mild speech articulation difficulties, difficulties in naming left and right, saying the days of the week, the months of the year, the alphabet and polysyllabic words.

It is only recently that some LEAs and some schools have recognised that dyslexia exists as a separate condition from generally poor reading (and spelling). This means that the more able dyslexic has been put into slower learning classes and groups and often with disruptive pupils. This treatment only increases the frustration and depression that they already have because of their problem and can induce behaviour problems. Support for learning may help them acquire subject knowledge and competencies but it cannot necessarily address their reading and spelling needs. Adding to their problems is the targeting of help only to reading. This has regrettably been reinforced in the Green Paper (DfEE 1997) where it states that dyslexics must be given reading support. The intense attention to reading does not appear to transfer in any substantial way to spelling (Montgomery 1997 b) and the same attention has never been given to pupils' spelling and they are very much aware of this (Peters and Smith 1986).

As each year slips by the pupil falls further behind until at transfer to secondary school he or she may be three years behind the rest in literacy skills. At 15 the able pupil may still have the spelling age of a six year old and a reading age at about the eight year old level. Although he or she can cope easily with the oral curriculum as soon as reading and writing are required the pupil is handicapped. Laptops and word processors are essential tools. Even at this stage, if an appropriate dyslexia programme is introduced (Montgomery 1997 b) there will be progress.

Highly able pupils, with IQs over 130, were found to be about a year ahead on both reading and spelling in comparison with age matched dyslexics with IQs from 95–129 (Montgomery 1994). They made up 10 per cent of a sample of 300. Their better reading skills tended to mean that they were referred much later than the other dyslexics and referral was usually precipitated by the development of problem behaviours so there could well have been an even larger number who were suffering in silence or compensating in other ways such as finding success and consolation in sport and hobbies (Edwards 1994). Giftedness and learning disability have been regarded until recently as mutually exclusive and many academics and employers still seem unable to regard as intelligent anyone who cannot spell perfectly.

In homes where educational success is unknown dyslexics' difficulties are generally regarded as part of the family pattern of low ability and little may be done about it unless the school takes the initiative and tries to break the cycle of low attainment.

The Code of Practice (1994) has ensured that many more pupils' difficulties are recorded but even when the Individual Education Plans (IEPs) are drawn up it does not mean that the real difficulties are identified and even when they are, that the appropriate remedial teaching is undertaken or made available. The remedial teaching given relies upon the interpretation by the 'specialist' of what a cumulative, sequential and multisensory method means. So many of these teachers claim to be interpreting programmes to meet an individual's needs and using a mixture of methods because training programmes to gain accreditation have had to be broadened and this has sacrificed the pursuit of knowledge of one specialist dyslexia programme.

Spelling difficulties – developmental dysorthographia

There are a significant number of pupils at all stages of education who have spelling difficulties from mild to severe without ever having had a reading difficulty. A 15 year old may have a reading age of 15 but a spelling age of 6.5 years. This is a seriously disabling condition and it is amazing that the pupil in this particular case had not been referred for special help until the age of 15. It is clear that the reading ability was sufficient to prevent him being statemented even in an LEA which did recognise the dyslexic condition. Reports from SENCOs confirm that it is particularly difficult to attract funding for spelling in a wide range of education authorities. In higher education it was noticeable that a significant proportion of students were limited by their poor spelling and their only strategy was to get a friend to proof read their course work and then to rote learn key spellings which might need to be used in exams (Montgomery 1997b).

As soon as misspellings seem to reach beyond two or three which might be regarded as slips of the pen, tutors and teachers can be observed to lower grades significantly. It frequently causes them to give more detailed attention to the form and content and so they begin to find further errors in understanding and reasoning which they might have otherwise overlooked (Moseley 1994). Early on some of these pupils have learned to write in such a way that with squiggles and contractions they conceal areas of error in their spellings. This can make the writing very difficult to read and errors can be overlooked. Some pupils may have had an earlier reading difficulty which the remedial strategies have improved to grade level and all that will be noticed is slow reading and slowness in using indexes and finding names in the telephone directory for example. The spelling remains poor and a handicap until specialist help is given. Attention given to spelling however does have a carry over into reading causing it to improve even when spelling is slow to respond.

Spelling difficulties may often be noted in children who have learned to read very early at two or three years old without being directly taught. It is then argued that they read so easily they missed out on the basics of phonic structuring. But there are at least as many who do not have such problems and so it must be inferred that in the early stages reading and spelling depend on different processes (Frith 1985) for their development and that the spelling route is in some way blocked at least temporarily in this group.

Handwriting difficulties – developmental dysgraphia

Some pupils may have handwriting coordination difficulties quite independently of having any reading and spelling difficulties. However hard they try to write neatly they will be unsuccessful and the writing will be scribbly with uneven pressure and is poorly formed. This will attract substantial criticism from almost all teachers who tend to regard poor writing and lack of neatness as lack of serious effort and in some cases an insult to their own efforts (Barrass 1982). A pupil with untidy writing may have been subject to continual harassment and become frustrated and depressed, even withdrawing from any writing activities whenever possible. In the more severe cases the pupil has such difficulty and pain with the writing activity (Sassoon 1989) that very little can be produced at any one time and so spelling gains little practice and they become pupils with spelling and handwriting difficulties. According to Alston (1993) 40 to 60 per cent of secondary school pupils in her sample complained of pain and difficulty with writing.

There are a significant number of pupils, more than 30 per cent in my studies, who had both dyslexia and handwriting coordination difficulties – dyslexia with dysgraphia. To overcome this all the specialist dyslexia programmes teach cursive handwriting in a multisensory approach with spelling and reading because it is recognised as both a special need and a support to the remedial teaching of spelling.

Developmental coordination difficulties (DCD)

Perceptuomotor and motor difficulties, developmental dyspraxia

In the past, children with these difficulties have been termed 'clumsy' children. They are mentally normal, without bodily deformity and with physical strength, coordination and sensation that is more or less normal. Their ability to form skilled and purposive movement however is impaired.

Praxis is the ability to motor plan. It implies the motivation to plan; the ability to produce the skilled hierarchies of movements; coordination between different levels in the brain such as the neocortex, the basal ganglia, the cerebellum and the brainstem; kinaesthetic and proprioceptive feedback; and facility with storage and retrieval. Developmental dyspraxia indicates that the function has not developed normally because of some neurological impairment or dysfunction. It only takes a very small disturbance of the nervous system to disrupt the smooth functioning of a motor skill or to cause it only to be learned with great difficulty and persistence. In the majority of cases there is a dysfunction rather than impairment. Impairment however may result from head injuries in accidents.

Motor learning difficulties is one of the range of terms used in this area. It is defined as a deficit in the acquisition of skills requiring fluent, coordinated movement, not explicable by general retardation or demonstrable neurological disease (Hall 1988). Identification should start as soon as the child enters school for it has been estimated by Henderson and Hall (1982) that at least 5 per cent of British children experience these problems.

Gubbay's (1975) research on 810 children of 8 years of age in Cambridge UK found that 5 per cent could be regarded as 'clumsy'. More recently, Laszlo *et al.* (1988) found that at least 10 per cent of the school population had a specific learning difficulty in this area. She recommended kinaesthetic training rather than the traditional training in motor skills and her training programmes of specific ball skills, once mastered, showed transfer to other skills, even handwriting. If a child can use a key to open a door but cannot pretend to do so when key and door are absent this would be an example of a dysfunction in planning and integrating movement.

An individual pupil may not have the full spectrum of difficulties. The problems may be in gross motor and locomotion skills, or fine motor coordination skills such as cutting and buttoning when handwriting may also be affected. Some unlucky individuals have both types of problem and it may also involve problems with articulation – the motor speech functions (developmental dysarthria); poor social skills; emotional problems and overactivity; and educational difficulties. Once again the difficulties are on a continuum from mild to severe.

In early childhood, clumsiness according to the researches of Gubbay (1975), is seen in mild slowness in the acquisition of motor skills such as walking and talking. In the latter the speech is often indistinct. There are frequent falls in learning to walk, a tendency to bump into objects, and he or she strikes the head repeatedly on tables and doors. There may have to be frequent visits to the hospital for patching up after cuts and falls. The first anxieties may arise when these children fail to be able to turn knobs and handles to get in and out of rooms, engendering much frustration. Only by extraordinary persistence do they learn to ride a bicycle, incurring frequent falls. The same difficulty is found in the skills required in games and PE at school where they usually become the butt of sarcasm and even bullying when teams have to be chosen. This can create endless misery throughout schooling. At home washing, dressing, cleaning teeth and mealtimes can become nightmarish for both the child and the parent. They drop plates and utensils and manage to get food over themselves and the furniture. Parents often resort to nagging or even beatings to little effect and the misery compounds.

At school if the children are tenacious and persistent they will eventually master the skills they require. However the timid, the temperamental or young child may readily become frustrated which can give rise to temper tantrums and aggravate an underlying tendency to hyperactivity. The difficulties and torments experienced lead to feelings of low confidence and self-esteem which can give rise to behaviour problems. In adolescence growth spurts can also lead to inconsistencies in skills development and many more may become temporarily mildly uncoordinated, but by this stage they will have developed more strategies for concealment and avoidance.

Gubbay (1975) devised a questionnaire to aid in the identification of children with Developmental Coordination Difficulties (DCD) as follows:

- Is the formation and neatness of the handwriting much below average?
- Is the sporting ability and body agility much below average?
- Is the child unduly clumsy?
- Does the child fidget excessively in class?
- Is the conduct much below average?
- Is the overall academic performance much below average for the age?

He then devised a screening test which consisted of such items as whistling through parted lips; skipping; throwing and catching a tennis ball; rolling the ball with the foot around obstacles; tying a shoelace; bead threading; piercing holes in graph paper and fitting plastic shapes into appropriate slots.

It used to be believed that clumsiness was grown out of by adulthood but more recent longitudinal studies (Cantell *et al.* 1994) have clearly shown that this is not generally the case. They found that those diagnosed as having motor difficulties at five still had delays and impairments at fifteen, their academic achievements were generally lower than these of their peers and they had fewer social pastimes and hobbies.

DCD in school age pupils studied by Schoemaker and Calveboer (1994) showed that compared with controls those with DCD were more anxious, lacking in self-esteem, more introverted and judged themselves to be less able both physically and socially even when as young as six years. They put this down to the importance placed upon proficiency in physical activities by the child and the peer group. Some put success in sport especially football as a higher goal than success in the classroom.

Speech delay was a most frequently appearing concern in studies by Chesson and McKay *et al.* (1991) with over 50 per cent of their sample having required speech therapy. They identified two distinct groups, those whose difficulties were identified before entry to school and those whose problems only became apparent after entering school. Half the group of 31 were doing well in maths at school but their problems in spelling and handwriting were hampering progress in other subjects. In all, 23 of the group were in receipt of learning support in mainstream and a further four required specialist provision within language units.

Attention deficit disorders and hyperactivity

The hyperactivity syndrome first came into prominence in the UK in the 1970s and was such a popular diagnosis that many teachers would label as 'hyperactive' any pupil who was overactive, tended to wander about the classroom and failed to sit down and attend to work for any length of time. This could mean that several pupils per classroom would be so labelled. It was at this time that diet, allergy syndrome, minimal cerebral dysfunction and biochemical imbalance were put forward as a range of potential underlying causes.

There has recently been a rekindling of interest in the subject after 20 years since it has come to prominence again in the USA and has been renamed *attention deficit hyperactivity disorder* (ADHD) together with a second related syndrome called *attention deficit disorder* (ADD) (Goldstein and Goldstein 1992). They found 5 per cent of school age pupils identified in the USA making up 3.5 million in the school system. The cluster of symptoms has not changed in the meantime and these are: cannot concentrate for more than a moment, acts and speaks on impulse, impatient, easily upset, explosive emotionally, restless, noisy, disobedient, highly distractible, rarely finishes work, clowning, talks out of turn, shouts out, destructive, antisocial behaviour, fidgety, cannot sit still, and given to fighting with other children. Just one such pupil in a classroom can be cataclysmic. The discipline problems are obvious but these are in fact secondary to the hyperactivity. The qualities of the hyperactive childs' behaviours are that they are inappropriate, non-directed, irrelevant in nature and the child is unable to control them. Action and response is haphazard. A closer examination of the behaviour shows that the hyperactive individual is incapable of maintaining *attentional set,* either postural or in looking behaviour. Even small digressions and dispersions in ocular control tend to scatter and divert attention. A composed slow moving child shows slow, controlled eye movements, steady ocular and attentional fixations. A hyperactive child tends to show very rapid movements, fleeting fixations and mercurial attention hence the new nomenclature – *attention deficit hyperactivity disorder.*

The hyperactivity is usually noticed at a very early age, and most mothers had noticed unusual behaviour before the age of two years (Stewart 1970). There was no history of birth difficulties in his studies and no significant socioeconomic patterns. There was however a history of feeding problems, disturbed sleep patterns, generally poor health in the first year of life and many were further handicapped by delayed development of speech and had poor coordination. Hyperactivity is an extreme condition which once observed would not be mistaken for an overactive disobedient pupil.

Not only do parents complain but teachers report that the child cannot remain seated and is always moving about the room. At meal times food is scattered about as well as crockery and tools and food seems to get all over the place as well as on the pupil. Stewart (1970) estimated that 4 per cent of suburban school age children suffered from the problem to some degree whereas Rutter (1975) estimated that 1 to 2 per cent of the population in this country have such problems. The ratio of boys to girls with the problem is estimated to be 5 to 1 although it may well be that as girls' behaviour generally is less aggressive they are not referred so frequently. More recently Taylor (1995) has stated that the incidence of ADD/ADHD is 0.5 to 1.0 per cent of prepubertal children although he thinks many cases go undetected. He opposes the widespread use of drug therapies such as in the USA but supports their use for some carefully diagnosed and selected patients.

In adolescence the overactivity often does not continue and may be replaced by underactivity, inertia and lack of motivation or drive. After the early history this may be seen by parents and teachers as a great relief but such a pupil will be likely to sink into serious underfunctioning and depression and desperately needs appropriate medical help. In all such cases the general practitioner is unlikely to be knowledgeable enough to advise and a specialist paediatrician should be consulted.

A treatment paradox

As early as 1950, Bradley had discovered a paradox in the effects of drug treatment on certain types of hyperactivity. He found that sedatives increased the hyperactivity but stimulants *calmed it* down. When the action of the *reticular formation* (R.F) in the brain stem was discovered (French 1957) which has the role of waking up the cortex to receive information as signals are routed through the facilitatory section of it the paradox began to be unravelled. The drug effects showed that *amphetamines* such as ritalin (methylphenidate) caused the release of the transmitter substance *noradrenalin* in the R.F. which had the effect of depressing its activity. Part of the way this was understood was the finding that when hyperactive pupils were sent for assessment to the educational psychologist their symptoms frequently disappeared and the pupil was sent back with a noncommittal report. In addition with some teachers many of them did not manifest the hyperactive symptoms. This was finally explained as the effect of fear on the R.F. which is to increase the release of noradrenalin so calming down the behaviour.

The drugs have to be used very carefully and are usually only given to help the pupil settle back into school in case drug dependence is developed. The effect of the ritalin is temporary, usually 4 hours. However 6–8 hour slow acting doses can be obtained to cover the school day. The pupil then has 16 hours at home off them and hopefully asleep for half that time. During the drug therapy parents, teachers and schools need to be trained to use behaviour therapy methods (see Chapter 13) to maintain attentional set when the drugs have worn off.

In addition to this developmental and possibly constitutional form of ADHD it is now well known that an increasing number of children show allergic responses to food additives such as tartrazines and monosodium glutamate. Others are allergic to certain foods themselves such as the glutins in all products containing flour, chocolate products, cows' milk and nuts. Peanut allergy can even be fatal. Avoidance of the foods known to cause the hyperactive response is the best method of treatment but accidents do occur and children have a love of soft drinks, crisps and sausages all of which may contain the allergen unless the brand specifically states otherwise. Teachers often need to advise parents to consult the child's doctor about these potential sources of problem.

After certain types of brain injury such as birth injuries, brain infections and in road accidents and tumours, the damage left can create a minor loss of inhibition over the general brain activity (Kraupl Taylor 1966). This can result in attentional deficits and hyperactivity in varying degrees. The form of ADD which could result would not be likely to respond to amphetamine therapies and nor would the dietary and allergenic forms, so very careful diagnosis needs to be undertaken before embarking on them.

Inconsequence and ADD

Stott (1966) gave the term 'inconsequence' to a behaviour disturbance when classifying 'maladjusted' behaviours and this was the basis of the British Social Adjustment Guides (BSAG). Inconsequence was defined as a syndrome of restlessness in which the behaviour was inimical to consistently pursued goals. The children had an inability to inhibit responses to stimuli at the primitive physical level. They did not give themselves time to carry through to completion the mental work which is normally performed upon sensory information preparatory to actual behaviour. They were for example unable to effect the cognitive rehearsal of the consequences of a proposed course of action. This is termed *lack of praxis* which is the ability to motor plan. Frequently they are the children who run out into the road in front of oncoming cars or jump off too high places. They do not test their hypotheses about the outcomes of their actions or run a mental model about the probable course of events ahead of reality. Their problem solving has a 'shotgun' character as they fire off a fusillade of attempts in the hope that one of them might be correct. The appearance is of a series of trial and error attempts without any evaluation of the differential outcomes so that they could select a more valid approach as reflective pupils might.

The preschool behaviour of these children showed continual uninhibited curiosity and trial and error meddlesomeness and they continually broke things. They were poor at social learning, had a proneness to accidents, wandered away from guarding adults and had a rash acceptance of strangers. Because the tolerance of parents, teachers and peers was so strained Stott and Marston (1970) found that they could become disaffected and disturbed by the rejection they experienced which in turn often led to hostility and antisocial attitudes. Out of a sample of 726 children they found 42 boys and 8 girls who showed the following list of maladaptive behaviours:

- does not get on with his or her work because is easily distracted by others;
- distracts others by provoking and interfering with them;
- is often the centre of disturbance within the classroom;
- plays the clown in order to raise laughs;
- shouts and speaks out of turn;
- does not heed correction and may play dense or show off when corrected;
- in general reacts very impulsively and does foolish and occasionally dangerous things.

New techniques for identification are available in the USA such as Single Photon Emission Computerised Tomography (SPECT) which records blood flow and brain metabolism. In the UK we have followed the American trend and in the last three years there has been the adoption of the new labels ADHD and ADD and a rash of conferences, courses, articles and books on the subject, but diagnosis is clinical rather than technical.

Ways in which pupils may conceal their difficulties

Any form of learning difficulties even of a mild and temporary nature which prevent pupils 'catching on' when others do or from working quite as quickly and learning as fast can lead to feelings of failure and fear of the learning situation. This can result in a progressive withdrawal from any learning experience with challenge to it and in some a refusal to participate in learning at all. This can also be seen in children with learning disabilities such as dyslexia. Pupils may use a range of strategies to conceal their difficulties and so defend their self-esteem for example: withdrawal; avoidance; evasion; distraction; digression; disruption; clowning; daydreaming; negativism; absenteeism; cheating. Clowning is a common response of able pupils. Similar behaviours may be observed in children with handwriting coordination difficulties where no matter how hard they try they cannot produce a neat infant print. Continual pressure to copy and write neatly will cause increasing distress and frustration leading to disaffection from school as a hostile learning environment. Much such distress in classrooms can be alleviated by teaching a fully joined hand from the very first and linking it to spelling (Montgomery 1990, Morse 1991).

Summary

Specific learning difficulties were identified in literacy, perceptuomotor, motor coordination and attentional areas. These are the specific difficulties which most intrude upon school learning. The difficulties occur in pupils across the range of ability and socioeconomic groups and are also on a continuum.

Severe difficulties in the literacy area can be the most handicapping and prevent access to a wide range of curriculum subjects which depend upon reading and writing skills for their development and so result in very low attainment often in the presence of high intellectual ability. If the response to these learning failures is neglectful or harsh and the pupil feels a loss of self-esteem then secondary behavioural and emotional difficulties are likely to appear (Kellmer-Pringle 1970, 1985, Montgomery 1995).

Although not generally difficulties which cause concern, it is noticeable that there are pupils who have disabilities in learning to draw and paint whilst writing is good, those who cannot sing in tune, appreciate music or learn to play a musical instrument, and those whose constructional and technological capabilities are very poor. All of these pupils suffer little discrimination for their lower attainments in comparison to the dyslexic at present but in the new millennium who knows how things may change.

Chapter 3

Lower attainment, disaffection and demotivation

Introduction

Although children with learning difficulties may be underfunctioning on a wide scale there appear to be an even larger number without learning difficulties who are also underfunctioning. The reasons for this are often complex and may lead to the accumulation of missed opportunities for learning which can hamper new learning and lead to further difficulties.

Some children may arrive at school already sure that education is not for them or they may come to perceive it as irrelevant to their needs given the way they are treated. For others, their social context may predetermine their first hostile reactions to education and these may be reinforced by some random early schooling experiences.

Others may have come from abusing and/or dysfunctional families and this can make school learning secondary to the satisfaction of their emotional needs as they withdraw from learning. It is not unusual to find pupils in all years who are difficult to manage and who are so distressed by events in and outside school that it may become impossible for them to concentrate fully upon learning.

Although teachers may work exceptionally hard to interest their pupils, what they offer and the way it is presented may give insufficient challenge to motivate large groups of children for long. Thus in some circumstances it can be the teaching method rather than the curriculum which is at fault. There may also be a tendency to underestimate pupil's cognitive capabilities so that they may be 'spoon fed' and lack sufficient challenge.

Able pupils are particularly vulnerable to underfunctioning where there is a lack of cognitive challenge. This has been a concern of both HMI (1977, 1992) and the National Association of Able Children in Education (NACE).

Children who have been ill in hospital or at home, who have been moved from school to school, who have had a succession of teachers in the same subject may miss important elements of learning. These omissions can prevent them from gaining access to the new curriculum on offer especially when it is hierarchically organised. When they are unable to break a task down to tackle it then they can become distractible and even disruptive. Patch or topic approaches as alternatives may enable these learners to achieve higher standards of performance. Uneven performance in subjects and across them can be a useful indicant of their difficulties and their potential.

In all these cases the progressive lowering of attainment in comparison with peers can lead to a lowering of the sense of self-esteem and self-worth. This in turn can result in the seeking of esteem in other ways which are attention seeking or disruptive and which will leave even less opportunity for learning and lower the attainment still further. Pupils exhibiting challenging behaviour can come to be regarded as working against the school goals and school ethos and when they do try to make an effort these attempts are not valued and supported and then further and deeper problems can arise.

This wide-ranging group have learning needs which may be summarised as resulting in or from disaffection from the learning environment. It may be progressive and lead to more extreme forms of alienation and to challenging behaviour. Underlying it is the progressive lowering of motivation and self-esteem leading to further withdrawal from any learning challenge.

Learning

It may well be that the skills and abilities many pupils bring to the curriculum are insufficient if that curriculum is delivered in an inappropriate mode. Inappropriate in the sense that information may pass by too quickly to be absorbed or it is given in such a way that all the sense of it cannot be grasped because it has not been planned properly and carefully structured. The sense of it also may not link with anything already known and so it can remain isolated and incapable of use.

What children 30 years ago found absorbing may not be so attractive to a modern class. If for example the mode of teaching is didactic, with long periods of teacher talk, explanations followed by closed questions requiring one word answers followed by long periods of writing, then it may be wholly unsuited to learners' needs.

Pupils in both primary and secondary classes complain that they have far too much writing to do. The education system for many years has been one in which hordes of pupils each day compile personal text books and so become copy scholars. In the rest of their lives they enjoy a far more exciting and interesting time gaining information in a myriad of different ways from dozens of different sources but seldom, except at University, sit down to listen to a lecture and take notes. School must seem a strange place to them and learning a passive process.

Since everyone has been to school there is an assumption that they therefore know all about teaching and learning and teacher education. Even the pupils hold similar views. Only recently a small class of pupils, in years 8–10, referred for special education because they were disruptive, were given a lesson consisting of a simulation game in geography about conflicting aspects of planning and land use using a problem solving approach. All of them undertook the task and six of them became very involved with it and collaborated well in their small groups and resolved the problem. The two girls who reported they could not see the point of it did the basic minimum but did not become disruptive or attention seeking as previously. The general view of the group was that it was not 'real' work as they had enjoyed it and had not had to write anything down. Most of them had severe reading and writing difficulties.

It is clear from this and other similar examples collected in the Learning Difficulties Research Project studies that pupils must have explained to them the *relevance* of what they are doing and how they are learning. On its own it would not necessarily enthuse the two disillusioned and alienated girls but they would listen and note and be more likely on a subsequent occasion to allow themselves to become a little more involved. They would be interested at least to monitor what was going on. Participation would be likely to make them feel too vulnerable at first but more detail and insight would appear in any written or oral work they undertook.

Relevance in the curriculum is frequently recommended but it was noted in the Scottish Education Department survey report (SED 1978) that pupils' failure to see the relevance of the curriculum on offer was a significant contributing factor in the development of their learning difficulties. It is indeed a problem to demonstrate the relevance of a great deal of what is contained in the National Curriculum to today's young people; nevertheless it is important for teachers to consider what is relevant and to share this with the pupils. Equally important is to demonstrate the relevance of all sorts of obscure content when it is used to improve intellectual skills and develop critical and creative thinking.

Delaying gratification by suggesting that the ten years of learning grind in schools is all contributing to some superior abstract master plan to make them an educated person, fit them for adult life and the world of work is a hoax that no longer can be perpetrated on most pupils.

It is frequently recommended that disaffected pupils' interests should be the locus for remotivating them and bringing them back to the fold. By this stage their interests may entirely be focused upon sex, pop and football stars, clothes, alcohol and drugs. The Spanish Armada or even the First World War may be too remote for them to feel interested. However, these and any other subjects can be used as vehicles for learning new concepts and skills relevant to contemporary issues and problems rather than as ends in themselves.

Interactive teaching – question and answer sessions led by the teacher now being recommended by politicians and DfEE alike have widely prevailed in education. They cannot however be regarded as effective teaching for learning. It will be the purpose of this book to show the range of teaching and learning options which are available for use.

Types of behaviour difficulties

Group management skills, according to the Elton Report (1989 S 3.23) are the most important factor in achieving 'good' standards of behaviour. The effective teacher is highly socially skilled, able to pour oil on troubled waters, senses difficulties and disruption before they arise and uses a mixture of styles and approaches as appropriate to the needs of the learner and the size of the group.

The most difficult pupils can be calm and sensible in a tutorial session withdrawn from the class. Put them in a small group and they can become a bit of a nuisance and produce half as much work, but put them in a class of 30 and they can cause havoc. The answer cannot, of course, be to give every such pupil individual tutorials. The cost would be prohibitive and in the end it would not be effective in normalising and integrating them. Giving each one an individual programme of work is not a realistic option in a class of 30 or more or even with 20, especially in short sessions of 35–60 minutes for it leads to long periods of time dedicated to worksheets which may in themselves do little effective teaching but simply serve to occupy the time hopefully in quiet activity.

Coping with difficult or 'challenging' behaviour can be a continual problem for teachers for Croll and Moses (1985) found that in any primary classroom there was usually one pupil likely to prove disruptive, another three who would be so if unfavourable conditions arose whilst seven might occasionally be disruptive.

Disruptive behaviour is that which interferes with the learning and opportunities of other pupils and places undue stress upon the teacher. . .

(DES 1979, Elton 1989)

There is a continuum of misbehaviour to be seen from mild attention seeking at one end to major upheaval and disruption at the other.

However, it is not usually that scale of problem with which the teacher has to deal. It is instead the continuous chattering when pupils should be working which presents them with the greatest challenge and which they find most wearing (Elton 1989). This can be regarded as the mild attention seeking at the lower end of the 'Richter Scale of Disruption'. Such a scale, like its progenitor, proceeds in geometric progression to a major cataclysmic upheaval around the 7 to 8 mark.

'Richter Scale'

Attention seeking 1-------2------3-----4----5---6--7-8!!!   Disruption

---

Figure 3.1

Common descriptions given by teachers and also derived from classroom observations (Montgomery 1985, 1990) of nuisance or attention seeking behaviours are:

They fidget, tap rulers, pencils or feet, whistle or sing ostentatiously, swing on chairs tipped dangerously backwards, roam around the room, crawl about under desks, snatch others books and pencils, and most irritating of all talk continuously. Sometimes they just engage in low muttering, at other times they call out answers to the teacher's questions and shout abuse across the room at peers.

It is little wonder that teachers become tired and irritable with the sheer effort of dealing with this continual harassment. In such a climate it is difficult to pursue curriculum goals in a steady and uninterrupted way. A teacher who does and ignores misbehaviour will find that before long it has escalated to major proportions with most of the class inattentive and several who have become disruptive. According to Mongon and Hart (1989) challenging behaviour is just the visible tip of a problem of *disaffection* which is widespread in the school population, becomes even worse in the secondary school and cannot be effectively tackled in isolation from a *systematic programme of school improvement*.

Although the Elton Report was a response to what was seen as a major increase in behaviour problems in schools as reported by the media, the surveys showed that only 2 per cent of 3,600 teachers reported that they had been the target of physical aggression at some time. Deliberate attacks upon teachers were rare although in 1996 there was a 50 per cent increase in physical violence towards head and deputy head teachers with 51 exclusions from schools for violent behaviour. Three quarters of primary teachers reported having to deal with the problem of aggression between pupils at least once a week. Nearly one fifth reported having to deal with such incidents at least once a day.

Other surveys (Rutter *et al.* 1979) have shown that whilst problems have increased in some schools in some areas, others remain the same with few difficulties and in yet others they have decreased. Of interest in recent years have been the widespread reports from teacher colleagues that violent tactics seen the previous evening on television are modelled next day by many primary children, especially boys, in the playground. They are adding to their behavioural repertoire and Piaget (1954) would have argued that in this fantasy play they were learning to exert cognitive control over it rather than learning to do it.

It is perhaps not so surprising that pupils will occasionally tend to make a nuisance of themselves when we consider their circumstances. It is a most unnatural thing to expect a group of thirty or more lively youngsters to be confined in a classroom for a whole day together for weeks on end and also to expect them to remain seated and quietly attentive. Any novelty effect will soon wear off. If the tasks they are asked to do are boring and mundane, presented in a vague or unstimulating manner, exact little mental challenge and do not seem relevant it is clear that the children will protest in the only way they can by chattering and being a nuisance as they try to entertain themselves in other ways especially in that well known game 'Get the teacher'. It is however very distressing to a well prepared teacher with a keen interest in the subject to find an equally noisy and inattentive class after ten minutes of best effort. This may have arisen because the previous learning experiences of the pupils may have led them to lower their expectations of all teachers.

Perhaps a helpful way of thinking about this is to consider the continuum of behavioural difficulties as being beset along its length by a range of 'at risk' factors which will act to make a pupil who sets out as attentive and positive at the beginning of a school career or a school day gradually switch off or go into negative drive.

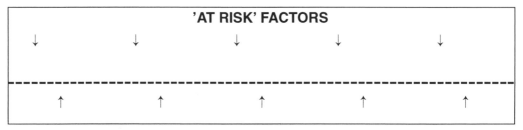

Figure 3.2

Such 'at risk' factors may begin when two teachers looking at the same behaviour treat it quite differently. A child shouts out answers in class and one teacher regards this as misbehaviour which if repeated after a warning, must be punished while another may treat it as high spirits which need to be calmed. The consequences of punishment can have a negative effect on the child leading to protestations, negativism and resentment whereas calming acts as a positive recognition of the child's energy and enthusiasm and gives a second chance to produce a considered response. The first teacher has put the child at risk since behaviour problems are very much a matter of social perception and this affects how we deal with them. This can be influenced by training but few teachers have experienced the substantial initial or inservice training needed to help them in this area (Hadfield 1989). Thus it is that schools need to develop consistent, positive discipline strategies which all the staff uphold. Just a few negative and punitive teachers on a staff or one with serious discipline problems can cause marked deterioration in general school discipline making it more difficult for all the teachers and their co-workers.

'At risk' factors which may predispose toward classroom problems

Social development and social context

Risk factors may reside within the social background of an individual child. Home discipline may be too severe or too lax. Indulgent parenting, accepting any behaviour, can thereby create a resistance to normal control techniques which have at their core a respect for persons and a willingness to listen to others and wait for turns. When the constraints of severe, punitive home discipline are released at school the child may not be able to cope with the new freedoms and can become very difficult to control. Inconsistent disciplining at home or at school may actually stamp in unwanted behaviour so that children learn to get their own way by persisting until the adult gives in. In the early years such inconsistency in giving rewards and punishments may lead children to have little notion of the meaning of praise and blame and right and wrong. They need then to have a very well-structured and supportive learning environment in their first years in school to overcome this. Assertive disciplining techniques (cited in Cantor and Cantor 1991) can prove effective in helping them become fully integrated into the classroom (Rogers 1991). These strategies are discussed in Chapter 13.

The child may have adopted models which are deviant and anti-school or belong to a subculture which is disaffected from school and society, seeking comfort and esteem only from its own peers and through the promotion of its own anti-authority subculture and goals. The gang may even become the substitute family.

Family relationships themselves might be disturbed and stressful with marital discord and violent quarrelling creating great distress amongst the children. Research over many decades has shown that such contexts can lead some of the children to become vulnerable to developing similar behaviours and relationships to those they have experienced, becoming aggressive and quarrelsome themselves at the least provocation (Jenkins 1966, Robins 1966, West 1982, Farringdon 1994) and acting these out in schools.

Some children might feel that others in the family are preferred and more respected than they are or there may be a new baby which is demanding of the parents' time, contributing to the feeling in the older siblings of rejection. All these can represent 'at risk' social factors which may predispose an individual to become attention seeking or a nuisance in class. If this is coupled with an awkward temperament or a mild difficulty, even temporary, in learning, then it is even more likely that a child can be set on a career in misbehaviour and disruption as the factors multiply or intensify some potentially trivial incident.

Schooling ethos

Schools and the schooling process itself seem to be able to create powerful 'at risk' factors. According to Rutter *et al.* (1979) and Hargreaves (1984) it was schools which gave an overemphasis to academic goals and neglected childrens' personal needs which disposed more children to fail and become a 'problem' in the school's eyes. These differences however could not be attributed to the catchment areas which the schools served (Galloway and Goodwin 1987). It depended more upon the school they happened to be attending than on the pupils themselves or their families. In addition, Mongon and Hart (1989) found that many pupils lived in a state of fear despite the good and kindly intentions of their teachers and that too many schools exerted a coercive rather than therapeutic educational influence. This is why it is so important for the ethos of the school and the classroom climate to be positive, constructive and supportive and then the most vulnerable children will have some protection and classroom work can proceed in a regular and orderly way. Difficult pupils with challenging behaviour have been found to respond far better to positive disciplining techniques (Scott MacDonald 1971; Wheldall and Merrett 1984; Montgomery 1990; Rogers 1991, 1994) than severe and punitive régimes.

Emotional factors

While it can be seen that difficult social, school, and learning circumstances can induce anxiety and distress and lead to behaviour problems it is also possible that some children are particularly vulnerable. There are two main and typical reaction patterns to emotional distress and these are to *act out* or to *withdraw*. Those who act out become the children exhibiting behaviour problems and are most likely because of this to obtain notice and perhaps some help. Those who withdraw tend to become passive, dreamy, self-absorbed and silent. If they are sad and weepy they might attract attention but otherwise their needs and distress tend to be ignored in a busy classroom.

Children who are emotionally vulnerable are likely to react more strongly and suffer greater distress than siblings and peers and they can even become emotionally ill. Others may already have inherited a vulnerability to emotional illness and it takes only a trigger experience to plunge them into a phobic, a depressive, a psycho-somatic response or into obsessional compulsive rituals which prevent them functioning in school or society.

Child abuse frequently leads to depressive symptoms even in the youngest of children, making them sad and weepy, often prone to tantrums, and to overt inappropriate sexuality and aggression in those sexually abused (Kempe and kempe 1984). Children who have been violently rejected by their parents are particularly sad cases and deeply troubled, frequently acting out their suffering in violence and aggression on peers, school and society at large. Their problems are deep seated and they need specialist psychiatric help (Kempe and Kempe 1984).

If children do show signs of emotional distress and illness then specialist help and support should be summoned immediately. The teacher can support the therapeutic programme by ensuring that the educational ethos is calm, secure and safe, positive and supportive. When the distress manifests itself it is important that the behaviour is understood and the emotions accepted and the pupil affirmed. This may even involve in rare cases, permitting the pupil to sit under the teacher's desk in the smallest safest place to be found whilst she/he grapples with the phobia. Teachers found that encouraging two such pupils – one phobic and one depressed and almost continually crying – to work together and have access to a small office where they could withdraw to work and play when they needed to helped them to help each other and kept them both in school.

Able but underfunctioning

It is more than 25 years since Mia Kellmer-Pringle, former Director of the National Children's Bureau first researched the subject of children she called 'able misfits'. It put the problems of quite a large group of individuals on the agenda of concerned professionals. She showed that there were legitimate concerns about the able and that they might be suffering, discriminated against and failing in school.

It was generally thought then and even now that ability is a gift which would enable 'bright' children to succeed against all odds whatever their circumstances. Her researches showed that able underachievers as a group showed a characteristic profile:

- a sense of inadequacy and limited ambition;
- a dislike of school work and book learning;
- poor work habits;
- unsatisfactory relationships with peers;
- a high incidence of emotional difficulties.

Teachers and other professionals working with schools will have met a number of such children whose early promise remains unfulfilled, those who will not work and those whose emotional difficulties come between them and success. It is often difficult to determine whether their emotional difficulties lead to their failures and poor relationships or arise directly because of them.

There are also children who may be highly intelligent but who fail to learn to read and spell, an extremely handicapping condition, which to some extent defies common understanding for people will wonder how a child could be termed 'clever' if he or she cannot do what even slower learners learn to do and some can do at three years of age self taught. These children too fit into the category of able misfit and of course there are others.

When we speak of the able, the talented and the gifted, clever or bright children, it must be realised that there are far more of them than most people think. In any classroom of mixed ability children there will be at least five who are able, one may be gifted and several are talented. Fifty per cent of them or more might have untapped gifts and talents if we can provide them with an appropriate curriculum which enables them to find or reveal their abilities.

Identifying the able has been shown not always to be simple and straightforward but identifying the underfunctioning able can be even more problematic. In a family one child may be of average ability and attainment, another may be of high ability doing very well in school and the third may be of even higher ability but functioning in school at a level lower than the average one. Parents very often know that such a child is underfunctioning but the school sees only the poor attainment and can conclude the pupil is of low ability or lazy and may refuse to investigate further. It can be difficult for parents to secure an assessment through the school as there are often many other children whose special needs seem more severe. Even if an independent psychological assessment is obtained there is no guarantee that it will show the high ability or if it does that any provision will be made. Parents are on hand to observe the challenging questions raised and the ingenious ways their children may solve problems and how quickly they 'catch on' when being given an explanation or demonstration. They can note the different profiles of development. Teachers with large classes do not always have the time to observe these nuances. Teacher judgment can however be facilitated where there has been inservice training in identification strategies (Denton and Postlethwaite 1985, Hany 1997).

In test conditions some highly able children work very slowly, others see uniquely different answers to items and problems and so their scores may appear artificially low until their performance and rationales are explored. A few children will deliberately exploit the tests and give wrong answers so as to remain with their friends or not appear to be noticeably different. If schools obtain high test scores and then pupils fail to shine in school subjects there is a tendency to perceive this as laziness and failure to pursue school goals. Pupils' reports read 'could do better', 'has good ability but . . .', 'must work harder' and so on. This negative stance adopted by the school can be very frustrating for the pupil who may not know why nothing seems to satisfy them – a scene set up to create an alienated able misfit.

Sometimes the promise seen in early years education is not fulfilled and once again a range of reasons is cast – misassessment, favouritism, burn out, laziness, challenge of the more advanced curriculum when quite often the reverse is the case. There may be insufficient challenge and a mundane curriculum with days of boredom stretching into infinity. Trapped in this 'psychic prison' (De Mink 1995) the pupil switches off and daydreams the time away. Others may seek the cognitive stimulation in that favourite pastime of all pupils – tormenting the teacher. Able pupils however are so much cleverer at this and think of many different ways to disturb others. They may clown and fool about enjoying the excitement and thrill of making their peers laugh and driving teachers to the brink of distraction without necessarily pushing them quite over the edge. This activity is interpreted by teachers as 'challenging' and misbehaviour and all too easily a pupil may become set on a career in disruption as people fail to recognise the signs and overreact in their disciplining techniques. Problem pupils such as this are said not to fit into the school regime and are excluded as soon as feasible. Nevertheless it must be said that there are many schools which go to great lengths to try to counsel and keep such pupils on track but it is so difficult to break these habits once they are well established and especially when they are driven by some inner emotional need or tension arising from personal or family conflicts and fears.

What we do know is that boredom and lack of cognitive challenge in the daily curriculum plays a significant role in causing pupils across the ability range to behave in this way. Where there is a pressure for so-called academic standards to the exclusion of a concern for individuals and their needs (Hargreaves 1984, Galloway and Goodwin 1987) then this will predispose many children to feel alienated from school work. We can also suggest that the more imaginative and creative the pupils the more likely they are to be switched off by a didactic form of curriculum and pedagogy. Even the most able and least creative after mopping up all the knowledge and skills of the primary and early secondary years may perceive increasing redundancy in the knowledge input or feel the brakes are permanently on. The disparity in ability and knowledge can become so wide that didactics no longer can reach them. Thus it is that differentiation has become an important consideration in curriculum provision for the able and endorsed by HMI (1992).

Able and learning disabled

While there are a wide range of learning disabilities (specific learning difficulties) the most common and the most detrimental to educational progress is dyslexia.

It has been a hard struggle for parents and dyslexia tutors to gain recognition for this severely disabling condition in which, often in the presence of high ability, there is a serious and unexplained decrement in reading and spelling skills. When pupils have high ability the fact that they can hardly read and write only seems to confirm the idea that they are really not very able at all. Imagine the frustration of a 6–7 year old with an IQ of 146 on the WISC – R and an inability to read and write. It is not surprising that he or she has become disruptive every time the class is settled down to these activities.

Career gifted

This group of able and underfunctioning pupils was first identified by Freeman (1991). In her longitudinal study she found the 'career gifted' had been nominated by parents or identification procedures as gifted at an early age. These children had enjoyed the aura that the title could bring but feared failure and also suspected that they might not really be worthy of it and would be found wanting so they would say that they could not be bothered to try with school work, that the work was too uninteresting and boring or that it was beneath them. By failing to involve themselves in school work they fell further behind so that eventually the only sign of high ability was on tests which required very little prior knowledge.

As can be imagined one of these individuals in the classroom could be a sore trial to the teacher. Because he or she is avoiding work there is much time which can be spent on other, sometimes disruptive activities. It is also upsetting for the teacher to be told that everything provided is 'boring' and it can also be catching so that other children may decide to tell the teacher this and so obtain some more attention or freedom to choose something different.

Gifted handicapped

This term first appeared in the literature in the 1970s. It included individuals with visual, hearing, physical, emotional and learning disabilities. Often provision had been made for them in special education and this led to the neglect of the high ability and talent which some possessed. In the case of hearing impaired pupils their very disability is not highly visible and there is a tendency to regard them as heedless and less able if they are unable to understand exactly what is said to them.

Where there is a stereotype that the highly able must 'look bright' (Karnes and Johnson 1991) then those who look different in some way may be considered to be less able than they really are. The UK stereotype is in fact of a white male, weedy, bespectacled, given to solitary reading, referred to as the 'little professor' by peers and often by teachers, sounding and looking old fashioned (Freeman 1991, p. 22). According to Yewchuk and Bibby (1989) the characteristics of high ability which teachers perceived in the gifted handicapped were found to be similar to those in the nonhandicapped. Thus we can use the same criteria for identifying them and be very much aware that failure to find them is much to do with misleading stereotypes and to structural or system induced 'blindness'.

Cultural difference and disadvantage

Being 'culturally different' refers to differences in racial/ethnic status, language, religious beliefs, values and the way in which children are socialised in families. Disadvantage is taken to mean to be brought up in homes or environments where financial resources are limited and educational traditions are not strong. These groups were found by Gallagher (1985) and Gallagher and Gallagher (1994) to be underrepresented in gifted programmes in the USA. Cultural differences and disadvantage are commonly observed in minority groups in this country and thus pupils from them can be doubly disadvantaged. Both groups are underrepresented even in the current expanded university system in the UK (Ashworth 1996). Creative curiosity, critical remarks and questions, physical activity and sociability may all be seen as a challenge and affront to teacher authority. It may seem particularly unacceptable when couched in the language of a subculture. In a disadvantaged area the school and environment may hold low expectations of its children and parents and teachers can become blind to high ability or talent of any kind. They may set the curriculum at a less challenging level in these areas and so compound the disadvantage.

Difference

One black pupil in a class of whites may be treated differently in a number of ways. Just being black may make them more noticeable whatever they do and can mean that the teacher is always finding them doing something 'wrong' even when they are not. The same can be the case for one white in a class of blacks.

Very small curly haired children both white and black with large eyes tended to be treated by peers and older children as dolls or babies to be cared for and may play the baby role in class and use it avoid challenging activities.

Differences in looks such as squints, spectacles, spots may all become a focus for other children's malice in some classrooms as may limps, mannerisms, tallness or fatness. Sometimes it becomes very difficult not to become a victim of childhood bullies and this is why bullying policies and conflict management are necessary.

Gender factors

Freeman's stereotype of the gifted child did not include images of girls and women in the national psyche. If the highly able girl does not achieve the highest grades in the curriculum then there will be little recognition of her ability. Often even when she does achieve them it is regarded as the result of very hard work and persistence but seldom for having flair or real ability. It is very easy for girls to underfunction because their patterns of behaviour tend to be quieter and they are therefore left to their own devices. Those who do 'act out' their frustrations will become regarded as problem pupils (Good and Brophy 1985) to be persuaded to leave as soon as possible. Being a girl can thus be a double handicap, and being a girl from a disadvantaging background or ethnic minority can be a triple handicap. Add dyslexia to this and the prognosis is very poor indeed. It has already been recorded that girls with dyslexia are underrepresented amongst those identified for remedial support. Girls are not significantly different from boys in their patterns of ability, creativity and talent but they may be more likely to be taught to underfunction in home and in school (Butler-Por 1987). Spender (1983) observed that boys gained two thirds of all the attention in class and regarded it as their rightful share. They complained of favouritism towards the girls when Spender and her co-workers tried to even out their attention giving. In Good and Brophy's (1985) research it was found that teachers would give boys more information when they asked questions whereas girls who asked similar questions were quietened, ignored or regarded as domineering. Although overt sexism is now less apparent, structural sexism is still in operation (Fawcett Society 1995) so that the sexes are not treated as equal citizens.

Deeply rooted stereotypical attitudes of any kind are difficult to change and lead to many forms of covert discrimination. In all arenas where attention should be equally shared between members in groups, committees or assemblies the contributions of females can be seen to be passed over. Both men and women discriminate against girls unfairly causing them to underfunction and creating a progressive weakening in their psychological makeup and frequently this can lead to a learned helplessness in all their decision-making.

Children in hospitals

Children in hospitals tend, educationally, to be a much neglected group. There is no obligation to educate them unless their stay is longer than ten days and now many hospital stays tend to be much shorter than this, an average of about three days. Long stay patients tend to be in hospital for an average of 4 weeks (Housby-Smith 1995). However, there may well be a strong need for education despite the shortest of stays. One of the reasons for this is that it brings the normal environment back into the child's life. It can also offer an opportunity for one-to-one tuition helping an individual over a learning block or learning difficulty especially where the child is in a children's ward or hospital school. Education in hospital which is educationally stimulating and valuable can be seen as educational therapy. It can truly take the patient's mind off fears and anxieties for a period of time and prove to be constructive in dealing with the problems of hospitalisation.

There are problems however in getting the education to where it is needed. Hospital staff, reminded of their own education, often regard attempts to resume education as punitive towards children and do what they can to encourage them to avoid it or try to subvert it. Often nurses and ward staff may be seen doing the work themselves rather than enabling the child to do it when the teacher has moved on. They may also be seen playing with the toys in the early years areas and doing the jigsaws – presumably satisfying some deeper needs of their own.

Schools may find it difficult to maintain contact with pupils in hospital. However the longer the stay the more important it is to establish contacts and visits and maintain curriculum continuity by sending work from the school. Some pupils have to spend long periods in hospital over a number of years and then it is essential that school and hospital teachers liaise to organise the educational provision they are going to make. This is made easier by having the National Curriculum which all pupils are following but even so there are many variations in what is selected so that hospital teachers need to be familiar with and have a key contact in the main schools in their local catchment area. 70,000 children can expect to have their education disrupted by hospitalisation (Housby-Smith 1995).

Summary and conclusion

There are a wide range of what have been termed 'at risk' factors operating in the home and school environments which can predispose pupils to underfunction and gain lower attainments. As the risk factors multiply they cause a progressive deterioration in motivation which can lead to disaffection and alienation from school and learning environments of any kind.

The term 'able misfit' has now been replaced with the concept of 'underfunctioning able' to refer to those who have high ability but are not demonstrating this in school subjects. They may have profound knowledge and interest in a subject outside the school curriculum or they may not. Their failure and frustration at school may lead many of them to become alienated and a problem to themselves and others so that the school may feel it can no longer contain the pupil safely and constructively and this can lead to exclusion. Others underfunction and pass quietly through the system without ever being noticed.

It has been suggested that lack of cognitive challenge in the curriculum can cause underfunctioning as well as a range of learning disabilities and difficulties which conceal learning potential. Stereotypic views of the 'good' pupil, gender, ethnicity, culture and the 'able child' can also cause pupil's abilities to be overlooked and lead to underfunctioning as expectations are lowered.

Having considered all these factors it becomes difficult to understand how anyone ever succeeds at school and avoids the complex mesh of damages and dangers to which they are exposed. It suggests the determination to succeed of some pupils can outweigh the negative effects to which they may be exposed. With a little support many more might achieve substantially higher levels of attainment.

Chapter 4

Differentiation: curriculum models and methods

Introduction

Differentiation in the UK has moved from a theme in special education for slow and disabled learners to a concern for all mainstream teachers. In 1992 Her Majesty's Inspectorate for Schools (HMI) came to see it as crucial to meet the needs of able learners. It saw differentiation as the key to making provision for able children together with the use of 'judicious questioning'. It found that able children, despite the introduction of the National Curriculum, were still not having their special needs met (HMI 1992). In fact it was often because of such an overfilled curriculum their needs now could not be met (NACE 1994).

The only teaching method however to which HMI had referred by which higher levels of knowledge, skill, understanding and thinking were achieved was 'judicious' and challenging questioning, now referred to as 'interactive teaching'. This would seem a rather limited prescription for action. Socratic methods are necessary but not always sufficient to achieve the goals of differentiation. Kerry and Kerry's (1997) studies showed that whilst many primary teachers did offer differentiated worksheets this was uncommon in subject teaching in secondary schools.

At the same time there has also been a pressure from Government for a return to more formal methods of teaching. The majority of teachers have however never used anything else (Skilbeck 1989). Didactics are particularly unsuited to groups with a wide range of ability and literacy skills but it is not impossible to teach such groups when appropriate methods are used (Montgomery 1990).

It would be a mistake to think that putting together classes of pupils of like ability, streaming or setting them for core subjects, particularly English and mathematics, means that differentiation becomes unnecessary. In fact these pupils will be found to be as widely different in abilities, knowledge, skills and interests as a 'mixed' ability class and can prove to be far more demanding to teach by any method.

Didactics may pass with the highly able but equally for them it has been found, in the controlled studies of Deci *et al.* (1983) to dampen pupils' learning and damage motivation and achievement for it permits no autonomy. In all learners there is a need to develop and practice the higher order skills of self regulation, planning and management (Brown *et al.* 1983).

Curriculum provision for children with general learning difficulties

Identifying the nature of the pattern of needs of each individual learner experiencing difficulties should enable an individual education plan (IEP) to be drawn up. However, the nature of the primary needs of the pupils with general learning difficulties are global in that developmental slowness in the areas of memory, language and thinking can slow down the acquisition of literacy skills and subject knowledge. There are methods of teaching and learning which are 'developmental' which can be used with slower learners in mainstream which are inclusive and ensure that all the learners in the mixed ability group, even the highly able, are stimulated and can work at their own levels (Montgomery 1990, 1996). Removing slower learners for remedial support is not an appropriate strategy for it further deprives them of the mainstream curriculum and as their needs are developmental a remedial curriculum which is compacted is hardly appropriate.

These learners can make up a substantial proportion of a class and so it is legitimate to give special consideration to their needs. Hegarty and Pocklington *et al.* (1981) found that this group were given more time and individual help by teachers to help them keep up with the general class work. Now they may also have learning support within the classroom. Although this is a widespread strategy there has been no formal evaluation of its effectiveness. It takes several forms such as reader and scribe, spelling dictionary, work sheet monitor, répétiteur, attention director, motivator, and calming influence. It could be argued that such support for learning is only required because the general teaching and learning on offer is inadequate.

After several years of literacy support in primary school Peters and Smith (1986) found that although reading had been given detailed treatment no such similar attention had been given to spelling. The literacy skills of pupils leaving secondary schools were found to be no more advanced than when they entered (HMI 1994). Such results show that, on a substantial basis, we are not meeting pupils' needs by the methods currently in use. It would therefore be a mistake to propose more of the same when it has already failed a substantial number of pupils.

What then do children with learning difficulties need from their education and how can this be provided within mainstream? They need opportunities to develop their speaking and listening skills so that they have a chance to enhance their language development and communication. They need to do some of this in group settings so that they can practice and develop social skills with peers. They need learning opportunities which will support memory and increase motivation to persist with tasks and to keep them alert, curious and attentive. As their vocabulary and comprehension skills advance these will aid the progression in thinking abilities. Teaching methods should focus upon concept development and attainment and the development of schemata or protocols for further learning in each subject area. These will have transfer possibilities and make learning more efficient and effective. Much of the learning of these pupils should take account of the fact that they are developmentally younger and thus methods traditionally used in early years education are more appropriate even well into secondary schooling. In fact some teachers in further education have modelled their teaching on primary methods and have found these enhanced the learning of their students. It was also recognised and recommended by the Further Education Unit (FEU 1989).

Such methods should include opportunities for experiential learning in the initial stages of a teaching series to ensure the pupils have the appropriate grounding. It may also be necessary to teach them what other pupils have picked up incidentally. Those with the moderate learning difficulties may need to be taught such things as the meaning of numbers on a bus, the meaning of maps, and why and where to put food in a fridge. In school terms it can mean that pupils have to be taught first how to read a worksheet and then carry out its instructions in the correct order. Text may not yet direct their behaviour and they may have to read the sheet aloud several times before they begin to comprehend what to do. Average six year olds have the same sort of learning needs. Characteristically they do nothing and the support teacher has to read the sheet to them to get them started. This however does not help them improve and a starting point could be to permit pairs to read the instructions to each other and decide how to proceed. Teaching, to be effective, also needs to encourage pupils to be reflective. Indeed Watson (1996) in her studies has shown the benefits of teachers encouraging pupils with moderate learning difficulties to reflect upon their learning and how to encourage classroom talk and develop challenging activities for them.

The second order learning opportunities for pupils with general learning difficulties should be in the area of basic skills of reading, spelling and handwriting. Teaching in all content areas in all years should ensure that literacy development is taught alongside and through subject content backed by a whole-school policy and approach. Number skills also fall into this category and teaching and reinforcement activities should be sought in, for example, art, science, geography, technology and language as well as in mathematics. Subject teachers must not assume that pupils will have the requisite knowledge in core skills areas for their subject studies.

The third order of learning needs are for pupils to learn how to study and to develop their study and independent learning, thinking and problem solving skills within curriculum subjects. It will require a more flexible approach to learning in classrooms but this will permit wider curriculum differentiation within whole-class teaching. The later chapters on speaking and listening, literacy skills and so on explain with practical examples how these problems of change and innovation may be addressed.

Curriculum provision for pupils with language disorders

The Association for all Speech Impaired Children (AFASIC) have studied the progress of children with language disorders and published a number of booklets designed to promote understanding of the needs of these children and how they may best be helped.

Their general recommendations are that these pupils need early *attention training* and a *consistently structured programme of teaching*.

Even if these pupils have an adequate perception and reception of speech they may not have learned to attend to it and develop the habit of listening. Thus early training has to consist of alertness training, developing the postural set of attending, looking at the speaker or source and so on. Mainstream teachers were found to be reluctant and even nervous of imposing such rules on very young children. However AFASIC found it to be essential if the pupils were to grasp the relations between attending, listening and success. One-to-one teaching and learning in very small groups was still found to be the only way in which they would respond to this intensive form of training.

At five years the pupils will have little grasp of language and so will have failed to learn much of the basic knowledge and experiences essential in schools. It is recommended by AFASIC that the teacher assumes the pupil knows nothing and sets out to teach all those things which others have learned incidentally. The words 'more' or 'less' spoken or written may hold no meaning for them although they may understand whether they want more chips and less salad in the presence of the real things. Thus all learning has to be based upon direct experience brought into the classroom and it may take a great deal of repetition to associate verbal labels with them. This structured teaching is essentially repetitive and rote training but once it is established and automatic it is then possible for the pupils to go on to education in the true sense. This intensive form of teaching is best undertaken in a special unit attached to a school where the teachers have had the appropriate training. Indirect methods and verbal expositions which all mainstream teachers use to a considerable extent, in fact they monopolise 70 per cent of the talking time (Flanders 1970, ORACLE 1980, LRDP 1998), do not work with language impaired pupils. They cause distraction and confusion. The field of study needs to be narrowed and thinking directed until the pupil has grasped the concept. The ability to generalise which is a facility easily available in all other children's learning and thinking repertoires from the earliest years is developed only very slowly in language impaired pupils.

Using support teachers in mainstream to pre-teach key concepts and story/learning sequences by *direct teaching methods* as for those with hearing difficulties can be an important aid to priming and facilitates learning. It also cuts down the need for in-class support in secondary school which can bring about derision and bullying from other pupils. Ten minutes daily teaching on a one-to-one basis using a step by step approach – *task analysis* (Englemann and Carnine 1982) will be more effective for language disordered children than group work. Visual approaches supporting early learning will also aid understanding.

Overprotection from adults can also be a problem and AFASIC recommend the identification of a significant adult or named key worker whose responsibility is to ensure that all adults involved in the child's education understand the needs and the difficulties of the individual. Obviously inservice training for all involved can help provide a network of support and increase understanding and awareness.

In all cases of learning disorders specialist developmental teaching programmes are essential. This specialist teaching and learning should begin in the home and be followed by placement in nursery classes which can offer specialist provision in small teaching groups. Early systematic specialist provision which continues into the infant and junior years offers the best chances for these pupils to join mainstream education later. Some may of course need specialist provision throughout their school life and further support as adults. When they are integrated later into mainstream education formal expository teaching will seriously disadvantage them and cause them to underfunction. They will then need the sort of education already described for children with general learning difficulties as do all children who have for a variety of reasons some mild developmental delay in the language area.

Curriculum needs of children with autism and autistic spectrum disorders

Wing (1981) recommended that the curriculum for these children should reflect the following principles:

- regular organised routine;
- careful communication with the pupil;
- modification of the repetitive speech and motor habits;
- use of behaviour modification sensitively;
- development and extension of special interests;
- highly skilled teachers;
- tolerant, supportive school environment.

It is likely that the majority of these pupils will be statemented and some schools have specialised in accepting them, particularly in the independent sector.

Brown and Taylor (1985) conclude that:

There is a need for the teacher to accept that many autistic children will resist any teaching programme when it is introduced because they resist change. This resistance has to be worked through until the new activity becomes part of their repertoire and therefore enjoyable. (p. 13)

It is clear from this that for autistic children to gain the best possible results from their schooling they need the help of experts especially in the early years. There are a range of approaches which may be used (NAS 1993) but the prime ones involve careful and finely graded task analytic approaches and behaviour modification. Both these techniques will be described in later chapters.

For those who can pursue academic studies there appear to be few problems in gaining a set of GCSEs especially if a considerable amount of the material relies on memory but it is their social behaviours which give rise to the greatest concern (Western 1996) and for which they may need continuing support into adult life after leaving the supportive and understanding structure of their school. Their extreme need for regularity and routine in which the slightest change requires them to be very carefully prepared is also of major concern for it can mean they find the simplest interaction in a shop is unpredictable. They frequently may ask for a detailed prescription or schedule for interacting with and gaining a girlfriend or dealing with others in a social setting.

More detailed discussions of the curricular needs of autistic children may be obtained from The National Autistic Society (NAS), 276 Willesden Lane, London NW2 5RB.

Curriculum provision for pupils with specific learning difficulties

Pupils with specific learning difficulties in reading and spelling become progressively handicapped as they go through the school years. This is despite the fact that they might have had five or six years of remedial reading and in class support (Montgomery 1997a). It is essential that these pupils with 'dyslexia' are identified in their first few weeks in school as 'at risk' so that a systematic and structured programme of *developmental spelling and reading* can be employed by the reception class teacher. Pupils who slip through this net will need a specialist *remedial programme* which is also structured, multisensory and cumulative. It needs to be given in paired tutorials as soon as possible, withdrawn from the classroom for at least two half hour sessions per week and reinforced by the class teachers. There are two such programmes which are recommended here: the *Hickey Multisensory Language Course*, 2nd edition (Augur and Briggs eds 1991) or *Teaching Reading Through Spelling* (TRTS Cowdery, Montgomery, Morse and Prince-Bruce 1983–1987, 2nd edition 1994). This is also based upon Hickey's adaptation of the Gillingham, Stillman and Orton Programme first published in the USA in 1940. Orton based the main principles on teaching methods he had observed in the UK in the 1920s!

Whatever the origins of the dyslexics' difficulties the only programmes which have been shown to give gains in literacy development over age are these programmes and others based on the same principles. They must be accompanied by the pupils learning *cursive writing* as many dyslexics have handwriting coordination difficulties. There are also those who are not dyslexic whose spelling and handwriting can be transformed by a cursive writing programme. Even those who have perceptuomotor difficulties can be helped to gain better mastery of these skills by training in one of them such as handwriting (Lazslo *et al.* 1988).

Pupils whose reading and spelling skills are generally poor as a result of their poorer cognitive and learning skills will also benefit from a structured Developmental Spelling Programme (Montgomery 1997b). This also includes cursive writing from the beginning, a programme of phonics and linguistics. The gradient of introduction for slower learners needs to be less steep with more opportunities for overlearning. Worksheets for drawing and colouring are not recommended for any of these pupils as they most often distract from the main points of the lessons which need the teacher to teach and to listen and observe the pupils' responses.

Curriculum provision for pupils with attention deficit disorders

Pupils with attention deficit disorders will benefit greatly from a highly structured and focused approach to reading and writing. If their successes are systematically reinforced this will help to keep them on target and preserve their self-esteem and motivation. Coupled with this they may need medication under medical supervision but especially they will need a structured environment with low extraneous stimulation and a behaviour modification programme such as is described in Chapter 13. An active learning environment is more suited to their needs and will be more beneficial than a passive and didactic setting.

Curriculum provision for pupils who are disaffected and demotivated

The different groups who make up disaffected and demotivated learners have several curriculum needs in common. They need to be treated with respect and fairness (Montgomery 1989) so that each has an equal opportunity with others to learn and take advantage from education. They particularly need cognitive challenge in the curriculum (Purkey 1970). How this is achieved can be built into the general teaching strategies of core skills and will be exemplified in the separate chapters in section two in which a general ethos as well as curriculum strategies will be developed.

Their second major need is to experience a supportive, constructive but controlled learning environment. This it will be suggested can be achieved by using a variety of strategies which have behaviour modification at their core and are variously described as 'assertive discipline' (cited Cantor and Cantor 1991) and 'positive approaches to teaching' (Wheldall and Merrett 1984, 1985; Montgomery 1989; Rogers 1991, 1994a.b).

A third and fundamental need is to gain cognitive challenge and enjoyment from curriculum activities for children of all levels of abilities. The area where this has been researched most widely is in the field of 'gifted' education. Some of the key findings in this area follow and will be used to underpin the teaching and learning strategies in section two for it is regarded as essential that all children are entitled to an enriched curriculum.

For those children who are emotionally distressed, bereaved or anxious a safe and gently calming environment needs to be provided. They need positive help and kind encouragement in an adaptable setting. They need to be offered more creative opportunities to play with materials and media away from pressure to achieve a particular result. Such experiences, particularly in drama, art, dance and music or PE can offer covert therapeutic experiences and opportunities in the hands of a sensitive teacher despite the presence of other children. A supportive school ethos and SPA – Supportive and Positive Approaches throughout the school can help disturbed children deal with some of their problems through this form of education as therapy. So easily, coercive school environments can disable and disadvantage them.

Curriculum provision for the highly able

During the middle decades of the 20th century research led to an expanded and multidimensional view of high ability then called 'giftedness'. Creativity, much more difficult to measure, was seen to play a more significant role in giftedness along with personal characteristics such as motivation and perseverance. Now Cropley (1994) has suggested that there is no 'true giftedness' without creativity. Intelligence tests are thus limited in their assessments because they test only the convergent aspects of intellectual functioning not broader aspects of high ability.

Giftedness now termed 'high ability' is generally defined as the capacity for the demonstration of high levels of performance in any potentially valuable area of human endeavour. Freeman (1991) concluded in her longitudinal study of nearly 200 highly able children that disadvantaged environments could constrain their achievements and realisation of abilities and then high quality schooling became crucial. It could be argued that for the average and less able it is even more crucial otherwise vast numbers of children are going to underfunction and perhaps do.

Incorporating creativity opportunities into the National Curriculum is particularly problematic despite Dearing's (1994) attempt to cut down the content. Opportunities to play with materials and ideas is characteristic of creative thinkers and producers and has little place in our current system of education.

Able and highly able children need a curriculum which is *cognitively challenging* and which provides opportunities for the development of talents and creativity in many different fields, they need an enriched and enriching experience (Passow 1990, Renzulli 1995). It has however been demonstrated that when slower learners and pupils exhibiting challenging behaviour (Montgomery 1990, 1989) are exposed to the same enriching experiences as the highly able, that with a little extra teacher support, these learners also become highly motivated and succeed in a way and at a level which is conspicuously different and higher than previously. Talents and new abilities and competencies are demonstrated.

Curriculum needs of children in hospital

According to a survey of responses by hospital teachers to a number of curriculum questions the following aims and objectives were agreed (Montgomery 1983). The aims were: to promote learning; to be a purposeful experience and to keep them in touch with normality (p. 22). The achievement of these aims could be achieved by developing 'learning capsules' packaged in such a way that they could be used efficiently in sessions of about one hour. They should have the possibility of being extended for further periods over several days and must be able to be carried about the hospital to the bedside. They also needed to be capable of being easily adapted to a reasonably wide ability range.

Apart from the normal school curriculum which each child would be following the teacher is required to have special skills to provide a secure and relaxed atmosphere where the children can express anxiety, fears, can ask questions and be reassured. They need to be able to construct an environment where the child can be 'normal', outside their 'hospital' selves and not the dependent 'sick' child of the hospital. In this sense education is therapy. Personal computers and work with CD-ROMs can extend the hospital horizons in a way today that was not previously possible and are essential educational equipment for every child in hospital.

According to the teachers children in hospital are likely to suffer a lowering of their sense of self-esteem because they are more dependent than normal on hospital staff and parents and from the regression which is likely to occur when the child is ill. To counteract this a near normal school setting is needed so that children can express their thoughts and fears about the hospital. The work the children produce needs to be especially valued and displayed. They need more creative work with materials, tools and instruments rather than stereotyped skills activities. They need more extensive opportunities for social interaction with peers and to be able to enjoy the activities and have fun.

Often the short stay patients find their experience the most disturbing and so they especially need the opportunity to make sense of their visit to make it a positive rather than a negative experience. Seriously ill children need help to talk about their feelings and to gain hope for a future. They often require a very wide range of resources and different media to try out and begin to find interest and satisfaction.

The liaison with the child's own school by telephone and fax if this is at a distance, is a very important part of the hospital teacher's role and necessary for the child's reintegration into mainstream. A special skill is the ability to take any material and match it to an individual's needs after a very brief diagnostic discussion; differentiation on a significant scale is thus part of the daily routine.

The nature of differentiation

Differentiation is concerned with the delivery of the curriculum and its assessment and has a variety of elements in it (Weston 1992). It seems to me that differentiation in practice can be organised under two main headings – Structural or systems approaches and Integral in which the basic curriculum is individualised and forms a whole life-style approach. The structural approach deals mainly with groups and it is less certain in that system that the same basic curriculum is available to all.

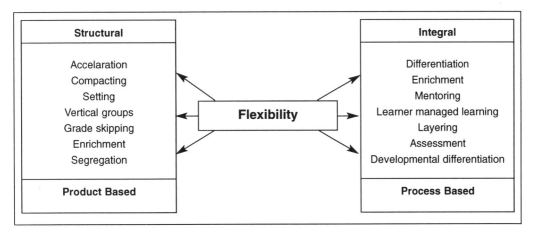

Figure 4.1 A comparison of models of differentiation

Structural methods all involve accelerating or de-accelerating the learner through curriculum contents in various ways. Even some enrichment materials merely teach what the learner could expect to learn in another phase of education. For example, primary pupils might be given sections of the secondary school or even university curriculum in the periods allocated to 'enrichment'. This form of provision is 'bolted on' to the normal classroom activities whereas a more sophisticated form which is integral to the normal curriculum is what is required.

If differentiation is integral or built in to the mainstream work all children can have an opportunity to profit from the enrichment. Most structural approaches tend to be product or content based whereas integral approaches have to be concerned with process, in particular cognitive processes in which there is both content and method.

The integral approach has the enrichment or the differentiated work built into the daily curriculum.

Three models of integral curriculum differentiation

- **By inputs** – the setting of different tasks at different levels of difficulty suitable for different levels of achievement (layering).
- **By outputs** – the setting of common tasks that can be responded to in a positive way by all students (assessment).
- **Developmental** – the setting of common tasks to which all students can contribute their own inputs and so progress from surface to deep learning and thus be enabled to achieve more advanced learning outcomes.

Of the first two perhaps the best that can be said is that they offer more than the formal or didactic methods of teaching to the middle but there are inbuilt disadvantages of which teachers need to be aware. In differentiation by inputs teachers provide some core work in which all pupils may participate but after that they provide different work within the same context at different levels – simpler conceptual and practice work for the slower learners and more complex problem solving extension work for the able groups. What has to be appreciated is that in this system the pupils doing the easier work can begin to feel lower in ability and value. The able students in this system may begin to feel special for they are doing the 'clever' work and can develop inflated opinions of themselves and their abilities and begin to look down on the other children even poking fun at them. All of these attitudes are destructive and wasteful so that none of the groups are motivated to develop their abilities and talents to the full.

A second problem is that it is the teacher who has to select who will do the advanced or less advanced work and thus too much hangs upon the teacher's diagnostic skills. There are in fact a number of studies which have shown that teachers need some training to do this successfully and that the majority of teachers do not receive any form of help in this area. In secondary schools Painter (1982) found that teachers left out a third who were highly able and misclassified as able a third who were not. Hany's (1997) extensive studies have shown that even experienced teachers referred to stereotypes for identification and used a few limited indicants to confirm their assessments.

A third problem is that the teacher has to provide three different lots of pupil work which can prove very time consuming day in and day out. Thus it is that publishers have stepped in and now provide schemes and topics in which they have laid out the differentiated layers of work. Asquith (1996) in *Geography Themes* gives some extension suggestions as follows. On Rivers: 'Carry out further experiments to see the effect of pebble shape on transport using flat and spherical stones. Which are the most easily moved? Additionally, identify dense and less dense pebbles of the same size and shape and examine the effect on erosion and transportation' (p. 56). For another lesson on rivers the extension suggested is to use a CD-ROM or encyclopaedia to find the names of the largest or deepest gorges, waterfalls and deltas in the world. Locate them on a map of the world and write brief notes on the different features in bubble diagrams connected to the maps (p. 59).

The suggestion(s) for support (the lower ability group) for this session are as follows: 'Children could make a three dimensional cardboard model of a valley, flood plain and river channel and use it to identify the landforms and processes on the slopes, valley bottom and river channel.'

As can be seen, the highly able at Key Stage 2 are not going to be intellectually challenged by these 'extension activities' and the others will spend lots of time with cardboard and glue and little cognitive challenge.

The second view of differentiation is where all students can participate in the same task but there are different levels of the assessment tasks set. The children may all do the same assessment tasks at which they progressively fail or the assessment criteria have different levels against which the work is marked. Often in this latter method at public examination time, some pupils are entered for a lower level qualification which is the first indication they may have been given that their work is not up to standard. Often when highly able students are set a task it may appear so mundane that they give a low level formatted response.

These two forms of differentiation are no more than a within-class selective education system with all the potential for social and political division which was witnessed before.

The form of differentiation by which higher cognitive abilities and skills have been achieved (Montgomery (1990, 1996) has been termed *developmental differentiation* and it was cognitive process methods which enabled a developmentally differentiated curriculum to be offered to all the class in a form which could be enriching for all.

The key features of developmental differentiation were:

- a respect for individual differences;
- the use of cognitive process teaching methods;
- a developmental use of positive cognitive intervention (PCI);
- assessment which was both formative and diagnostic.

It is termed developmental differentiation because pupils gain access to the curriculum at a level suited to their linguistic, cognitive and other developmental levels. Through their studies the activities enable them to progress towards higher levels of skills both in the curriculum and in child development terms.

In order to effect change it was necessary to design materials and methods at two levels – teaching materials with built-in cognitive process methods for the teachers to use with the children so that they could feel the different effect and the strength of the positive response (Montgomery 1985, 1996). To do this the training courses also had to be redesigned to enable teachers to develop the methods and materials for themselves (Montgomery 1994). Fortunately it was possible to find some enrichment materials which illustrated some of the methods teachers should use. Paramount amongst these were the project packs produced by the Maidenhead group of primary teachers chaired by Johannah Raffan, in particular the 'Motorway Project', 'The Village of Eddington' and 'Townscapes' There were, however, many other 'enrichment' materials available at that time which were decidedly not cognitively enriching providing most frequently accelerated content – content which the pupil would meet at a later stage in his or her school career.

Critical thinking theory as a background to cognitive process teaching methods

Critical thinking is the art of thinking about your thinking so as to make it more precise, accurate and relevant, consistent and fair (Paul 1990). This had been described as metacognition by Flavell in 1979. He argued that thinking about how we are thinking and learning whilst we are doing so contributes in a major way to intelligence. Thus if we can promote metacognitive activities especially in those who would not normally use them we could in these terms be likely to be promoting and enhancing peoples' intelligence or at least their intelligent action.

Apparently most education world-wide is geared to inducing monological thinking which is single track and context defined because of the overuse of didactic teaching methods whereas critical thinking is recommended (Chapter 11).

In schools and colleges around the world instructional practice presupposes a didactic theory of knowledge and learning and literacy. Despite the fact that we know that these methods are particularly unsuitable for pupils, according to Rogers and Span (1993) they are still widely used. This is also despite the fact that employers in the developed nations now realise that they must increasingly produce workers who can think critically, who can reason and work in a flexible and creative manner (Stonier 1983).

The nature of cognitive process pedagogies

Cognitive process pedagogies are the core of developmental differentiation and enable it to be achieved. Cognitive process teaching methods are based in critical thinking theory and are the means by which higher order thinking and metacognitive skills can be developed through the curriculum. However before change could take place the central objectives in teaching had to be re-evaluated and were redefined as follows:

- to enable students to think efficiently, and
- to express those thoughts succinctly.

The Cognitive Process Pedagogies:

- Games and simulations;
- Cognitive study skills;
- Real problem solving and investigative learning;
- Experiential learning;
- Collaborative learning;
- Language experience methods.

In order to assess the cognitive level achieved by the methods and materials which were developed for the classroom trials Bloom's (1956) taxonomy of cognitive objectives was used and an emphasis was placed upon operations at the three higher levels of analysis, synthesis, and evaluation.

Games and simulations

Over the last 20 years there has been a growing acceptance of games as a teaching technique particularly in High School and in Business Studies and Management Programmes at Universities. They are, however, equally valuable in schools although they are mostly used in remedial education for literacy difficulties. Recently, however, computer program games have been developed which encourage and develop thinking skills through the pursuit of a game e.g. Dungeons and Dragons.

In the non-simulation game students work in groups and have to know certain facts, perform skills or demonstrate mastery of specific concepts to win or be successful. The participants agree objectives and there are sets of rules to obey. Typical of this form is the card game which can be adapted to educational purposes such as 'Phonic Rummy', 'Alphabet Snap' and so on.

Simulation games contain the elements of real situations and students individually or in groups interact with and become part of the reality. Role playing is often an important feature of the game. For example, in working with a class of children on the problems of bullying or stealing it is often very useful to organise small group work role play so that individuals can practice expressing their own and others' feelings about the subject as well as analyse the issues and suggest solutions or resolutions of the problem. Characteristic of all games is that they must be followed by a debriefing session to discuss what transpired so that educational and metacognitive objectives are achieved (see Chapter 11).

Cognitive study skills

The following examples can apply to textual, visual and performance material.

- Locating the main points and subordinate ones;
- Flow charting;
- Completion activities;
- Prediction activities;
- Sequencing;
- Comparing and contrasting;
- Drafting and editing;
- Organising – tabulating, classifying, ordering, diagramming, categorising;
- Drawing inferences and abstractions;
- Recognising intent, bias and propaganda;
- Planning;
- Managing one's learning and keeping it on task and on schedule.

Cognitive study skills are a form of self directed learning and frequently involve active work on textual material. Although reading skills are taught in primary school it is not usual to teach higher order reading and cognitive skills there or in secondary school, although they are considered to be essential to the educated person and a requirement for success in higher education. Even able children do not automatically develop them.

However it is very important to incorporate study skills into all curriculum subject areas rather than try to teach them as a separate skills course. Bolt-on provision has been shown to be ineffective and non-transferable (Thomas, *et al.* 1984, Meek and Thomson 1987, Weinstein *et al.* 1988). Examples may be found in Chapter 9.

Real problem solving and investigative learning

Human nature is such that if you present a person with an open-ended situation in which the answer to a problem is not given the mind automatically tries to solve the problem and make closure unless it is ill. This notion of the human as scientific problem solver and investigator from birth was put forward by Kelly (1955). Although not everything can be converted into a problem there is considerable scope for doing so across the curriculum.

There needs to be plenty of content material around to research to help develop ideas and strategies or verify solutions. Because the activities start from the children's own ideas and knowledge each is building up their own cognitive structures and knowledge hierarchies and can interrogate the various sources. The teacher in this setting is not only the interactive resource but the manager and facilitator of learning (see Chapter 11). Some examples are:

- Design problem solving and technology – Using one broadsheet newspaper and half a metre of sticky tape, design a house big enough to sit in.
- In Physical Education – Using four different parts of the body move from one side of the room to the other and over one piece of apparatus. Then with a partner use four parts between you to get back again.
- In History – You are a master builder in mediaeval England. A local merchant would like a house built on the main street, consistent with her wealth and status.
- In English – Pairs of children were set to produce a holiday brochure for their town or suburb. They began with an analysis of the style, content and format of typical holiday brochures.
- In Science – In the context of the study of solvents and solutions the children were given an envelope whose contents they must investigate. It is clearly a mixture, but of what? (sand and salt). Could it be harmful?

Experiential learning

It is suggested that learning is not circular, returning the learner to the same point each time, as in the Kolb (1984) learning cycle. Instead, at each turn, the experience, the talking about the experience and the reflecting upon the learning and doing adds to the sum of knowledge and changes the processes and the understanding in an additive way. In the first cycle the talk is about the content and method of what was learnt and in the second cycle the learners reflect upon the ways in which the learning was accomplished, this is the metacognitive level and the result is a *learning spiral* (Montgomery 1994), progressing from surface to deep learning (Marton and Saljo 1984).

Experiential learning involves learning by doing or *action learning*. It is surprising how much students in schools and colleges remain passive in the learning process and yet how much more effective their learning could be if they were direct participants.

Although learners may often learn without direct experience by observing and modelling others, and able learners can be particularly adept at this, this does not mean that direct experience is not useful. The experience does, however, have to be cognitively challenging otherwise it is no more than other mundane activities.

Collaborative learning

Collaboration means that students work with each other towards the framing and design of problems and strategies as well as in their resolution or solution. Each contributes some part to the whole. Quite often the process is called 'cooperative learning'. Either term is appropriate but frequently what is meant to be cooperative or group work is no more than pupils sitting together doing individual work. In Britain it is common to find students sitting in groups of four to six working round tables in both primary and secondary schools. Research studies showed that interactions within the groups were mainly between children of the same sex and not related to the task in hand (Galton *et al.* 1980, Bennett 1986). Pupils in groups on average spent two thirds of their time on individual work interacting with no one. Only 5 per cent of the time was spent talking about the task and then it was likely to be requests for information. It was in fact the exception rather than the rule to find a group working as one. Bennett's studies which recorded the task in detail showed that little of the talk which did take place was task-enhancing. The influence of peer tutoring and constructive peer tutoring can thus be said to be negligible. This does not devaluate collaborative group work. What is at fault is the method of pedagogy used by the teacher which does not induce or create a need for group problem solving or group work.

Using a computer programme to provide decision making tasks Bennett observed triads of children in homogeneous and heterogeneous groups and found that the high attaining children understood the decisions and attained 95 per cent success rate whichever type of group they worked in. Thus working with average and low attainers did not damage their capacity for achievement, a concern which has frequently been raised.

Language experience methods

Many strategies may be used here. The common theme is that the learners explain, recall, dictate or scribe the material from their own experiences which then becomes the subject or topic for discussion and reading material as they write their own books. Students find it motivating to hear, read or see their own work performed and are encouraged to develop it further extending their language skills on a number of fronts. See also Chapter 8.

Summary

It is proposed on the basis of research and development work in schools and colleges that in order to meet the needs of all children in both heterogeneous and homogeneous classes more attention should be paid to methods of curriculum differentiation. The methods should directly address the development of higher order cognitive and metacognitive skills within all curriculum subjects and be developed as a whole-school policy. The key method of differentiation proposed was developmental differentiation which was found suitable for whole-class teaching in more formal settings.

Bloom's taxonomy was proposed as a useful assessment tool in association with the development and use of cognitive process teaching strategies based in critical thinking theory. These methods did offer cognitive challenge in ordinary curriculum contents and this was verified by both the pupils and the teachers.

Overall if provision were more flexible and not locked into age cohort progression and teacher directed study it would be possible to plan for wider differences in learner's needs. It ought to be possible for any pupil in school to follow not only the mainstream provision but also where needed remedial, distance and self-directed programmes of study. The organisation of rooms, resources and tutelage would need to be better integrated with programmes of study negotiated between teachers and learners rather than being wholly teacher directed and curriculum led. The crucial factor here would be to find time in already over-filled programmes. How this can be achieved will be considered in later chapters.

SECTION TWO

The nature of effective learning and teaching

In Section Two *general curriculum principles and practices*, drawn up from the needs identified in the underfunctioning groups, are applied to the teaching and learning of the *core skills* in speaking and listening, writing and reading, study skills, thinking and problem solving, number difficulties and social and behavioural difficulties. There are separate chapters on each of these subjects.

Lower attainment and underfunctioning, it has been suggested, is a much more widespread phenomenon than has generally been perceived and has many different origins. A range of approaches is therefore necessary to address the problems. In particular these approaches need to be undertaken across the curriculum subjects by staff working as teams from an agreed policy base. These approaches are described and applied in cross curricular skills.

A modest change in teaching methods will be required from interactive teaching to a mix of methods, the cognitive process pedagogies and tactical lesson planning. The majority of the methods may be applied in whole-class teaching illustrating developmental differentiation. Some strategies are also applicable to individual and small group work and can be undertaken as the teacher goes round the class engaging in PCI – Positive Cognitive Intervention.

Effective learning

These notes illustrate the nature of learning and learners' needs of which the teaching methods described in the following chapters have to take account. Significant advances have been made in the theory of acquisition of learning which show the kinds of learning processes we need to elicit and keep running in order for learners to attain competent performance. De Corte (1995) identifies seven key principles:

- *Learning is constructive* – the most fundamental. This means that pupils are not passive recipients of information. In order to learn they have to participate in the construction of their own knowledge and skills. This he contrasts with the implicit view current in teaching practice that it is the transmission and passive absorption of knowledge gained and institutionalised by past generations.

- *Learning is cumulative* and it is on the basis of what they already know that pupils construct new knowledge and derive new meanings and skills.
- *Learning is best when self-organised.* Here de Corte relates this to the metacognitive nature of effective learning especially the managing and monitoring of learning activities.
- *Learning is generally goal oriented* although a small amount of learning is incidental. An explicit awareness of and orientation towards a goal facilitates effective and meaningful learning especially when the learners can choose the goal and define their own objectives.
- *Learning is situated.* This means that learning essentially takes place in interaction with the social and cultural environment (Resnick 1994). It follows that learning which is collaborative is more effective because the interactions can induce and mobilise reflection and thus foster the development of metacognitive knowledge and skills.
- *Learning is individually different.* Individual differences in ability, skills, needs, interests and learning style mean that we each construct our learning of the same experience in different ways. Different learning styles, for example whether a deep approach or a surface approach is adopted (Marton and Salgo 1984), can mean very different learning outcomes. If a deep approach is adopted, in which the student searches for meaningful relations, this learning will be more effective than if the learner had focused solely on memorising the information – a surface strategy.
- *Effective learning is usually collaborative.*

Teaching methods which have bound into them an automatic recognition and fostering of the principles of human learning as described above will be far more effective than didactic methods and will provide greater opportunities for differentiation at all levels of ability. In the following chapters an attempt is made to show how these principles can be applied in the practice of *teaching for learning.*

Chapter 5

Speaking and listening

Introduction

The Bullock Report (1975) first indicated that there had been insufficient attention to speaking and listening skills in classrooms at both primary and secondary level. In 1987, The National Oracy Project was set up to help teachers improve pupils' skills and the more recent annual reports of the Chief Inspector (Woodhead 1996, 1997) duly state that there have been some improvements.

In 50 classroom observations by experienced teachers using a modified Flanders Classroom Interaction Analysis it was found that teacher talk was still at a level of 70 per cent of the time, that there was very little open questioning and mainly one word answers from the pupils (LDRP 1998). Little would have appeared to change since the 1970s in this small but diverse sample.

Despite requiring more pupil talk in classrooms the problem of how to achieve this by increasing legitimate talking is rarely addressed. If for example there are 30 pupils and they are all to have an opportunity to do short presentations to the rest then it means that an awful lot of listening has to be done by the other 29, probably when they would learn more from listening to the teacher. The preparation and the presentation is usually the best quality learning experience for the one doing it. Pupils do like hearing each others' presentations and are generally prepared to give each other a chance to be heard but then the talk has to be interesting and not go on for too long.

Similar problems can exist with respect to questioning. Teachers are asked to engage in more open-ended questioning but if they do they will get extended answers and some very long ones indeed so that even the best behaved of the other pupils can become restive. The more disadvantaging the environments from which the pupils come the less likely it is that they have had any training in listening, inhibiting their impulsive responses and turn taking. The more likely it is that the longer anyone else talks, including the teacher, the more they will become frustrated and will shout out or switch off and do other things.

Teachers who do not maintain good discipline can cause normally well behaved pupils to regress to these immature and egocentric levels (Montgomery 1984).

The lower the pupils' self-esteem the more they need the opportunity for talk for it is when people listen that we become significant and have meaning and purpose in our own eyes. There is nearly always someone to listen when we have a real problem to disclose but children and adults need the comfort of the active listener. It is particularly sad that many children are not given opportunities at home every day to be listened to. It is therefore not surprising that many of them spend a great deal of their time in school and in class in what is termed 'social talk' unrelated to any aspect of the curriculum. In this off-task talk they are satisfying very basic emotional needs.

What all these pupils need is an opportunity to engage in legitimised talk directed towards curriculum activities or towards personal and social skills activities where this is appropriate. Such talk is not possible where the teacher uses interactive or expository methods and then gives individual work to complete such as note taking, question answering in writing, narrative or imaginative writing. In didactics the communications are all routed through the teacher and only one person can be listened to and responded to at any time, a unichannelled communication system. However, where expositions are short and pupils are frequently paired for work activities there can be many listeners and many speakers and a quiet working noise. Reframing traditional curriculum presentations can also contribute to an increase in pupil talk and can be developed for different audiences.

The wording of some of the History curriculum exemplars indicate very clearly through the vocabulary used the speaking and listening intent but words like 'retell' may really mean, 'write it down':

Level 1. Retell the story of the Gunpowder Plot.
Level 2. Explain why Boudicca fought the Romans. Talk about life in a Viking village in comparison with today.
Level 3. Describe changes over time. Give reasons for an historical event.
Level 4. Describe different features of an historical situation.
Level 5. Distinguish between different types of historical change
Level 6. Understand that change and progress are not the same.
Level 7. Recognise that peoples' ideas and attitudes are often related to their circumstances.
Level 8. Understand the relative importance of several linked causes.

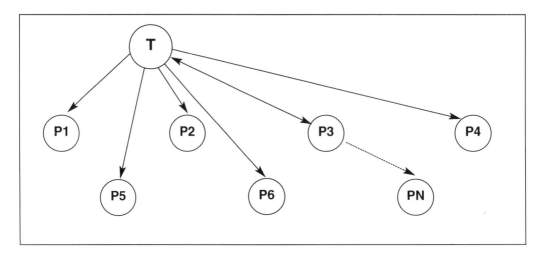

Figure 5.1a Unichannelled communication situation

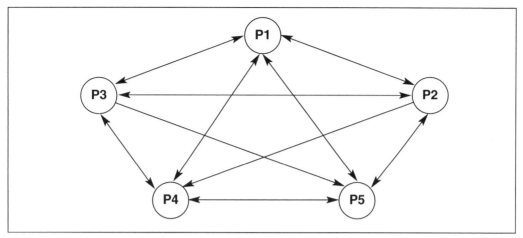

Figure 5.1b A complete communication network of a small study group

In Figure 5.1a only pupil 3 is being allowed to answer and all the responses of the rest are being suppressed by the teacher or inhibited by the pupils. If the question was 'retell the story of the Gunpowder Plot' then we should get a digest of some of what had been learned and the teacher might go as far as asking the same question of two or three more if the first answer had been very brief. Next he or she might ask for additional details and reasons before setting the pupils to write it all down, to answer the set questions on the worksheet or in the text book at the end of the chapter. The pupils might question why after hearing it, reading about it, and speaking it they are asked to write it all down. After all there is a very good version in the text book already. The question of 'what relevance is all of this to me' might very well be raised.

Despite good intentions it is possible for some pupils to spend days and weeks in formal classrooms without participating orally. Nicholas was such an example. He was an average 13 year old who had a mild speech impairment and needed opportunities to extend his verbal capabilities without being taunted. He was shadowed for a whole day through eight lessons with different teachers and the only occasion on which he was spoken to was at 3 o'clock in the afternoon when a teacher tetchily told him to pay attention. At no time was he asked a question and only put his hand up to answer after another pupil had been selected.

Listening skills may receive even less attention than is given to speaking since there are few indications that it is taking place. Even if the pupils are silent they may be somewhere else in their heads. Some may sit in silent, vacant reverie. Even when they do listen the main ideas may be missed. It is quite amazing, when asking a group of pupils or adults to listen to a short extract and then identify the main points, how many different main points, so called, they can come up with and defend in some way. In fact it is marked that so often the main point we think we have made so carefully is entirely missed. Listening is to a large extent selective. We pick out those things we want to hear or which have some appeal to us.

Learning to listen can begin or be lost very early on in school. When asked a question young children and immature or undisciplined pupils find it very difficult to inhibit their first, often motor response (Luria 1973). The science teacher explained to his difficult year 8 group that they needed to pound the fibres in the pestle and mortar in order to start making paper. Immediately six of them banged their fists on the table to imitate the pounding act and broke out into an excited babble.

Luria gives the example of the typical six year old's response to the following problem:

If Jane has 3 apples and Jack has 3 more than Jane, how many have they together?

The first response is usually '6' until they are asked to think again about the three conditions of the problem rather than the apparent two. The sum is 3 plus 3 plus 3. In learning to inhibit their first response they are on the early stages of the development of thinking skills in which they pause and stop to think around the problem and look at all the conditions, in this case the key word 'more' has to be identified.

Some examples of speaking and listening activities

Story

Listening to a story every day is a good training for listening especially when the teacher uses prediction activities and open ended questions to encourage thinking about what has been heard. Pupils of all ages can enjoy story sessions.

Target – Expand – Contract (TEC)

There are many ways of using this strategy across all curriculum areas and it can be used in part or in full. De Bono (1983) illustrated the technique by suggesting as a training strategy that individuals in a group are first asked to talk for thirty seconds about Noses. The others are asked to listen and then identify the targets in the speaker's thinking. For example the speaker will often describe a selection from the physiognomy of noses, their function, their shapes, animal noses, noses in history, physical anthropology of noses and even their friend's or husband's nose. Several pupils can be invited to do this even as young as five years old and as each does so their targets can be elicited and noted on the board. The list of targets can then be individually examined and further information gathered on each one. This can be recorded as a concept map for example (Figure 5.2). In topics on the senses, mammals or people TEC can be a useful way of starting from where the pupils are and what they know so that it is all brought up to consciousness ready for new information to be integrated into it.

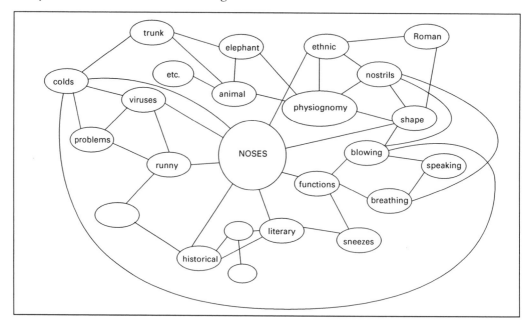

Figure 5.2 Example of a concept map on noses (partly completed)

The Expansion stage can be appropriately extended by individuals and pairs electing to pursue research into three of the targets. The first two could be teacher supported with information on structure and function and the third might be a target of their choice which is textually, video and/or CD-ROM based so they can learn or practice their research skills. The final section, Contract, is where the main points of what has been learnt are summarised. Here the general targets can be recorded as well as some key specific targets from within each.

Oral presentations

The range of topics for practising the speaking, listening and thinking skills is endless. Some examples are: Fish, castles, feet, roads, rivers, water, money, idols, totems, kings, suns, stars, violins, paints, colours, light, paper, news, cars, settlement, television, trainers, tribes, weather, etc.

When pupils are set to research material for a topic they very often approach the task at a superficial level looking for clue words and then writing notes from the textbook into their own work books without any of the content making an impression on them. They can even talk about something else entirely. Note taking therefore needs to be taught first as well as how to give a short presentation. They can then assemble notes under side headings such as topic title, main idea/theme supporting information, conclusion.

Goldisocks and the three bears; aural cloze

Rawlings (1996) provides a useful example of a listening game which can be played with children as young as three years old and up to seven. It can be a model for other games using curriculum material. The story of Goldilocks and the three bears is well known to young children so that when errors are introduced into the story such as: deciding to go for a pork; Goldisocks; 'who has been eating my potatoes' and so on, they can easily identify the errors. As the pupils identify each error a piece of a cardboard cut out of a bear is put up on an outline of a bear. By the end of the story the whole bear should have been reconstructed on the outline.

As well as stories, any description of an object such as a boat, a fish, a leaf, a mammal, a chair, a map and so on can become the subject of such an exercise. It is a more amusing variant of the use of *cloze* procedure, in which words are omitted at regular intervals such as every fifth or seventh word, and not only helps develop careful and consistent listening but also gives an indication of the level of comprehension especially where the pupil's response is to note down the correct words in their books for checking later.

In story time the teacher frequently uses a *prediction* strategy to ask 'What do you think is going to happen next?' Older pupils might be encouraged after such an introduction to take an extract and in discussion with a partner try to develop some amusing errors of their own. This can lead on to a study of humour in text, on radio or TV.

Feelie bags and taped sequences

These techniques have been used by teachers for decades but deserve a wider application than in a few infant and junior classrooms.

Feelie bags may contain several items. The pupil plunges in a hand to feel an object and has to guess what it is he or she is holding. If instead the pupil is asked to describe the object being held to the group or class so that they build up the clues and can guess what the object is, this can help extend their skills. Young pupils enjoy taking turns at this and can with practice become efficient at giving good descriptions. This can be followed up by using the description given to weave into a story about some adventure. The story may be better developed if having described their items pairs work together and design a story round their artifacts. This shared experience can then be transferred at the appropriate moment to drafting the story on the word processor together.

Maths teachers often put shapes into feelie bags for pupils to describe and practice accuracy in the use of new mathematical vocabulary.

Taped sequences are also a popular item for developing listening skills and developing story lines. Brooks *et al.* (1987) for example produced a commercial tape for this purpose in their workpack on oral skills. It is fairly easy to produce a tape with three to eight sounds in sequence on it. The sounds might include a running tap, a door banging or creaking shut, and owl noise, a car starting or driving off and screeching to a halt, a siren coming and then going into the distance, a car horn, a bicycle bell, a cup being put down in a saucer, a bottle being emptied into a glass, a seagull crying, a cat purring and a dog barking and so on.

The pupils are asked to listen to the chosen selection and as each occurs try to write down the name or nature of what they heard. Young children will need to say aloud what they have heard if they are not yet able to write. The tape can be repeated until they can identify all the sounds and they can count the number of tries which they needed to get the whole list correct. They may then weave a story round five out of the selection of eight using the strategies suggested.

Circle time

Circle time (Curry and Bromfield 1994) has become increasingly popular in schools since the early 1980s. It involves the pupils sitting round in a circle on chairs without desks or tables in front of them. This was frequently the discussion-seminar format chosen in higher education. Notes can be taken if necessary but the purpose is to enable all the participants to have eye contact and to have direct communication in the complete communication network. Pupils cannot hide behind desks and all their body attitude can be seen. Because each is sitting side by side with peers and not exactly opposite a single individual the face to face encounter which can precipitate confrontation is dissipated. Confrontation is also dispelled by the widest distance being between those who are more or less opposite each other.

General rules for the conduct of circle time workshops need to be established, for example:

- Everyone has a right to be heard and a duty to listen.
- There should be no 'put downs'. In the first stages it may be that the rule should be that all statements made should be positive.
- Everyone has the right to pass.
- Everything said should be confidential unless otherwise agreed.

The Personal and Social Education (PSE) curriculum might be the focus for some circle time activities in which a bullying subculture might be the target. It might also be used to help gain insight into general dealings with people and their roles; to gain and maintain mutual respect amongst peers; to raise self-esteem through affirmation, understanding and support; to develop positive discipline; to give training in social skills, problem solving and conflict resolution. It has a wide range of applications in the school and work context for creating a friendly forum for any participant to discuss problems as and when they arise and to develop resolution strategies and examine their effectiveness.

Bowers and Wells (1988), and Rawlings (1996) in working with and developing their circle time materials for inservice education have trialled and demonstrated their effectiveness in a variety of primary and secondary schools. In various funded projects they have shown that their strategies were effective in gaining and improving positive discipline; improving pupils' social, communication and collaborative skills; facilitating problem solving and conflict resolution. Many of these changes were not amenable to the measuring devices of the researcher over short test periods (Saunders 1988) as in the Headstart programme (Weikart 1967). Even where the possibilities for measurement of improvement were not available teachers recorded the benign effects on their classes so that their LEA funded further training in a wider range of schools.

At the simplest level circle time might begin by asking the pupils to form a circle with their chairs facing inwards and then sit on them, no desks between. Can they achieve this on another occasion in complete silence. To get them concentrating, if they know the alphabet they can then be asked to arrange themselves in first name alphabetical order round the circle from a point the teacher fixes as A. The rules are that it must be done in silence, with only one pupil moving at a time. To signify intent to move a pupil may stand up but only three may stand at any time.

After the task is completed an open discussion should be encouraged so that they can reflect upon their strategies for doing the task, and also to share their thoughts on what they were thinking as it was going on. Discuss what were the difficult aspects and what were the easy ones.

Complete the circle time session by ending on a positive note and ask each person in turn to say one positive thing about the person next round in the circle. In the next session it might be possible just to call 'circle time!' for a fairly quick assembly of the whole group in the ring. The session might then begin with a positive statement from each pupil about him or herself. Some pupils find this really difficult and others may want to criticise. This should be prevented and the discussion on this occasion should focus around the self image. Suggest, for example, that everyone is a mixture of good and bad but if we focus only on their bad parts they can come to believe themselves to be bad and then act that out. They might think about counting the 'positive strokes' and smiles they get in a day from others. They could then record how many positive strokes and smiles they give to others and look at the relation between them. They can discuss how they feel when they receive some genuine praise and what its general effect is. From this it can lead on to a circle time in which they share a best success event.

The key strategies in circle time are based according to Bowers and Wells (1988) on the Iceberg Principle in which *conflict resolution* or *problem solving* is the tip of the iceberg (an island, or hippopotamus in other cultures according to Rawlings 1996). The other three are the submerged, supportive base and are: *affirmation* – valuing each other; *communication* – understanding each other through speaking and listening or writing and reading; and *cooperation* – helping each other. These three are also the essential bridge building skills in conflict resolution and to make these points they can be represented in various ways pictorially so that the pupils can have some record and reference points.

At the level of conflict resolution there are important *problem solving* questions which are asked and there are definite steps in the problem solving procedure. These questions are in order:

- What happened?
- How do you feel about it?
- What would you like to see happening?
- What could you actually do?

People in general tend to move straight from the problem to the solution or resolution without ever examining the feelings and the options. Having established this protocol with the pupils it provides a schema for more general problem solving which can be useful. For example some pupils did use the strategy with peers to help resolve playground conflicts. There are indeed schools which have developed mediators in each class who will take on such a role in minor conflicts in and outside the classroom and this is much appreciated in particular by their younger peers. They also are trained when to refer a problem directly to the coordinating member of staff.

Mediation

The mediation process has a defined series of steps and has come to prominence recently to help in cases of disputes between neighbours and in marital breakdown rather than introduce the lawyers and further conflict. Mediators in these more formal settings must have had specific training. The general stages followed are similar to the problem solving steps: defining the problem; expressing feelings; creating options; setting goals; and evaluating outcomes. The mediator in this formal situation is an outsider, a neutral third party whose job is to conduct the session and move the participants through the stages rather than giving advice and taking sides. At the end, after all the options have been considered and a particular course is agreed, it is recorded and made into a specific plan with a time frame. The parties sign the agreement and a date is set to evaluate what has happened subsequently. This strategy may be used in schools in cases where a pupil's behaviour has become problematic and a behaviour contract needs to be established to define what behaviour is acceptable and will be engaged in.

In addition to teaching problem solving schema through circle time and resolving some real world problems of pupils the general activities require other very important higher order thinking skills such as creative and analytical thinking, reflection and critical judgment, these are discussed in further detail in Chapter 11.

In classroom mediation the teacher models respect for the pupils and their views, working for change in prejudicial and unthinking stereotypes by gradually opening these up for discussion in a non-confrontational way. Pupils then do not fear 'loss of face' and loss of self-esteem through being wrong or sharing something half thought out; others will help, they will rephrase and help clarify the group's ideas and goals.

Rawlings (1996) also emphasises the importance of *play* as a valuable learning experience and learning strategy for adults as well as children. Through play individuals can relax and act more spontaneously. They may then be encouraged to broaden and deepen their range of skills and intellectual activities and being relaxed be enabled to make more creative and imaginative responses so that better solutions can arise.

Tactical organisation for increasing speaking and listening

In a five minute explanation the teacher sets the scene and asks the pupils questions. They are asked to think of a situation in which they, class X, hold some very valuable information about a gang's plan to introduce a computer virus which will cause all the banks to download their databases. In the turmoil the gang will withdraw millions of pounds from false accounts. They found the plan in a wrecked car. When they go to the police and various other authorities and the banks they are laughed at and sent away.

In groups of three the pupils are asked to discuss and note down the moral and ethical issues of doing nothing, joining in with the gang's plan, and preparing an action plan to do something which will prove effective.

After about 15 minutes the different groups can present their ideas on each of the issues, taken one at a time and after each presentation the topic can be opened up for a general discussion. By this strategy the pupils have more individual time for talk especially where the 'buzz' groups are kept small, and they can clarify their ideas and formulate a way of explaining them with their peers before sharing them with the larger group. The action plan is open-ended and offers some good opportunities for creative and analytical thinking and can bring in further discussions about the legal framework for our protest behaviours.

A similar strategy can be used but based upon current information about issues and topics contained in the newspapers and textbooks or from historical sources such as in the example which follows. Another valuable resource for discussion material and thinking strategies is de Bono's (1983) CoRT Thinking Materials which are discussed further in Chapter 11.

Situated learning

A typical way of introducing a study topic in English or history may be to ask the pupils what they might know about the forthcoming events on November 5th. Having elicited that it is bonfire night and that most of them will have some fireworks to let off or be going to an organised display close to the key date the next questions will try to probe their knowledge of why they will be doing all this. Amongst the group there will no doubt be some information for instance that the Guy burned on top was the so-called Guy Fawkes and he tried to blow up the Houses of Parliament and that was why he was burned at the stake. They may not know it was something to do with a catholic plot or in which century it occurred. Even after several teaching sessions the majority of pupils by the end of the year may retain little more than this outline. The methods of study, teacher exposition, textual research and written summaries may fail in many instances to connect with deeper levels of understanding and so it might be helpful to try some different tactics such as the following.

Ask the pupils to imagine a situation in which they belong to a religious group or sect. The group meet on a regular basis and they are becoming very concerned that the rest of the community who are not at all religious are beginning to behave aggressively towards them. As they become more fearful about the future they begin to believe everybody is against them and that the whole nation is going to the devil and is becoming evil and persecuting them. They decide that they must do something to put the situation to rights.

The pupils can then be asked in twos or threes to discuss how the group might genuinely feel, then to put themselves in the position of the majority and think how they might feel. After an open discussion of these issues ask them to return to their small group discussions for another brief period and discuss what the sect might legitimately do and what they might illicitly decide to do. When their suggestions have been drawn together and the main ones noted they can be asked to think of situations in the real world where one group, not always in a minority, try to assert their rights over others unfairly and by use of arms. There are of course many examples and it is helpful to collect these as they arise from the newspapers to supplement their reading.

Having primed them in this way it is then easier to bring the historical subject of the Gunpowder Plot into focus. It will help them analyse the political and religious context of the period and gain some understanding of the people's attitudes and actions as being a product of their time and circumstances. They might also consider what prevents a country from being torn apart today by those with different religious, or political viewpoints. By these means it is possible to help pupils move away from surface levels and superficial learning about 'the plot' towards deeper levels of understanding. Once the introductory lesson has set the scene in this way other lessons may follow the more traditional pattern but it is important to refer back at intervals to connect with the deeper levels. Moving from what pupils know and experience in their own time and comparing this with historical events aid understanding of both the past and the present.

As others see us: events seen from another standpoint

Mrs Brown (Bowers and Wells 1988) (who appears as Gatria in Rawlings 1996) is described as the nurse who looks after patients with care and kindness and is seen as an angel of mercy; the wife and mother of a family seen by her children as a nagger; seen by the children's friend Tom as ' the best cook in the world'; and by the husband as the 'girl he fell in love with'. The pupils may offer suggestions for different roles for this woman. The questions that are suggested are, Who is the real person behind these roles? What makes this same person seem so different to the different people?

After these have been discussed it is then opened out to cover such issues as: How do you think other people view you? How many different roles do you occupy? They might select one person to describe who views them in a particular way and then describe this to the class or their partner. The listener then has to decide who it is who sees them thus.

Having practised different ways of looking at the same person it may be helpful to extend this idea to looking at a new situation or event from different viewpoints. This can translate to examining the front pages of four different newspapers to examine the way they treat the same story to draw out facts, opinion, propaganda and bias (Montgomery 1985, 1996).

In each example it will be seen that the teacher begins with a model and then the pupil's own experience before moving to external relations and issues. From here, or more directly, it is possible to move to looking at historical events from different human perspectives and different social, economic and political perspectives. In support of this it is often possible to draw on literature of the period to add contextual detail. Thus Defoe's description of the plague, later reworked by Camus in *La Peste*, and Pepys' description of the Fire of London and his work at the Admiralty can provide useful contemporary data. Much of this may be found on audiotapes at the local library as well as illustrated and described in collections of historical sources and artifacts.

Sacheverel Sitwell wrote revised versions of a number of well-known stories in which the behaviour of the key person was quite different from that in the original story. For example he wrote about Cinderella as always moping about and complaining, crouching over the kitchen fire whilst her kindly stepmother and stepsisters tried to help her and persuade her to enjoy herself. In the Ways and Means books, Bowers and Wells (1988), and Rawlings (1996) give the example of the Maligned Wolf based on the story of Little Red Riding Hood. The wolf is good and kind and busy keeping the forest clean when he sees a suspicious looking little girl all dressed up in a weird red outfit . . .

Observation, accurate reporting and stereotypes

It has long been known in psychological experiments that people of all ages are very inaccurate when reporting something they have actually seen. It is usually studied under the title of the 'witness phenomenon'. Only recently on Radio 4 a broadcaster described attending his first lecture by an American professor who in an introduction on the law, truth and the witness, had arranged to start the lecture and then a woman would walk into the room up to his desk, fire a blank from a starting pistol and then make a quick exit by the same route. When the students were asked what they had seen occur their reports varied widely. Three men, two men, a man and a woman were seen to enter and run about to different areas of the room issuing all manner of threats. They discharged a rifle, shot at the professor, all fired hand guns, and left by various doors and windows. Not one student training for the bar was able to give an accurate description of what had been seen. The broadcaster had apparently decided to quit the profession there and then in despair.

Many of us have arranged similar demonstrations in psychology and education classes in which the well known faculty secretary comes in and hands over a life-like dummy gun to the tutor or two students rush in and grab the lecturer's notes and make off. Video clips may also be shown of hostile events on a tube train, and extracts from audio tapes or films may be run. On each occasion there are similar reporting results from the audience, a general failure to note the critical turn of events. If the tape is rerun the chances are that the information given will be more accurate but much of the intermediate detail is still wrong or in the wrong order. Subjects will then tend to fill this in from their imagination rather than say that they cannot remember. Similar results are found in memory span experiments where items may be remembered in the middle but their sequence is lost. As information overload increases whole segments may be lost. After the reporting phase subjects may truly believe what they said they saw. Other settings may derive from incidents in shops, the playground, coffee bars, and so on.

Simple demonstrations of these propensities may be built upon and the principles extended to any levels of scientific, historical, geographical, artistic, technological and literary levels of the curriculum. By these discussions it is established that what we see is often more what we know or wish to see than what actually happened. It can also be used to illustrate that we are all to some extent psychological prisoners of our culture and our time in history.

Each session should, however, contribute in some measure to improving a pupil's powers of observation from events, pictures, texts, videos, and tapes. The first part of the strategy is to attend carefully and not to allow the mind to drift. Extracts from critical sections of detective stories on audio tapes from the public library can provide the material for this and even capture the pupils' interest sufficiently to borrow the readings for themselves. Learning to *remain alert* when listening to a description and then *flagging the main cues* and key aspects of a *sequence* described can help support later recall. When the basic outline is correctly remembered then other items can be attached to this basic structure being careful only to report *fact* rather than opinion and imagining. Further work may be found on this aspect in the chapter on study skills.

Analysis of rumour

This is an extension of the witness phenomenon. Three pupils are asked to volunteer to sit outside the classroom or in another room for five minutes to wait for their turn to listen to a piece of prose and repeat it. Inside the classroom another volunteer is identified and the piece of prose is read to him or her. The following passage can be used or something shorter for primary age pupils. The essentials are that it should contain some specialist terminology and details a little outside the majority of the pupils' experience.

The story should be read fairly slowly and only once. No questions for clarification should be allowed. When it has been read to the first pupil, one of the other volunteers should be brought in and the first pupil should retell the story to the next person giving as much detail as possible. After this number three should be brought in and is told the story by number two and so on.

The Thames Sailing Barges and 20 smacks were all assembled off Osea Island for the Blackwater Barge and Smack Race of 1997. There were three different classes of spritsail barges, with the start being staggered so that the slowest ones went first and the fastest last. The course was down the river and out into the North Sea and round the Bench Head outer buoy and back. The starts took place every 30 minutes and the smacks went last as a group. They also included a set of Bawleys, Winkle Brigs and other 'old gaffers'.

I say 'assembled' but we were sitting out on Nellie, a stumpie rigged barge, near the start and there were barges and smacks going in all directions trying to raise their sails and beat up to the start line between the official boat and Osea pier so as to arrive at the 'mark' on time without gaining penalty points for slipping over it too soon. The warning gun came for the final barge class and there were only two in the race. Our skipper called us aft to look. She said there was something strange going on between the two ninety year old 'ironpots'. Daisy, big and black with huge tan sails was seeming to go in short dashes and semicircles in front of her grey sister Ammonite. Each time Ammonite was driven further out from the start and almost onto Osea pier. As the start gun went off, Daisy was ahead but Ammonite was coming up on her quickly on the windward side piling on all canvas.

We watched the smacks set off and then followed them ourselves at a more sedate pace. As we passed the end of the island we were stunned to see Ammonite completely stuck in the middle of the river on a sand bar which had caught her on the fast ebbing tide. She had been 'luffed up' by Daisy and was now stuck there for a further 10 hours to wait until the tide came fully in again. Her crew and their paying punters looked very glum.

As each listener repeats the story the pupils will notice that it becomes significantly shorter and all sorts of errors creep in. Certain facts which the listeners latch on to may be retained throughout and come to have greater significance than in the original. As the individuals try to make sense of what they hear the meaning, the sequence and the facts may be changed. Some subjects in order to give the tale some extra interest may add their own embellishments and actually make up whole sections. Thus it is with rumour. A good discussion can usually be developed from this example.

Prisoners of time, culture and stereotype

The well known failure of the scientific and medical communities to understand and appreciate scientific leaps of creativity can be discussed and exemplified and also the bias in historical texts.

The ethnic and sexual stereotypes which have prevented all but the artistic work of white middle and upper class males to be valued until recently can be used to introduce these effects. Pupils might have heard of Holbein but although in her day Angelica Kaufmann was equally famous and earned as much money from patrons it is unlikely that any have heard of her. Tufts (1974) for example, describes five centuries of this hidden heritage illustrating it from works by Sofinisba Anguisola, Lavinia Fontana, Artimisia Gentileschi and so on.

These points about hidden heritages can be further illustrated by asking older pupils to write a list of three names of famous men painters and then three women, the same for musicians, writers, politicians, social workers, warriors, Nobel prize winners, infant prodigies and so on. Even their teachers when asked to write down six of each find it very hard to compile the list of the women in each category. The pupils' attempts can provide good discussion material and set them off on personal research to try to find a balance. Their researches can enable them to form collections of their chosen artist, designer, or musician from a particular period and then enable them to give a short presentation to the rest of the class on what they have uncovered. A class reference book can also be put together using new digital imaging, computerised techniques.

Sharing experiences and personal problem resolving in PSE

A technique often used as a a means of getting people to know each other and listen carefully is to ask them to get together in pairs and then arrange their chairs so that they can sit on them facing each other. They can be organised in a line or in a circle with a chair's space on each side to cut down interference. The pupils should then sit in their facing pairs so that their knees just touch. Their task is to tell their partner about themselves for three minutes which the teacher times. They then exchange roles of listener and speaker. Because pupils in a class may know each other very well and rely on past knowledge when they have to report back what they were told the same format can be used to ask them to describe something which caused them a problem or something which made them very happy. Alternatively they may be asked to tell their partner a story and make it fit exactly into the three minutes. They may be asked to select a film story to relate or an episode from a TV soap or saga which the other person has not seen.

Another way of using this format without sitting knee to knee but at their desks to practise speaking and listening is to ask pupils to read a section of text about a curriculum topic and then describe and explain it to their listener who may ask three questions to clarify the account when it is finished. They can take it in turns to prepare alternate sections. While one of them is doing the reading preparation the other can be writing down the key points gleaned. After two turns each the teacher can ask individuals to explain what has been learned to check that all have the main points.

Once pupils have some experience of circle time and supportive listening they can move on to a simple form of counselling support. In groups of three, pupils can be invited to share something such as an event which upset them or a problem they need to resolve. The second person in the group takes the role of listener and the task is to offer only supportive listening responses. For example, nodding and smiling at appropriate points, giving *onward* responses such as rephrasing and repeating to check understanding, summarising and saying such things as 'And then what did you do?', 'And then what happened?', 'What do you think you could do?'. The third member of the group has the role of observing the interaction and giving feedback on the types of support and listening responses given by the listener and its effect on the speaker. At the end of the session which may be kept quite short – ten minutes – the groups of three should then examine what solutions arose out of the sharing. Some groups will want to share their experiences with the larger class and perhaps gain further suggestions and support so time should be left for this. Others will not wish their shared experiences to go any further but will still be able to contribute to discussions about feelings and processes in the listening session. Each member of the triad should be encouraged to experience each of the different roles during a tutor period.

Role play and the use of drama in everyday curricular activities

Drama and role play are techniques well used in English, PSE, and Performing Arts areas and some useful examples may be found in Taylor (1993). However, these strategies can be used over wider ranges of subjects such as trust building activities in PE when peers lead, guide and catch and bear their colleagues. They can also be extended to performance based activities in history, geography and science. Just occasionally with younger pupils in science a session can develop new insights and stronger memories when the pupils act out the different densities of molecules in substances or become the blood corpuscles gathering oxygen from the lungs and delivering it via capillaries into the organs. Revision sessions might occasionally consist of groups of three or four pupils selecting a process or an experiment to act out for others to guess.

After a series of sessions on expansion I don't think we ever laughed so much as when seven, 11 year olds put sugar paper on the floor and threw themselves down onto it and then rolled and jumbled and jumped about attempting to explode all over the place to demonstrate unpricked sausages being heated in a pan and the air inside the skins expanding and exploding them. This was followed by scene two when on this occasion the cook had learned the lesson and poked them all with a ruler when they tried to keep very still, roll all together and simulate shrinking.

In other sessions when their individual work had been to write up an experiment or describe a process they would volunteer to read them out whilst the teacher or other pupils would try to follow the instructions as read. A favourite was 'you get a beaker and stand in it'.

Other strategies may begin with talks on 'How to build a . . .' or 'How to make a . . .'

while a listener has to follow the verbal instructions. The instructor may be shielded from the sight of what the listener is doing.

Compare and contrast

Very often pupils are asked to compare and contrast the approaches of different people in history or in literature; they may have to do the same task in relation to facts about, buildings, clothes, foods and so on. It can help to give some training first in these techniques. Most often the required response is to write their information down but it can be an interesting change to bring two different bicycles, rabbits, motorbikes etc. into the classroom for a compare and contrast session. So often all the ordinary detail which the listener needs is omitted whilst the observer and speaker focuses on what he or she considers the important aspect such as the differences, so that it may never become clear that it is bicycles which are being discussed.

Smaller objects can easily be shielded from the rest of the class, the listeners, but a sheet or a screen can serve equally well and create just the right amount of interested anticipation, and just occasionally there may be no need to write a report of it all but to discuss the effectiveness of verbal description as opposed to having a picture or the real object. Expertise can also be drawn upon for one bicycle may look very much like the other until the specialist intervenes. The principle of describing first what is observable before going on to similarities and differences can be a useful schema on which to build in other forms of curriculum reporting: practice such as this is often taken for granted and this leads to poor results.

Formal talk and debates

Pupils at as young an age as possible can be introduced to aspects of formal debate with proposers who speak to a motion or for a particular viewpoint and opposers against. There can also be first and second speakers and so on. Balloon debates can be a useful way of helping develop speaking and listening skills especially where something topical is selected. An example might be to identify eight characters with brief descriptions all of whom are in need of a liver transplant but there is only one available. The class then have to put forward reasons for a particular individual having the transplant. An alternative is to assign the written pen portraits to individuals in groups of eight to discuss why each one of them might be the one who should have the transplant and then gather together the points from three of four groups on each person.

Other variations of this are survivors on life rafts, food shortage on a trek across the Arctic, famous scientists and their contributions to humankind and so on.

Interviews

Families are prime sources of data for all sorts of school topics such as historical studies when older members have lived through important events in the 20th century and some may recall what their grandparents experienced in the late 19th century. Many different jobs and roles will have been undertaken by family members and some of them have spent time in other countries and can give accounts from first hand experience. Fishing families have tales, for example, which frequently go back to the days of sail and can provide a great deal of valuable information and insight into the rise and fall of the fishing industry and the pursuit of the herring and mackerel. Similar wealth of data is available in all ports around the country and in settlements on rivers. There will also be farming, and mining communities and in the towns and cities other ways in which people form identity groups such as in cultural and religious groups, sporting and social clubs, work and area groups. Pupils need first to plan what information they need to know and then to identify the questions which will reveal this information. If they plan their work in pairs then this will facilitate speaking and listening as they discuss and plan.

They should also discuss ways in which interviews may be conducted and how they can be set up formally and informally. They need to learn to understand the use of and include both *closed* and *open questions* so that in the latter they can gather up a much wider range of information which they might not have covered in their closed questions. They should also learn how short questionnaires can be constructed to obtain much of the factual data or used as a guideline to give the interview some structure. They will need to be able to sort out the relevant from the irrelevant data which they will collect and the embellished yarn from the factual account, opinion from fact and so on. All of these are useful topics for discussion as they start to sort and analyse their data.

Summary

In this chapter on speaking and listening it has been suggested that more opportunities need to be provided for talk in classrooms and that this cannot be done in the traditional formal class arrangement where only one person can be speaking at a time. Turn taking is a valuable lesson to learn but pupils need more turns if they are to begin to clarify their thinking. Because we do not always know what we think or know until we try to explain it to someone else, talking and listening can be regarded as prime learning experiences.

Some of the strategies described such as Targeting in thinking can be organised upon formal lines but many of the others require different tactics where the teacher briefly introduces the task and then pupils, usually in pairs, discuss or plan their next activities. They may then come together as a class whilst they are questioned about what they have done or they may then make a brief presentation to the rest before going on to the next level of the task. Coming together at intervals under the direction of the teacher ensures that the activities make forward progress.

Strategies such as circle time, problem solving, problem resolving, supportive listening, questioning and interviewing, role play, personal presentations, the exploration and use of artifacts are used to give examples of ways in which more speaking and listening can be planned in classrooms.

Chapter 6

Handwriting

Introduction

It is probably true to say that almost every child beginning school at five years has a problem with spelling and handwriting whereas there are a number who arrive able to read fluently. With appropriate teaching and plenty of practice the majority of pupils can become fluent writers. Whether they do or not will vary according to their interest and motivation, the method of tuition, and whether they have an additional learning problem.

There are various estimates of how much time is spent in writing in schools with many pupils thinking they spend too much time. Other than in practical subjects, pupils may spend up to 80 per cent of the school day in tasks requiring handwriting. Thus it is an important skill to be acquired and as such it has not always received adequate attention to help young writers become fluent.

The system of handwriting widely taught in England and Wales in the 20th century is a modified form of print introduced first in 1913 (Jarman 1979) which revolutionised handwriting teaching. Before this and often up until the post war period in the 1940s a form of cursive, a joined script, had been taught which Jarman termed 'civil service hand'. This was a simplified form of copperplate writing. Almost all other countries still teach a joined script from the outset of schooling whereas in England and Wales it is still common for cursive only to be introduced in the Junior schools or when the pupils become eight years old and can 'write neatly'. This means that our pupils at eight have to learn a whole replacement set of motor programmes for handwriting and because of this, in a significant number, a fully flowing cursive is never achieved. In addition there are 10 per cent or more of pupils who will have had problems in coordinating the fine motor skills required for print handwriting, who have very little chance of ever being permitted to learn cursive as they can still hardly write a sentence which can be deciphered much less write it neatly.

Developing handwriting

Although there has been a significant amount of research into the teaching of handwriting which shows that teaching cursive from reception is the most effective and efficient system (Morse, 1991; Alston, 1993; Montgomery, 1997b) very little has changed in this direction in the practices and policies of some schools. Many infant schools still teach print script, a few add ligatures to assist joining, only a few teach full flowing cursive from the outset. Those who do teach cursive from the beginning have been shown to enable the majority of their pupils to reach level three at Key Stage 1 (Morse 1991). The learning of Morse's 'Kingston Cursive' (see Figure 6.4d) was not only found to improve handwriting in the 18 schools in which it was used but it also increased the fluency and speed of the writing, enabling the pupils to express their ideas more fluently and enhanced their spelling abilities (Morse 1992). Cripps (1988, 1995) has reported similar results although the form of handwriting training he illustrates is not a full cursive with lead-in strokes.

Teaching cursive handwriting to all the pupils can thus have more widespread positive academic effects than just on handwriting. Speeding up the writing enables more thoughts to be written down and increasing fluency increases speed and reduces the physical and mental effort needed to be put into writing. As writing also involves spelling this too becomes more fluently recorded and automatic. It is therefore important that spelling teaching is also linked with handwriting and that there are developmental, and remedial strategies available for this.

Handwriting is a motor skill and benefits from being taught as such with training in speed and fluency. It is often too closely linked with news and story writing based upon early tracing and copying techniques without being given a chance for some separate development. Too often it is also treated at a later stage as an art form, as calligraphy or 'beautiful writing', rather than as a means of recording and communicating ideas. Teachers may not infrequently refuse to read the poorly formed writing of older pupils or require work to be rewritten neatly. There is in fact a tremendous pressure in classrooms at all levels for neat writing even at the expense of content. The so called 'neat' writing required is usually a version of modified print such as we might read in infant textbooks, or use to fill in job application forms.

Pupils on the whole do not deliberately write poorly and untidily (Cotterell 1985). Illegibility is an indication of their handwriting problems and various illegible squiggles may also help conceal spelling difficulties. Pupils with handwriting coordination difficulties may have such problems early on that they have experienced little practice and this of course also inhibits their ability to spell. Each spelling may have to be thought out each time instead of appearing automatically in writing. As all this engages a considerable amount of brain processing power it results in the content of the narrative being diminished. It is therefore crucial that all pupils very quickly learn a fluent style. Wedell's (1973) research showed that pupils with a coordination problem *must* use a joined script.

The print script usually taught, however, will never produce a fast flowing and efficient style because of the way in which it is constructed. Compare the examples in Figure 6.1 and try writing them first with eyes shut and then with eyes open.

Print script is more laborious to make than a continuous running hand and so less can be written in a given time. In the developmental stages of learning it is also harder to acquire. The reasons for this can easily be observed because to form the print a b c it is necessary to start each in a new place, usually 'at the top' but not always. At the finish of that letter the pen has to be lifted slightly from the page before repositioning it for the start of the next letter. Ball and stick form is even more disruptive of the act of writing. Pupils frequently regress to it as they try to 'draw' the letters the teacher gives them to copy.

For a beginner the high precision skills of positioning the pencil on an imaginary line, starting each new one afresh and making them all lie in the same direction with equal

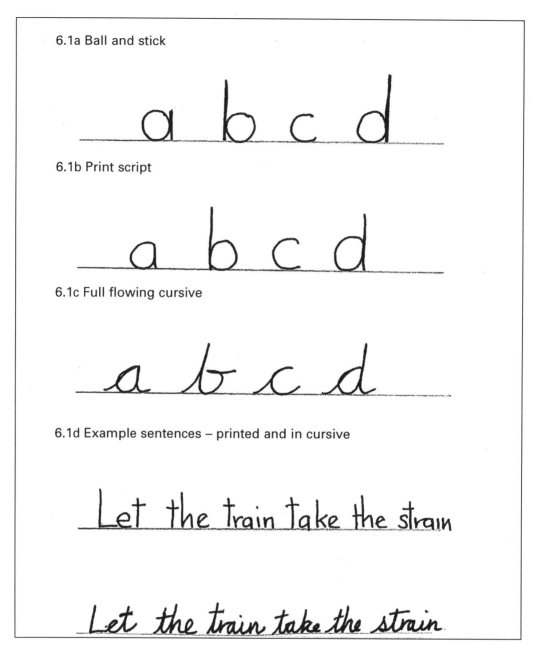

6.1a Ball and stick

6.1b Print script

6.1c Full flowing cursive

6.1d Example sentences – printed and in cursive

Figure 6.1 Examples of letters and sentences to be written first in print and then in cursive

spaces between them are not available with the results seen in Figure 6.2. Likewise pupils with even a mild coordination difficulty can find this perceptuomotor task well nigh impossible. Being made to use a print form until the pupils can 'write neatly' can result in them never acquiring a running hand and so they are handicapped by the writing curriculum and this handicaps spelling and both problems can damage learning in all subject areas where writing is required. Even the seven year olds reflecting on writing consider they are given too much of it (Figure 6.3).

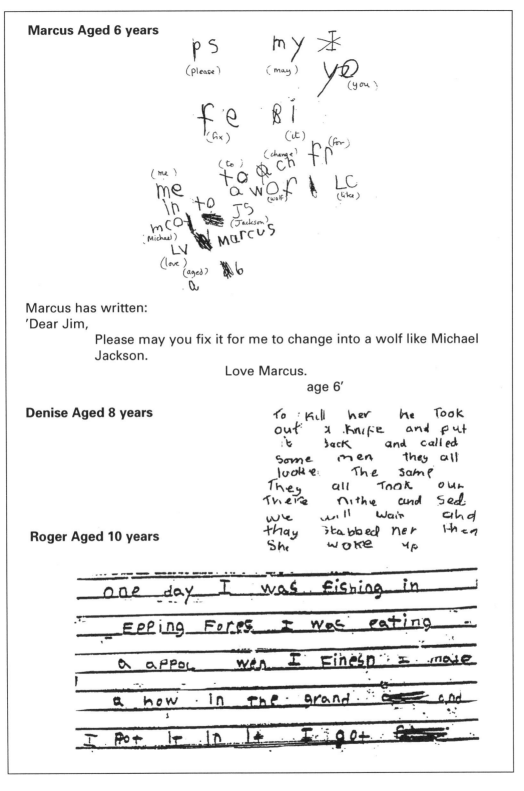

Marcus Aged 6 years

p S (please)   m y (may)   ✳ y☉ (you)

f ͬe (fix)   ß i (it)   fⁿ (for)   (change)

(me)   (to)   ͨh   (for)

me   ᵢn to   a w☉f (wolf)   ᴵ   L C (like)

m C☉ (Michael)   J S (Jackson)

L V (love)   Marcus   (aged)   ℔6

Marcus has written:
'Dear Jim,

    Please may you fix it for me to change into a wolf like Michael Jackson.

               Love Marcus.
                    age 6'

Denise Aged 8 years

To kill her he Took
out a knife and put
it back and called
some men they all
looke The same
They all Took our
There nithe and Sed.
we will wait and
thay stabbed her then
She woke up

Roger Aged 10 years

one day I was fishing in
Epping Fores I was eating
a appol wen I Finesd I made
a how in the grand and
I Pot It In It I got

Figure 6.2 Writers handicapped by learning print script (reduced in size)

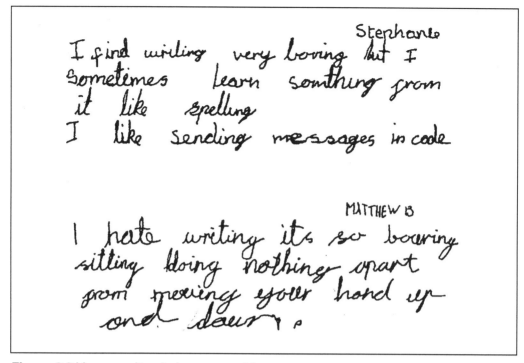

Figure 6.3 Young writers' views on writing

In a survey of secondary pupils' wrting in one school Roaf (1998) found 25 per cent of pupils unable to write faster than 15 words per minute. These were the pupils who were struggling in all lessons where a lot of writing was required. The survey suggested a close link between self concept and handwriting presentation. The majority of the slow writers showed difficulties with – motor coordination, spelling, and letter formation. A speed of 25 words per minute was regarded as a successful rate.

Thomas (1998) describes a policy adopted in her Kent infant school that the creative aspect of expressing children's thoughts is, in the first instance, developed only orally. They spend a longer time than before on developing an automatic joined hand. As a result they have seen a new quality in the creative written work. The teachers do not act as scribes and the pupils do not engage in copy writing. She compares the usual system in the UK with that which operates in France where cursive writing is a lengthy process, has high priority in schools and teacher training, begins on entry to school and takes precedence over reading, and suggests there is much to be learnt from the French experience. As the TTA supported the investigation it is likely that all schools will be involved in a similar change of practice.

Reasons for teaching cursive handwriting

Using a cursive style:

- aids left to right movement through words across the page;
- eliminates reversals and inversions of letters;
- eliminates the need to relearn a whole new set of motor programmes after the infant stage;
- induces greater fluency in writing which enables greater speed to be developed without loss of legibility;

- the motor programmes for spelling whole words, their bases and affixes are stored and so improve spelling accuracy;
- space between letters and between words is orderly and automatic;
- a more efficient, fluent and personal style can be developed;
- pupils with handwriting coordination difficulties experience less pain and difficulty;
- legibility of writing is improved;
- it reinforces multisensory learning linking spelling, writing and speaking.

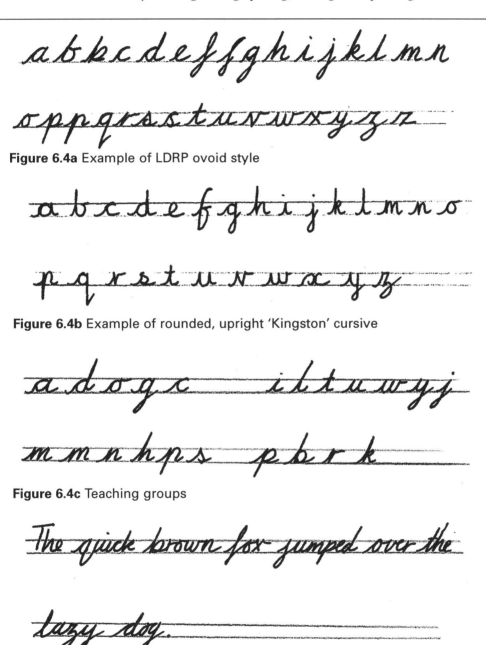

Figure 6.4a Example of LDRP ovoid style

Figure 6.4b Example of rounded, upright 'Kingston' cursive

Figure 6.4c Teaching groups

Figure 6.4d Examples of writing form

Guidelines for cursive writing teaching

- Teach the basic letter shapes as a single fluid motor movement not in copy writing or tracing.
- Teach the letters singly but encourage joining immediately in syllable units not meaningless patterns.
- Teach the letters in use order with sounds and names not in alphabetical or shape families.
- Use lined paper from the beginning and until pupils can write neatly and fluently without them and then always offer the choice of lines.
- Sometimes use double lines as above to help develop stability in body size of letters and the appropriate length of ascenders.
- Start each letter on the line with a lead-in stroke.
- Teach joining as soon as two letters with their sounds and names are known.
- Teach base words, syllables and affixes as one writing unit (phonograms) wherever possible.

Assessing first marks on paper

Put some crayons and pencils in the centre position on the group table or place them in the midline in front of the pupil. A group session rather than a class one will enable a record to be made of which hand the pupil uses for taking a writing tool and the sort of hold or grasp which is naturally used. Some may even include letters in their first scribbles.

Now ask them to copy four shapes onto the back of their paper which the teacher draws on the board as follows:

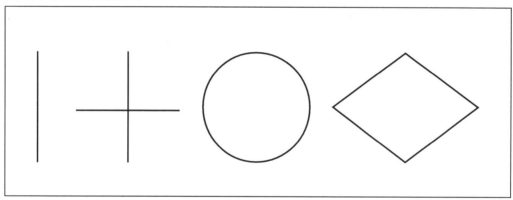

Figure 6.5 Four shapes to diagnose developmental levels of drawing other than letter shapes based on Gesell norms

These tasks give some baseline developmental assessment information to show what a young child brings to learning from home. The four shapes represent what an average child at 4.5 to 5 years can be expected to be able to draw having been shown the model. If they are unable to draw the circle and the diamond it is unlikely that they are ready to begin writing letter shapes and they will need much more scribble and pencil holding practice first.

Check to see if they can write their own names. Next tell the pupils to 'Take a pencil and make me some writing marks on paper like you have seen in the story books'. 'Write me a story or a secret message'.

Note which hand is used to take the pencil. Is this consistent? 'Now let us see if you can write your own name again.' Later they can be told, 'This is your first piece of writing. We are going to keep it and make a book. We are not going to help you with it, we want to see what you know first'. When they have finished, give praise. Encourage daily sessions of scribble and name writing as this will strengthen pencil control and develop fluency in pencil movement.

Indicators of developmental level

Hand preferences and whether established; inconsistent selection; pencil grasp; firmness of grasp or lack of it; shakiness of marks or fluency; real alphabet forms if any; ability to follow instructions; tendency only to follow or imitate others; lack of understanding of what is required are all significant indicants of where the pupils are in their development. It is then possible that each can be led to the next developmental step such as having their grip modified to the correct triangular grip or being given a pencil with a moulded grip to assist their pencil control. Hand preference can be reinforced and pupils can learn about the nature and feel of fluency.

After they have written their 'story' write the name of each pupil on their paper in cursive and ask them to try to write it underneath and observe each day whether there is any development in this ability. To do this ask them to cover up the copy and try to write their names 'from inside their heads'. This is important for them to learn and they might like to spend some time using this *look – cover – write – check technique*. It will help them scrutinise the key parts of their names and facilitate the learning of the motor programme. Some names are difficult to learn and so syllabification and short forms can be used initially.

Ask pupils to study their name carefully and then try to make it themselves without looking at the model, first of all with the forefinger in the air and then on the paper with finger paints and/or with a pencil. Let them repeat this aerial tracing (Fernald 1943) several times or more if they wish. The idea is to develop a mental image and motor programme of their own name. Tracing and copying do not necessarily do this. Some may just succeed in writing the first letter and part of the next by the end of a week. Each succeeding day this can be built upon.

Teaching for fluency in handwriting

All pupils in the early days will benefit from fluency training and strengthening exercises. Young pupils often have very bendy fingers and flexible joints. Too much pressure put upon pencils will emphasise problems but fluency training will lighten pressure. A start may be made on this process by having daily practice in finger and brush painting. In these sessions the pupils can be trained to produce rhythmical flowing lines based on hand and arm movements. It is important to ensure they use the nonpreferred hand to hold the paper still and build this habit in. In some sessions play music and try to get them to move their writing and painting strokes to the rhythm of the music. Nursery rhymes and songs can also be used to develop fluency. Especially encourage the skill of forming circle patterns as these are fundamental to writing. Help them develop the triangular grip with all the tools.

Some children will have difficulty organising their scribble to these forms. It is helpful therefore if during PE and music and movement the floor work can be directed to turning and circling. This can be further reinforced with singing games involving arm movements such as 'The wheels on the bus go round and round'.

Introducing the letter forms

After name writing practice some easier letter patterns can be given repeating letters in their names or letter-like forms. Give them lined paper on which to do this so that they can feel that it really is part of writing practice. Lines improve the look of the writing and help the pupils locate the position on the paper where they should begin the letters. It does not harm their creativity or style (Burnhill *et al.* 1975).

In a class teaching session each letter of the alphabet can be introduced for writing, not in alphabetical order but in *use order* for spelling. The most frequently used letters with power to build words quickly (Fry 1964) are **i, t, p, n, s**. These letters are those introduced first in all the APSL dyslexia remedial programmes (Hickey 1977, Cowdery *et al.* – TRTS 1983 et sequel). As well as teaching a full flowing ovoid style cursive, a multisensory training technique as shown below should be used:

- Show the cursive form of lower case letter **i** on the board.
- Explain how it is made by talking them through the letter e.g. 'Start on the line and flow up then back down and round a little. Now add the dot over the top'. Repeat this several times and ask them to join in the talk through.
- Give them the *sound* of the letter unless one of the children knows it (**i**). Talk through the letter once more and get them to do so too and say its sound as well.
- Now demonstrate the formation of the letter **i** in the air with your back to the children. Repeat with left hand for left handers.
- Each time the letter is written its sound should be spoken, that is, the short vowel sound (**i**). Introduce the idea of a key word to remember the sound e.g. imp, ink.
- Ask pupils to imitate the movement in the air altogether once and then trace it with forefinger on the table saying the sound at the same time. Repeat the sequence a few times with the class and table groups so that every pupil can be observed.
- Individuals can be asked to come and show the rest of the class how to trace it in the air.
- The teacher then writes the cursive **i** on the board and pupils can volunteer to come and write **i** next to the model but the model is always covered up, and then uncovered for matching. Small pupil sized blackboards can be very helpful now for practice.
- When pupils have the feel for the letter they can be encouraged to try it on paper.
- When they have the correct form they can then try a joined group of **i** letters, murmuring the sound as they write it (a phonological approach).

As each letter in the programme is introduced (Montgomery 1997b) in use order, this same format should be used. Other aspects of these lessons are described in the section on spelling to form the handwriting linked with spelling programme.

The right handed pupil should hold the paper down with the left hand. The paper should not be vertical but should be *tilted* at an angle of about 25–30 degrees to the right (between 4 and 5 o' clock).

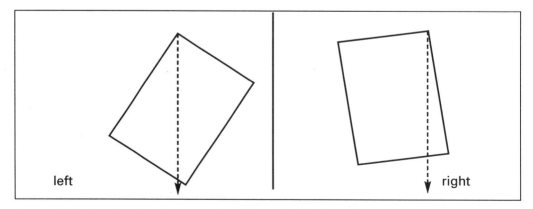

Figure 6.6a. Angles for the paper for left and right handers

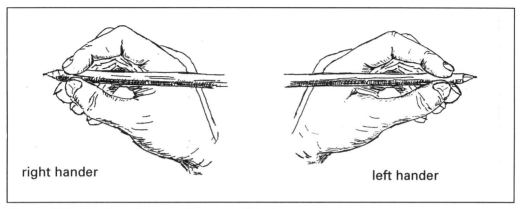

right hander

left hander

Figure 6.6b To show handwriting pencil hold

Teaching left handers

When beginning writing lessons it may be best to teach left handers as a group if there are enough of them. It is then possible to model all the activities with the left hand so that there is no confusion. Ensure that the pupil is comfortably seated with feet on the floor and both arms able to be laid on the table from the elbows. Having the correct size of furniture is essential.

The left handed pupil should hold the pencil or pen *slightly further* from the point than the right hander so that their writing is not obscured.

The paper should be held down by the right hand and should be tilted much more than for the right hander. A tilt of about 40 degrees is common. Some pupils need a tilt of 90 degrees so that their writing flows downwards. Over time each pupil will gradually find the most comfortable and legibility inducing position for themselves.

They should be encouraged to be free to experiment and take an intelligent interest in the skill.

Seating arrangements for left handers are crucial. In pairs seating, the left hander needs to sit on the left hand side of the pair to allow both pupils room to wield their pens without interference. This is more problematic where there is group seating and the chairs need to be given more space to the left of the left hander to allow for freedom of movement.

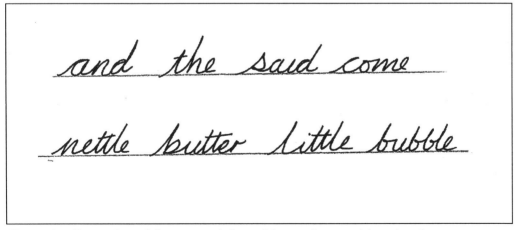

Figure 6.7 Examples of fluency training with words as writing develops

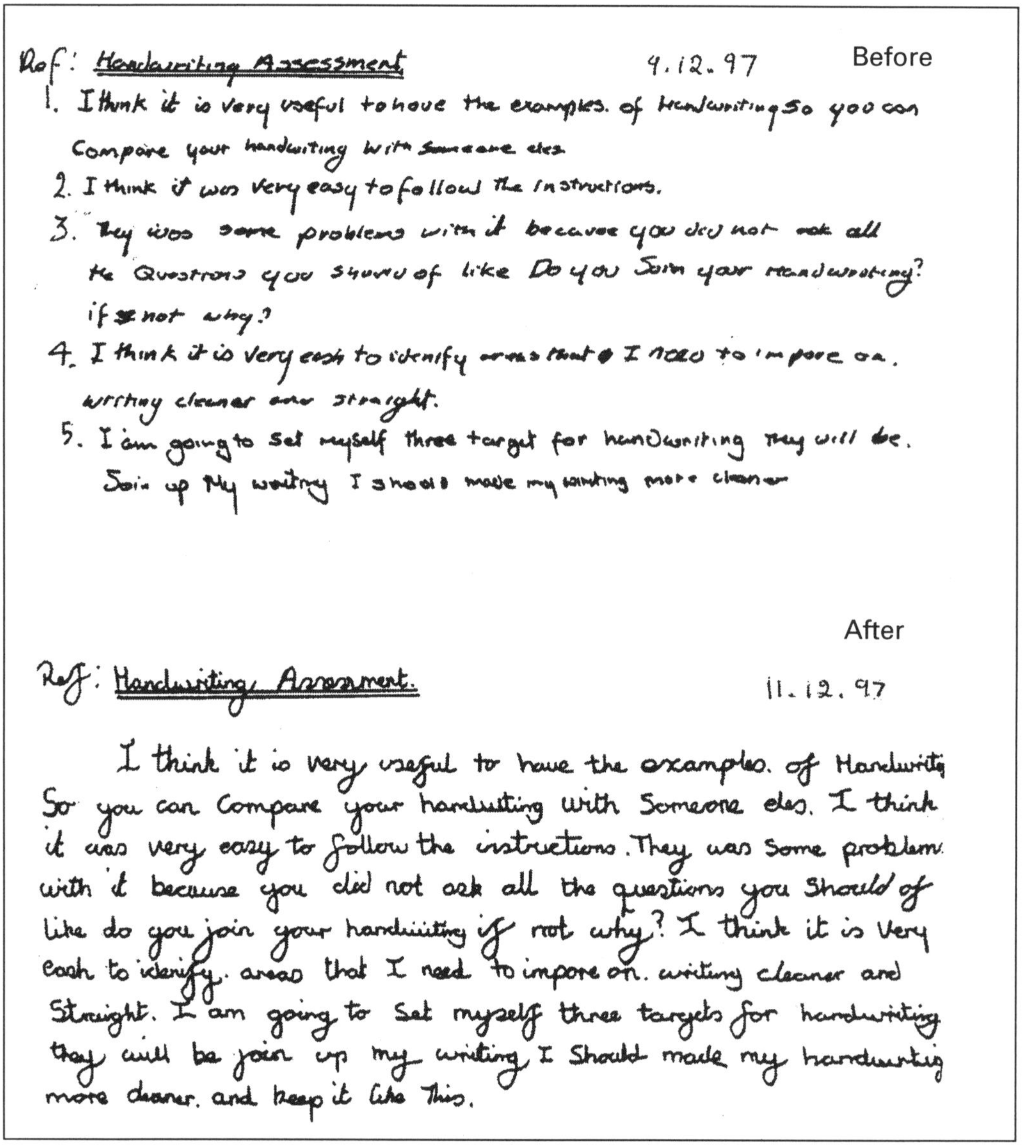

Ref: Handwriting Assessment   9.12.97   Before

1. I think it is very useful to have the examples. of handwriting so you can
   compare your handwriting with someone else.
2. I think it was very easy to follow the instructions.
3. They was some problems with it because you did not ask all
   the questions you should of like Do you join your handwriting?
   if not why?
4. I think it is very easy to identify areas that I need to impore on.
   writing cleaner and straight.
5. I am going to set myself three target for handwriting they will be.
   Join up my writing I should made my writing more cleaner

                                                             After

Ref: Handwriting Assessment.   11.12.97

I think it is very useful to have the examples. of handwriting
So you can compare your handwriting with someone else. I think
it was very easy to follow the instructions. They was some problem
with it because you did not ask all the questions you should of
like do you join your handwriting if not why? I think it is very
easy to identify. areas that I need to impore on. writing cleaner and
straight. I am going to set myself three targets for handwriting
they will be join up my writing I should made my handwriting
more cleaner. and keep it like this.

Figure 6.8 Marks' handwriting before and after cursive training

Corrective approaches to handwriting

Mark at 12 years old makes typical errors. He was either not taught to form his letters
correctly in the infant school or missed out on learning to write early on and so formed
his letters as best he could and these were now thoroughly fixed as motor programmes in
his brain. He was becoming distressed and fractious because his current teacher continually
complained about the illegibility of the writing and often would not accept it for marking
as it was not neat enough and poorly spelled. He was also given veiled warnings that when
he got to secondary school he would be in trouble if he handed work in like that.

As Mark was not given any help on how he could improve his writing and spelling he
was beginning to avoid writing whenever he could and was depressed about it. Then his

Special Needs coordinator, Joy Hastilow, decided to test out the suggestions made here as part of her MA course work. She devised a handwriting analysis which he used to analyse his errors and then after just two lunch time sessions on how to form **i** then **t** and **p** and make words Mark asked to have a copy of the full cursive alphabet, an upright one, to take home and practice. From learned helplessness in which he believed he could not change his writing he was galvanised into action with the above results achieved in a week. His teachers who did not know about the secret programme started complimenting him on his written work and his parents noticed the difference in him, in attitude and motivation and offered to help support his writing too.

Identification and analysis of handwriting errors

A list of the general types of errors made may be found below in Figure 6.9.

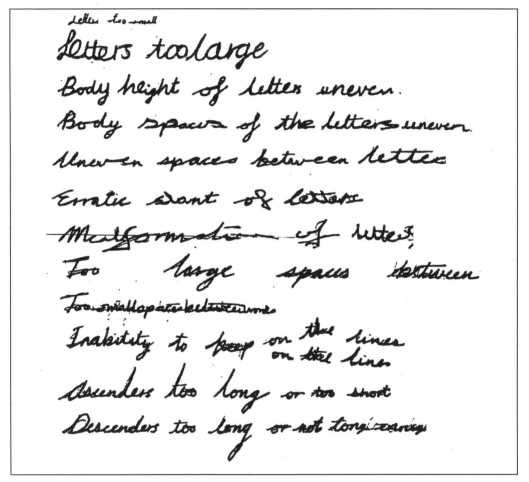

Figure 6.9 Examples of fluency training with words as writing develops

With the pupils' help make an analysis of errors in a sample of the handwriting. The more opportunity the pupils have to discuss the errors they find, the more likely it is that they will have the interest and motivation to try to improve their own handwriting. The key points to address first are *body size* and then *slant*. Begin any intervention with practice using double lines to get the body size of the letters all the same. Next address the slant of letters to get them all sloping the same way whether forwards or backwards. All letters should have a *lead in stroke* and this should begin on the line for every letter made separately. All words should be practised with a lead in stroke to help override previous learned motor programmes.

Changing from print to cursive should not include half measures in which arbitrary groups of letters are connected because they are easy to join and are in small groups.

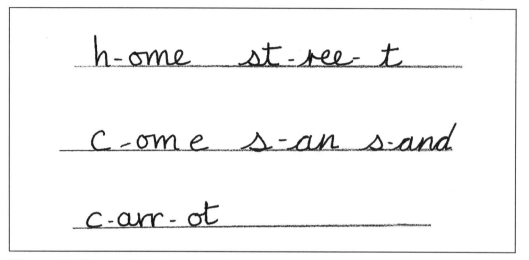

Figure 6.10 Types of joining to avoid

Remediating handwriting difficulties

There is a significant minority of pupils who will actually have handwriting coordination difficulties. Estimates vary from Sassoon's (1989, 1993) report of 40 per cent of boys and 25 per cent of girls at age 15 stating that they found writing painful and avoided it whenever possible, to 10 per cent in other studies where the fine motor control itself was examined (Gubbay, 1975; Laszlo, *et al.* 1988).

Alston (1987, 1993) found that 21 per cent of 9 year olds in some Cheshire schools were ill equipped for the writing demands of secondary schools and this does not appear to be uncommon in other schools. However, there is no need for writing to be painful and a significant proportion of such difficulties are brought about by bad posture, incorrect writing positions, inappropriate furniture, and wrong positioning of the paper (Sassoon 1987). These, as will be seen, can be dealt with by a more careful consideration of needs and a more flexible approach to provision.

Difficulties will become handicapping if a print script is insisted upon until the writing is neater. For those with handwriting coordination difficulties such a time will never come *unless* they are taught cursive. Even so there will be the rare occasion when a pupil with spidery shaky writing cannot improve whatever style is used because the underlying difficulty is not amenable to training. This may be the case in motor impairment when the effort needed to write is excessive and then the pupil should be given a laptop and there must be a classroom computer on which the work can be downloaded. In some such cases it may be sensible only to introduce some limited handwriting skills as the pupil gets older for signing and form filling.

Even so a tiny minority of pupils with severe difficulties should not be made to learn to form handwriting at all and some should learn much later. These children need to have a word processor to use from reception class with a portable laptop. Ben was such a pupil. He had general problems with locomotion following a difficult birth and the impairment also affected his ability to write. It took him 50 minutes to write the story below as his writing was so laborious and often the effort would reduce him to tears especially when his teacher gave it back to him to rewrite neatly. His distress was becoming of great concern to his parents as he was beginning to have temper tantrums about going to school.

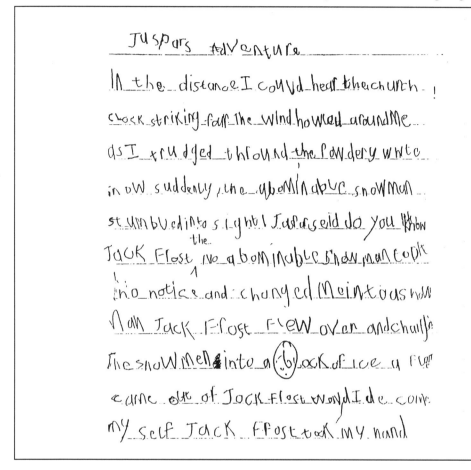

Figure 6.11 An example of Ben's writing

Motor coordination difficulties in handwriting

Examine the piece of writing in Figure 6.12. It contains a number of clues to the pupil's mild motor coordination difficulties at the checklist.

Checklist of motor coordination problems

- Writing pulling in from the margin towards the midline.
- 'Rivers' of spaces running down through the writing.
- Apparent capital letters spotted about but which are really large forms of the lower case out of control, especially of **s**, **w**, **k**, and **t**.
- Writing which looks scribbly or spiky.
- Shaky and wobbly strokes on close examination of letters.
- Writing which varies in 'colour' sometimes dark and in other places very faint indicating variation in pressure.

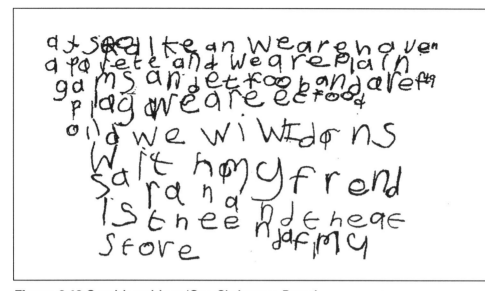

Figure 6.12 Sarah's writing: 'Our Christmas Party'.
Chronological age: 7 years 6 months; Reading age 7 years 2 months; Spelling age
6 years 9 months. it took her three quraters of an hour to write and she copied
most words from the dictionary in front of her.

- Writing which produces ridges on the reverse of the paper and even holes in it due to pressure exerted.
- Inability to maintain the writing on the line.
- Difficulties in copying fluent letter shapes in one fluid movement.

Summary

Whatever stage and level of handwriting has been reached by a pupil if it is made in a print script then an attempt needs to be made immediately to switch to an ovoid cursive to increase fluency and speed. This can make the difference of a degree classification at student level or a grade level in school subjects. Not all pupils will want to transfer to cursive and may have parents who refuse to let them even when provided with relevant evidence. Most however will be willing to try even though for a while their writing may not look so neat to them or feels less under their control.

Beginning writers should be taught to use a joined hand from the outset with lead-in strokes and pupils with handwriting difficulties and dyslexia *must* be taught a joined hand for the perceptuomotor reasons already given.

Only when a pupil has developed a fluent style should any calligraphic variation for art form be introduced. For pupils with handwriting problems such as graphomotor dyspraxia or developmental dysgraphia calligraphy may not be a suitable study.

The essential factor in changing handwriting is to involve the pupil in the evaluation and the redevelopment strategies as motivation to want to change is a key factor and some may be frightened to change at first given the difficulties they may already have experienced.

It is important to teach handwriting and spelling together so that one skill can act to enhance the development of the other and so make give the practice activities in handwriting added value.

Chapter 7

Spelling

Introduction

The Government has pledged to raise literacy standards so that by the year 2002, 80 per cent of pupils at eleven years will reach level 4 in literacy Standard Attainment Tasks (SATs) and so will be fluent in literacy skills when they transfer to secondary schools. By September 1998 all primary schools must introduce a literacy hour into each school day and 200 advisors have already been appointed to help train teachers in underfunctioning target schools.

Turner (1991) ascribed what he said was evidence of a lowering of reading standards to a lack of basic phonics teaching. Teachers however claim to use mixed methods in which phonics plays an important part. 'New' methods introduce phonics in the form of phonological training but neither these nor phonics teaching overcome specific learning difficulties (Chall 1967, 1987, Hurry and Silva 1997). Many dyslexics have in fact been switched to phonics programmes several times over as a remediation technique as soon as their difficulties are identified but this has not helped them over their dyslexic problems.

Multisensory teaching derived from dyslexia remedial teaching schemes (Gillingham *et al.* 1940) may now be given to all pupils and regarded as 'a new method' but the time may be wasted for a significant number of them for Hulme (1981) found that although it helped those with specific literacy difficulties it did not enhance the skills and abilities of those without such problems. A new long-term study by Hurry and Silva (1997) followed 180 pupils over a five year span who were given specialist support when they were six. They found that the Reading Recovery training programme (Clay 1989) costing about £1,500 per pupil and involving specialist training for teachers, and one-to-one teaching over a period of 20 weeks, produced gains in which five years later the pupils were six months ahead of others from similar poor backgrounds and with acute reading problems. They also found that a cheaper phonologically structured approach to reading was equally effective with deprived children but this phonics course was no help to those who could not read at all at six years old. Clay (1979) in fact screened out such children, about one per cent of her samples. The gains made by other pupils faded with time and therefore it was concluded that Reading Recovery was not effective when used as a general remedial method for children who are slow in reading. This is not surprising as slower learners need developmental rather than remedial teaching (Montgomery 1997b). After four to five years Hurry and Silva found that Reading Recovery children had a three to four month advantage in reading but this was not statistically significant and there was no effect on spelling or on the children who were complete nonreaders at six. Those on free school meals had the six to seven month advantage.

The Phonological Training, a phonics based approach, produced a spelling advantage but no overall reading benefit again with the six month advantage for those on free school meals but no advantage to those who could not read at six.

Recent surveys by HMI (1996, 1997) have shown that more than a third of pupils at eleven are unable to read and write adequately for their studies in secondary schools. The 1997 SATs results for eleven year olds have shown that standards in basic skills have in fact risen this year by five per cent. However, as the first results were published before the tests had time to bed down, improvements such as this are bound to be achieved as teachers learn to teach to the tests.

Good literacy standards at an early age will be difficult to achieve if a balanced approach to literacy is not adopted. Teachers and researchers focus most of their attention upon reading reserving rote learning for spelling and handwriting. This bias is reflected in literacy teaching surveys such as that of Gorman *et al.* (1993) which dwell entirely upon reading and rarely mention spelling and the Green Paper (DfEE 1997) which regards dyslexia as entirely a problem associated with reading.

In teaching some phonics in the course of reading plus a few spelling rules such as 'magic e' teachers often think they are teaching spelling but this is only a minute part of what they might be doing (Montgomery 1997b). There is perhaps still a fear of what used to be called the 'spelling grind'. Pupils used to sit in rows chanting spellings, learning sections of the Bible and whole books of poems by rote (Barnard 1961, Chambers 1987). The reaction has been to drive teachers towards 'meaning emphasis' methods, particularly the Look and Say approach to teaching reading and then various whole books and apprenticeship methods during which spelling was mainly 'caught' during reading (Peters 1967, 1985) and reinforced by copy writing. In addition a generation of teachers has grown up in a system where the linguistic aspects of the language were not divulged.

Spelling

Spelling is a recall skill in which the correct letters have to be given orally or in writing in a precise order. In our writing system 26 alphabet letters represent about 44 speech noises in which all the vowels have two sounds – short, and long when the vowel 'says' its own name. There are also consonant digraphs where two letters make one sound e.g. **ch**, **sh**, **th**, **th** (voiced), **ph**, and **wh**, and this is different from each of the constituent sounds. The double vowel **oo** has a short and long sound of its own and acts as an extra vowel and **y** may be a vowel or a consonant. There are four diphthongs in which two letters in one syllable are blended to make a completely new sound, these being: **oi**, **oy, ou** and **ow**.

Before the age of printed books and the introduction of the dictionary by Dr Johnson, English words were spelled with a much closer correspondence between symbols and sound. There was also a wide variation in spellings made by individual clerks even within their own scripts. Over time the relationship between the sounds of speech and its phonetic transcription has also slipped as pronunciation has changed. Now the majority of words used by beginning spellers can be represented by 80 phonograms according to

Spalding and Spalding (1967) in their Writing Road to Reading scheme. Different phonograms may represent the same sound, for example **i**, **ie** and **igh** may all represent the long vowel sound of letter **i**.

According to Hanna *et al*. (1966) at least 85 per cent of the English language is regular in that the spellings follow an ordered pattern of sounds and linguistic rules. A computer given the basic sounds of the alphabet can only produce a correct spelling once in five words but Henry (1995) has shown that an understanding of the nature of the spelling of 14 key words can give the correct spelling of the majority of words pupils need to write in schools.

A regular word is one in which the the alphabet symbols correspond exactly to the sound represented, a system of basic phonics, e.g. *pin, bag, stop, trust*. When beginning spellers or those with spelling difficulties such as dyslexics have cracked this alphabetic code a system of 'skeletal phonics' can be seen e.g. 'mi mum got me a cmputa fr mi bthde'. Typically medial vowels are omitted or wrong vowels are inserted even in relatively regular words. Irregular words such as *come, said* and *women* may be represented as they sound e.g. *cum, sed*, and *wimmen* or *wimen*.

Adults looking at children's spellings often forget that it takes time to learn and the wider the vocabulary used the more potential for misspellings can occur. Even when pupils appear to have learned to spell well, whenever a new vocabulary is introduced mistakes will be made. Such weaknesses arise even in the first year of undergraduate programmes because the original learning strategies have been by rote. This is frequently why it is argued by some that their ability to spell was only developed through learning Latin or a modern foreign language which gave them insight into their own language. This is of course a very circuitous route for learning to spell well.

As well as a lexicon of correct spellings which most people carry in their heads there will be a number of errors also securely stored. Some common ones are: *seperate, accomodate, dessicate, potatoe* and so on. Errors once ensconced are particularly difficult to eradicate and no amount of writing them out neatly five times will correct them otherwise they would not still be there.

Pupils vary in their ability to develop good spelling without help. There are some who are generally poor and some who for a variety of reasons may have severe, persistent and specific difficulties such as dyslexics. Poor spellers do not appear to have specific difficulties but are generally slow to develop literacy skills and because of this may miss out on many key teaching inputs for they may not be ready for them. Others have had unsatisfactory opportunities for learning and carry forward with them a range of basic errors which are unable to correct alone and which handicaps their progress later.

The dyslexics' difficulty in the majority of cases has been found to be an inability to establish verbal codes, especially in the phonological area (Vellutino 1979, 1987). This means they have a difficulty in 'cracking' the alphabetic code needed to develop reading and enable them to spell. This is why so called 'new methods' include phonological approaches to teaching. However, these have already been found to be insufficient if by six years the pupil has not yet learned to read (Hurry and Silva 1997). This does not mean that the theory is wrong only that the method of teaching called phonological is clearly not working (Montgomery 1997b). Normal readers learn their phonics for spelling whether directly taught or not (Chall 1967; Francis 1982) during learning to read. Dyslexics' problems begin when they fail to break this alphabetic code in the reception class and then fail again even at six when they are given extra help and fail again at seven when they are given remedial phonics so that by the time they reach junior school they are already three time failures.

However, the majority of pupils in mainstream only need a corrective and developmental programme whilst beginners need a developmental programme *per se*. The next sections therefore begin with corrective techniques and are followed by lessons in developmental then remedial spelling.

Corrective spelling strategies

There are a number of words in common use that most people will spell wrongly. Sometimes they know they are prone to misspelling them but forget each time the correct spelling. The area of error is usually only over one letter.

Pupils should be asked to give some words with which they have such difficulties to see if they can learn to use the corrective strategies. Younger pupils tend to make lower order errors such as articulatory, phonic and syllabic errors so that the strategies can straightforwardly be directed to these. If they make higher order errors then they will need to use the full protocol which includes the dictionary work.

Spelling errors tend to be made early on in spelling development and once stored in the brain they cannot be unlearned but they can be overridden. What is seen is misspellings popping up under duress in examinations, appearing in different error forms in general writing and appearing in the same piece of work with the correct spelling so that it looks as though the pupil has just been careless.

The pupil may be fully aware certain words are problems and may have tried to correct them but now is totally confused as to whether there should be **e** or **a** in the middle of *separate,* or two **ms** or one in *accommodate* and so on. They often cope by alternating between the two.

Twelve cognitive process strategies for spelling

The cognitive process approach focuses all the attention on the area of error to identify and correct it. This attention gives it a higher profile in the memory and sounds warning bells as the spelling approaches and then the strategies can be applied. After a while the pupil experiences the heightened awareness and writes through the word giving the correct spelling. Eventually the correct motor programme is elicited on every occasion. Thus it is essential that all corrections are written in *full cursive* to establish the automatic motor programme.

- Articulation – clear, correct speech, 'chimney' not 'chimley'.
- Over articulation – parli(a)ment, gover(n)ment.
- Cue articulation – say it incorrectly, Wed - nes - day.
- Syllabification – break it down into syllables, mis - de - mean - our.
- Phonics – try to get a comprehensible skeleton of the word's sound.
- Origin – the word's root in another language may give clues.
- Rule – the **l-f-s** rule and **i** before **e** except after **c** can help.
- Linguistics – syllable structure and affixing rules govern most words.
- Family – *bomb, bombing, bombardier, bombardment* give clues.
- Meaning – to *pare* or *part* helps spell *separate* correctly.
- Analogy – 'it is like *braggart*' helps spell *braggadocio.*
- Funnies – 'cess pit' will help me to remember how to spell *necessary.*

Using the full cognitive process protocol to correct misspellings

- The pupil proof reads to try to identify misspellings.
- Teacher also proof reads for errors.
- A composite list of all misspellings is made by the teacher.
- Pupil selects with teacher two spellings to work on.
- Pupil looks up the words in the dictionary.
- Pupil puts a ring round the area of error – the wrong letter or omission.
- The words are studied in the dictionary for clues to meaning and origin.

- Teacher discusses with the pupil two cognitive strategies from the list of twelve for dealing with *one* of the errors.
- Pupil applies the strategies and checks to see if they have been successful using SOS.
- Pupil now addresses the other word identifying two strategies which can be applied.

Identification of developmental levels of errors and interventions

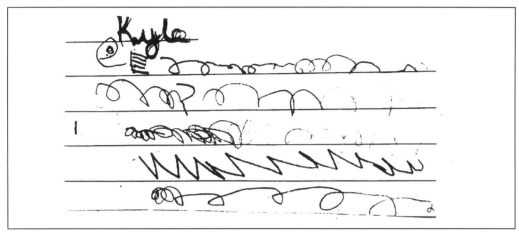

Figure 7.1a

- Random letters and scribbles – start at the beginning of the programme (Figure 7.1a).
- Single lower and upper case letters, letter groups and sometimes words representing spellings. Start at the beginning of the programme. Focus particularly upon syllabification and word building. (Figure 7.1b).
- Most common words correctly spelled but a rough phonetic equivalent given for some of the more infrequent or irregular ones. Undertake an error analysis to find out what is not known and begin there. This is often blends and digraphs. (Figure 7.1c).
- When the majority of errors are to do with *basewords* and the addition of *prefixes* and *suffixes* these are the errors of more mature writers and make up 75 per cent of all misspellings of normal adults.

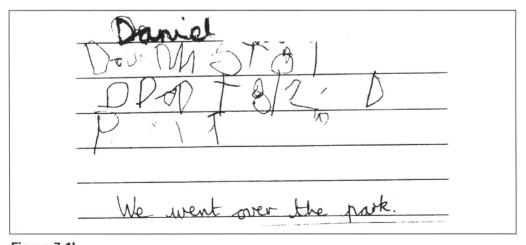

Figure 7.1b

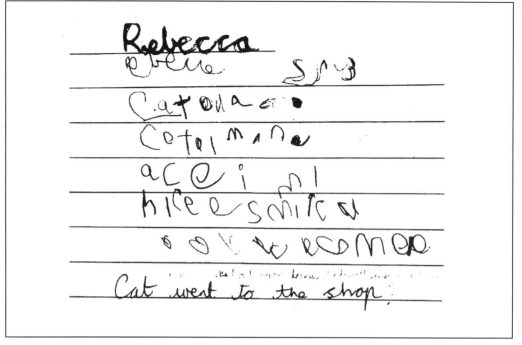

Figure 7.1c The cat went out of the shop because he didn't know what to buy

Early identification

In the first few weeks in school screen all the pupils in the class as follows:

- find out which letter names and sounds they know and can recognise;
- take a sample of their writing and spelling:
    ask them to write their names on a piece of paper;
    ask them to copy their names and a short sentence;
    ask them to write you a message or a story. It is helpful if this follows some discussion of say, a storm and what they saw.

It is essential not to give any help with writing or spelling and to collect with pleasure all their scribbles. Undertake an error analysis as follows.

Error analyses

After marking the writing for content, copy down each spelling error or photocopy the page and underline every spelling error. Some pupils may make a lot of errors because they are trying to use a much more extensive vocabulary. Others will play safe and only write words they think they can spell. Dictation exercises are thus also needed at times to identify their problems.

Creative misspellings and miscues analysis: five year olds

William, five years two months: '*teh tre fel on to f ten ottn telfn pol riu*'; (the tree fell on top of the other telephone pole wire).

Faye, five years two months: '*my littl sid is in bed bkos se is hafi hi tosls oot*'; (my little sister is in bed because she is having her tonsils out).

Interventions
- Both are promising spellers, continue introducing sounds for spelling and teach *the* and *and* as writing units.
- Teach William to spell *tree* and Faye to spell *little* as these are already nearly correct. Use a writing strategy so that they learn to add the final letter that they have missed. Remind them of the Look – cover – write – check strategy for this.
- Sit with them and ask them to read their sentences articulating clearly for spelling to see if they can improve some of the other spellings e.g. Faye should then identify the two syllables in sister.
- Explain that this is what real writers do they *edit* and *redraft* what they have written, often many times so that they get it right.
- Teach syllabification for spelling to begin to correct *telephone* and *sister.*
- Now ask them to produce an edited and final version of their pieces of writing. Put both pieces of work in their assessment file for reference.

Error analysis of the collected misspellings of two seven year olds
Maxwell seven years:
yeserday, traveld, underneith, mooved, wich, past (passed), satsoomers (satsumas), papper (pepper), quikly, writeing, arived.
Miranda seven years:
moter, envent (invent), ruber, wheele chairs, washing micine, dumy, vacum clener.

Interventions
- Teach Maxwell **-st** blend checking for clear articulation, focus with him on the feel of this blend in the mouth. Give him some other words to spell which check that he has absorbed the information e.g. *stop, stand, stem, pest, fist, rest.*
- Explain the use of **-ck** in words. Refer to the **-ck** lessons on this. (Montgomery 1997a)
- Give corrected spellings of *underneath* and *satsumas* and praise the close approximations to the correct version.
- Introduce syllable structure, short vowel sounds and go on to affixing rules (see appropriate lessons in this series) to correct in time the spellings of *pepper* and *writing* then later *arrived, passed* and *travelled*. These types of errors will then disappear.
- Teach Miranda articulation for spelling *invent, vacu um* and *ma chine* plus digraph **-ch**.
- Give the correct spelling of *wheel* and *motor* using a writing strategy for relearning.
- Teach syllable structure, short vowel sounds and begin affixing rules and linguistics programme to correct the other errors such as *rubber, dummy* and *cleaner.*
- The pupil now reports to the teacher on progress.
- A day or two later the teacher asks the pupil to spell orally both of the words as a check that they are still remembered.
- When these words have been learnt it is then possible to tackle two more. After a while the pupils will be able to manage this process themselves.

Some examples of the use of the protocol for correcting higher order errors

The typical problem words as spellers become more advanced are:

separate – usually misspelled *seperate*
accommodate – usually misspelled as *accomodate*
opportunity – usually misspelled as *oppertunity* or even *oppurtunity.*

- First look up the spelling in the dictionary.
- Next put a ring round the region of error e.g. the second **e** in *separate,* the omitted **m** in *accommodate* and the second vowel in *opportunity.*
- The meaning of *separate* is to divide or *part*; the prefix is *se* (aside) and *parare* is from the Latin meaning *to put.* Learning to apply the meaning 'to pare or to part' to the words's spelling usually sorts out the problem.
- The origin of opportunity is from *ob* (before) and *portus* (a harbour) which can be linked to port to make *opportunity* which has the meaning of qa timely event like coming upon a harbour or port in a storm. *Ob* is assimilated to *op* before *portus.* After the short vowel sound in *com* the consonant **m** is doubled. Other examples are in *ad -gression, agression, ad-cumulate.* It is therefore important that the common prefixes and their meanings are learnt.

Older pupils can be asked to

- write their name and address;
- write a short story in their own words without help/bring a piece of narrative writing from a subject area;
- write from dictation, (Peters and Smith 1993 provide a set of these for different year groups).
- do a spelling test such as that of Schonell (A or B) or Daniels and Diack's. The spelling test errors and all the errors on the other tasks should be subject to an analysis so that an appropriate programme can be selected or drawn up for example:

Error analysis of Kevin's writing
Kevin was an undiagnosed dyslexic; aged 14 years (year 9).

> The candall flafm flickered and sundily the Daor creked open the wind blow the candall out and I saw a figer standn at the Doar with a gegos knife in his hand and then I saw a nather and a nathe. the window smashed and a man came and I stept back and I fell bown a trap Doar into a pasig whay. Ther was a spidr her whet in a masif web andI ran on and on in tell I came facr to facr whit a masif monser he was just about to eat me then my mum woke me up

The teacher's form of marking was as follows: Spelling: creaked, another, front walked – too numerous to list.' Punctuation: no full stops or commas.
   It is clear that this English teacher felt powerless to help Kevin when some basic in-service education could have helped both. In fact there is some punctuation in the work. The protocol would be:

- List the errors: candall (2) flafm sundily Daor (3) creked blow figer standn gegos a nathe(r) (2) stept bown pasig whay ther her whet masif (2) in tell facr (2) wiht.
- Calculate an error count e.g. 27 errors in 103 words gives an error rate of 26 per cent. The rate for different words is 20 per cent. Noting error rates can be encouraging to pupils as their spelling improves.
- On this occasion it might be helpful to read back to Kevin what he has written so that he can use the same articulation strategy for editing his own work.
- Words which would clearly come out wrongly would be: flafm sundily Daor creked gegos bown her facr wiht.
- A decision can now be taken about which errors should be addressed to make most sense, which have frequent need of use and which have powers to generalise to other spellings. Select on these grounds: *sense, frequency* and *power.* Try to satisfy all conditions in the selection of first and second choice errors.

- Here the choices might be:

  teach cursive writing so that **d** and **b** errors will no longer occur;

  teach articulation and syllabification for spelling (*sundily*);

  check and teach consonant digraph **th** to correct *with;*

  check if he knows the short vowel sound and closed syllable structure; if yes (unlikely) move on to the long vowel sounds and also the effect of silent **e** to correct *flame, creaked* and *face*. Leave *gegos* except to syllabify for spelling.

Error analysis of an advanced speller's work

The advanced spellers' errors on this page were collected from the final year examination papers of Teacher Education students. There were 250 student scripts on Special Needs subjects over a period of three years.

The error rate was very small, under 0.01 per cent and 75 per cent of all their errors were confined to errors in basewords and affixing. A small number of errors were slips of the pen, mostly corrected, and a few were slips of the brain in that homophones were written. The rest were occasional but more basic errors in verbs, nouns and phonics. Basic errors were mainly confined to a few individual scripts indicating students with problems in spelling:

anonomously	anonym	incorrect base word
agressive	ad – gressive (agg)	prefix error
arguements x2	arguments	suffixing error
attatchment	attachment	not a -tch word
advise (ce) x2	advice	noun – verb error
allert	a-lert	wrong prefix a- not ad-
appart	a-part	wrong prefix a- not ad-
advantagous	advantageous	softening g

The error types indicate how the correction should be addressed, in some cases for a base word it may simply be to correctly articulate it.

Developing spelling

Most schemes deal with phonics but provide many worksheets which can be completed without using phonics leaving out the multisensory and articulatory nature of the training needed.

Fourteen example developmental lessons on linguistics

1. Syllable beats

Syllabification is one of the most basic spelling skills and therefore it is important to establish the concept and the strategy early on. Older poorer spellers may have entirely missed out on this useful piece of learning. This can easily be a class lesson and pupils can all participate in the beating. Chime bars, triangles and other percussion instruments can be used,

Ask the pupils to listen to the sound of a pupils name. Find out if they can hear the beats e.g. *Ritson, Jason*. Tap the beats as you say them.

2. Word building using i, t, p, n, s

These five letters are some of the most frequent letters used in words (Fry 1964). They are also useful since a good range of words can be built with them and a wide range of strategies can be demonstrated in the process. Developmental spelling requires pupils to be explorers in the world of letters and then to reinforce what they have discovered by writing training.

Each letter needs to be introduced separately as in the handwriting lessons. When they have learned the first two sounds and names they should put them together in word building. When they have learned the first five letters **i**, **t**, **p**, **n**, **s**, they should be shown how to construct words with onsets and rimes as in: *s/it, p/it, sp/it* and so on. After five or six words have been offered and written down ask them in unison to read them aloud as you point to them.

Next show them how to segment the initial sound for reading by covering up the rime and when the onset has been given reveal the rime for them to say and then to say the whole word.

Show them that if they make the mouth shape of the letter without sounding it is impossible to read words the wrong way round (no reversals). Encourage them to generate new words from the five letters.

3. Basic closed syllable structure

When pupils have learned the terms 'vowel' and 'consonant' and have some notion of their meaning then linguistics teaching can really begin. So far they will have been learning phonics, the correspondences between symbols and sounds, and phoneme assembly and segmentation. These strategies only apply when there is a simple one-to-one correspondence between sound and symbol. This leaves out a large number of words for which other strategies have to be developed.

The point of learning strategies is that they can be generalised to a wider range of words thus saving memorising every one individually.

The work on syllable beats should be revised, then explain that the syllables or beats make up all the words we use. Give them some example words and ask them to identify something they all have in common. They should tell you they have **a**, **e**, **i**, **o** or **u** in the middle. Ask them the special class name of all those middle letters i.e. vowels. When they see the simple structure consonant – vowel – consonant (cvc) they should remember that the vowel makes its short sound as in *bad, beg, rib, hop,* and *run.* Later initial and final blends can be included to teach ccvc and cvcc structures.

4. The long vowel sounds or second sounds of vowels: A E I O U

Pairing short vowel and long vowel sound learning can easily create confusion so they must be separated. There are two approaches to teaching about long vowel sounds and the teacher must judge when each is appropriate. One way of dealing with this is to teach the long vowel sound as the vowel 'saying its own name' first. As pupils grow older they can be talked to about the long and short sounds where the long sound is in fact the name of the vowel. Being able to recognise the differences between the pairs is an essential for spelling and word building using rules.

5. Silent e as the clue to the long vowel sound

Teachers very often call this the 'magic e' but 'silent e' is more accurate and establishes a principle that there are silent letters in a much wider range of words. There is often a tendency to teach 'silent e' as a rule very early on, but this can lead to confusion, pupils must understand the concept of long vowel sounds first. Where they are unable to tell the difference between them they will over generalise the rule and put silent **e** on many short vowelled words as well.

6. Open syllables

Open syllables end in a single vowel. There is no consonant to hold or close the vowel in. When this occurs the single vowel has the long vowel sound, or says its own name e.g. *me, she, no, so, to, flu, my, why.* When there is a long vowel sound at the end of a syllable then this sound is spelled with a single vowel e.g. *a-corn, stu-pid, le-gal, e-ven, o-pen, u-niform* etc.

7. Base words, affixing and suffixing rules 'drop-and-double'

A stem is a part of a word to which inflexional suffixes are added e.g. *com -ment. Com* on its own is not a word. A base word is a full word to which prefixes and suffixes are added to alter its meaning e.g. *form, forming, reform, reformed.* Inflexions are variations in endings added to words which change them in relation to gender, case, numbers, person and tense etc. for example: *waiter, waitress; dog, dogs; pass, passed.* Prefixes are syllables added to the beginning of words to change their meaning e.g. *re-, ad-, con-, a-* and so on. Suffixes are syllables added to the ends of words to change their meaning e.g. *-ing, -ed, -es, -le, -ment.* Prefixes and suffixes together are called affixes and each has a meaning. Ask the pupils the difference in the middle vowels of the following word pairs:

hop, hope; run, rune; plum, plume; can, cane.

Get them to write down underneath the letters which is vowel and which consonant e.g. cvc, cvce. Introduce the suffix -ing and its meaning – to be in the process of something e.g. hoping. Give them a single instance of the suffixing rules *add* and *drop*

e.g. hop, hopping; hope, hoping.

Find out if they can propose a rule from each. The rules are: After the short vowel sound in a closed syllable we must *double* the final consonant before adding -ing. After the long vowel sound, *drop* silent **e** and add *-ing.*

8. The suffixing 'add' rule

Introduce the new rule which is *add.* In this case the suffix is simply added to the base word without any changes being made: *bend-ing, farm-ing.*

Once again give them an opportunity to look at a sample of spellings and to try to infer the rule from them. This problem solving approach will help them to think more carefully about spelling and to make more careful observations of variations and patterns.

9. Suffixing different forms of the past tense: *-ed, -d, -t*

The *-ed, -d,* and *-t* are inflexional suffixes. Each of these three forms changes the tense of a verb from present to past tense e.g. *pass* to *passed, spell* to *spelled* or *spelt, send* to *sent.*

Discuss the concept of 'verb' as a doing word and ask the pupils to provide a number of examples. Show them some other ways in which we can change a verb such as *walk, walking, walked, will walk; speak, speaking, spoke, will speak.* Explain that these changes are called changing the tense of the verb. Can they explain what a 'tense' is?

Help them to formulate the occasions when *-ed* is used rather than *-d.* This is when a whole word exists before adding *-ed,* and the word has the short vowel pattern e.g. cvc, vcc, or the pattern vvc, as for *ing.* Single *-d* is used after 'silent e' words e.g. *hope, hoped. In sent, bend, spelt* etc. they need to feel and hear the final letter *-d* and *-t* in order to spell the words correctly.

10. Suffixing rule 'change', when words end in y

The suffixing rule 'change' most often applies to the use of the letter y in a word. For example the ending **y** in the word *mystery* is changed to *mysteries* when we want to make it into a plural form. In verbs ending in **y** such as *say, pay* and *lay* the **y** is changed to **i** before we add the suffix *-d* to convert it to the past tense form, and when we add *-s* to convert it to the passive form as in *tries* and *flies* with exceptions such as *says* and *pays*, *saies* or *sies* would not preserve the original sense.

Even though we now pronounce '*said*' as '*sed*' in earlier centuries the form 'sayed' was used. If we want to change the form of a verb ending in **y** to third person singular we use a similar strategy, remove **y**, CHANGE it to **i** and add *-es* e.g. *tries, cries, flies, replies, dries.*

11. Suffixing with vowel and consonant suffixes

There are two types of suffix, vowel and consonant. Suffixes are added to a complete word or base word e.g. *farm, farming.* They are also added to parts of words called stems or roots. In each case they change the meaning of the completed word.

Consonant suffixes can be added to any baseword without changing the spelling of the baseword e.g. *care + less.*

Vowel suffixes obviously begin with vowels. The base word does not change its spelling, e.g: *looking* (cvvc+*ing*) and *walking* (cvcc+*ing*) unless it has either the short vowel closed syllable (cvc) pattern or the silent **e** long vowel pattern (cvce), e.g. *hop+p+ing*, and *hoping.*

Give the pupils a list of common suffixes to write down in their books such as the following: *-ed, -er, -ful, -ish, -less, -ness, -s, -y* and ask them to try to explain their meanings. Introduce the *exceptions* to the 'silent e' rule where the **e** is retained to preserve the original meaning or where **g** has to be kept as soft **g**, e.g. *dye+ing, hoe+ing, canoe+ing, singe+ing* and *whinge+ing.*

Different suffixes have come to us from different languages. An example of an Old English suffix is: *-ship* as in *friendship* and *seamanship.* Ask the pupils to hypothesise on the meaning of *-ship* (a skill or status). Get them to write down the suffix and its meaning and then collect some *-ship* words. A suffix from Greek is *-scope* meaning a watcher or an instrument for watching. They can now generate some scope words e.g. *telescope, horoscope, stethoscope.* Latin suffixes are: *-ary, -able* and *-ible, -ous, -ject.* Their meanings: are belonging to or connected with (*dictionary, library*); able to or fit for (*readable, edible*); full of (*joyous, dubious*); and to throw (*eject, reject, object*).

12. Common consonant prefixes and their meanings

Prefixes are meaningful words and syllables placed before base words or roots which alter their general meaning, for example: something which is legal can be converted to the opposite meaning by the addition of the prefix *il-* to make '*illegal*'. There are consonant and vowel prefixes. When a prefix is added to a word the word to which it is added does not change its spelling, e.g. *mis + spelling* gives *misspelling.* People often tend to leave out one **s** which would not follow the general rule and would give *mi + spelling*, '*mi*' is not a prefix. Another example would be *necessary* to which *un* is added to make *unnecessary.*

Some common consonant prefixes are:

ab, circum, dis, ex, il, im, in, inter, ir, sub, trans, en, mis, over, out, post, super, un, under.

13. Suffixing -able and -ible

The endings *-able* and *-ible* both mean the same – able, to be able or capable of e.g. *readable* and *legible; -able* is the more common. There are some clearly defined situations in which one is used instead of the other. Give the pupils two lists of words to study and to propose a rule to account for when -able and -ible are used, as follows: *comfort able, clean able, read able, poss ible, horr ible, incred ible, cruc ible, vis ible.*

The answer is of course that after a whole word we use *-able* and after a part word or stem we use *-ible.*

14. Suffixing the stable final syllable (-shun) -tion, -sion

Whenever (-shun) is heard at the end of a word nine out of ten times it will be spelled *-tion.* Therefore when the pupils are in doubt they should write *-tion*, as in *attention, satisfaction*, and so on.

Introduce the pupils to the stable final syllable *-tion* (shun) and teach it as a cursive writing unit. Ask them to think of some words to which *-tion* the stable final syllable may be added e.g. *attend, except, attract, dictate, act, complete*. Tell them to study the base words and propose some general rules which might govern the addition of *-tion*; later introduce the exceptions.

Remedial training approaches

The spelling samples will also provide enough data to do a handwriting analysis. A significant proportion of dyslexics also have a *handwriting coordination problem*.

Their special needs demand:

- a spelling linked with handwriting cursive handwriting programme;
- a multisensory training approach to alphabetic phonics in spelling and reading;
- a multisensory mouth training programme to ensure the link is made between grapheme, phoneme and writing unit;
- a carefully structured programme of linguistics;
- training in writing schema and study skills.

Two specialist dyslexia programmes are recommended and briefly outlined below. Even if specialist teaching for dyslexics is not available the most important first step is to identify their educational problems and level of development so that they can be supported and not made to feel a failure. A key worker should then be identified to work systematically through the dyslexia programme in consultation with him or her so that they can learn together. There must be no short cuts and no pick and mix approaches with other schemes the tutor knows better. There should be no attempt to hasten the pupil through the stages. Nor should there be any attempt to move on to the next 'lesson' until the teacher is absolutely sure that the previous one has been learnt even if the first few steps take a month to learn. Progress will speed up after this.

Identification

- Give a standardised spelling test such as Schonell A or Daniels and Diack.
- Analyse the errors on the test given as already shown. Words correct may simply be whole word knowledge.
- Check to find out what initial sounds and blends and final blends are known. This can be done by randomising the letters of the alphabet and asking the pupil the sound and the name of each presented. The blends can be drawn from their own spellings.
- Obtain a sample of the pupil's open-ended writing and identify the level of intervention needed as in the examples already given.

Dyslexics' spellings contain no more reversals than other normal spellers with the same spelling age. Their spellings only seem bizarre because they are so much older and would normally be expected to know the conventional spelling. Often their spellings are possible to read if they are pronounced as written. If they are undecipherable this is because they have not learned the requisite grapheme-phoneme correspondences.

Caroline has only learned to 'spell' with some letters in her name. She does have a notion of words with spaces in between and uses capitals and letter like forms. She has learned her early reading books by heart and can copy a sentence. She needs help from a specialist teacher in a tutorial withdrawal group of two, at least three times a week for half an hour at a time until she begins to be able to use skeletal phonics, then withdrawal can be reduced to twice a week and kept under review. She needs to be brought up to grade level before entering Junior school or too much of the curriculum will pass her by.

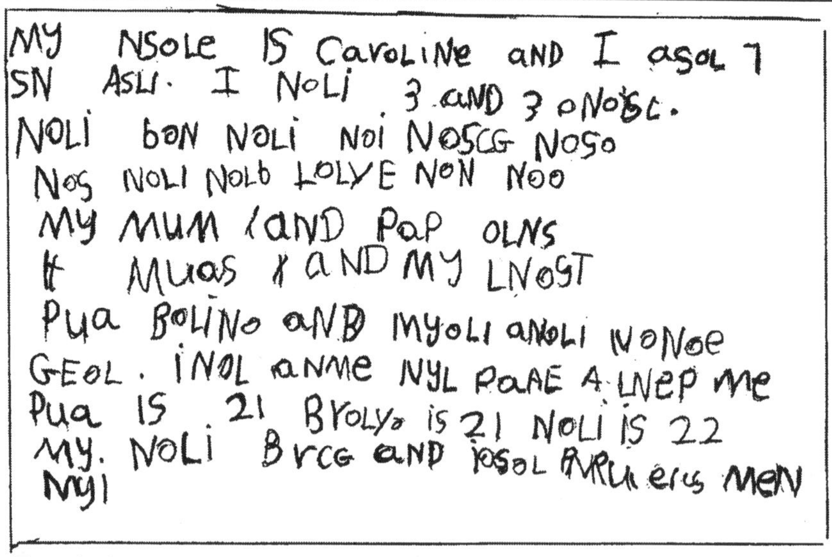

Translation:
'My name is Caroline and I am 7 years old. I have 3 brothers and
3 sisters. Some of them live at home and some of them do not.
My mum and dad live at home and so do my goldfish...

Figure 7.2 Caroline's own words (aged 7½ years)

Multisensory mouth training to help overcome a particular dyslexic awareness problem e.g. with cursive t and sound t

Demonstrate the letter shape of cursive t with sky writing and then by writing it on the blackboard as before. Each time give them the sound of the letter.

Talk them through the writing movements and use a multisensory mouth training method for reinforcing the sound e.g. say, 'Listen carefully. The sound is (t), say (t)'. Make sure that an intrusive 'uh' or schwa sound is not introduced e.g. 'tuh'.

Ask them to produce a sequence of **ttt tttt**'s in rapid succession. This causes them to sound the **t** without **uh** and represents the way they should learn to say it. Mouthing and sending out a puff of air without voicing.

Ask them to close their eyes and make the **t** sound and to think of whether their lips are open or closed. Teach the meaning of this if necessary.

Ask them what their tongues are doing when they make **t**. Spend some time on helping them to get the feel of this letter. This completes the multisensory quadrilateral-vision-sound-articulatory pattern and kinaesthetic writing pattern. Now give them plenty of practice in making letter **t** on their paper whilst sounding (t) and noting the articulatory feel. This may be the concrete clue to spelling dyslexics need to crack the alphabetic code.

The nature of specialist dyslexia programmes

The remedial teaching required by dyslexics, frequently those unable to read and spell at six years old, is a specialist alphabetic – phonic – syllabic – linguistic (APSL) programme. The improvement rate once on the programme needs to be about twice the developmental gain in age if the dyslexic is to be brought up to grade level. In a study of 38 dyslexics on the TRTS programme described later showed that in a period of 1.3 years with two one-hour teaching sessions per week, they made average reading gains of 2.45 years and average spelling gains of 2.01 years (Montgomery 1997b). Hornsby and Farrer (1991) reported gains in the order of 1.5 years with the Alpha to Omega programme which is phonic and linguistic. The Basic Skills Unit (1997) in a recent survey found that some 6 million of the adult population between 16 and 60 were barely literate. Most of them could not for example follow a simple cookery recipe. It is not therefore a new problem. The failure of the Look and Say methods of teaching to help a core group of pupils with problems in the USA in the 1920s resulted in Samuel Orton, after visiting the UK, adapting the methods of phonics teaching and handwriting which he saw there to see if they would meet the needs of the group we now call dyslexics. With his researcher Anna Gillingham and the experienced teacher Bessie Stillman he developed the Gillingham, Stillman and Orton programme (1940) to remediate reading, spelling and penmanship. It went through several volumes and Kathleen Hickey and several colleagues visited the USA in the 1970s to learn more about it.

In 1977 'Miss Hickey' as she was always known, published a modified and anglicised version of their programme. In 1991 a second and revised edition of this was published as the *Hickey Multisensory Language Course 2nd Edition* edited by Jean Augur and Sue Briggs. Both had had dyslexic children and had only finally found help for them when they found Miss Hickey. The revision of the original programme had already been started four years before her death in 1984. Training courses became a regular feature once a secure base had been established at Staines. The organization became the basis for the Dyslexia Institute and branches have been established round the country. The Dyslexia Institute has also published its own version of the Hickey original as *DILP – the Dyslexia Institute Language Programme* available only to those who attend its courses.

The Hickey second edition divides the programme into three sections as follows: Part One: Chapters on the theory and background to the multisensory approach to teaching and the basic techniques of the programme such as how to introduce the phonograms using the stimulus – response routine in 9 steps; the first 12 phonograms are detailed as follows **i, t, p, n, s, a, d, h, e, c,** (k), **k,** and **-ck** (k). To these are added concepts, spelling rules and vocabulary, the basic language programme, alphabet work, cursive handwriting training, reading and spelling, story writing and self-directed learning activities. These chapters are essential reading before embarking on the teaching programme, according to Augur and Briggs. The book remains true to the ideas and principles of its originator.

Parts Two and Three are both divided into three sections and demonstrate in a carefully ordered sequence the teaching of the 84 phonograms which make up the programme and the associated rules and structures. A range of teaching games are presented and each section is carefully cross referenced. Teachers with an interest in the area could well follow the programme even if they had not had the benefit of a training course. The danger as always would be the tendency to try to take short cuts and move the pupils through the course too quickly.

Teaching Reading Through Spelling (TRTS) Cowdery, *et al.* 1983–1987, second edition 1994. Three of the authors were trained by Hickey. The TRTS programme is presented in a series of slim A4 books originally published as Series Two in the Learning Difficulties Research Project and now by Frondeg Hall for the authors.

Book A details the process of making an assessment and compiling a case profile under the title of *Diagnosis.* The profile contains interview data, criterion referenced, norm referenced and diagnostic data from tests and information from reports. Much of the book however is about trying to gain a direct insight into the young person's needs and difficulties from direct observation with the test data as a background to this.

In the *Foundations of the Programme,* Book B, the four essential elements of the programme are described – alphabet work, the reading and spelling packs and the cursive handwriting style and training method.

The alphabet work (Cowdery 1984) is similar to that found in Hickey and other APSL derivatives. It consists of using wooden capital letters which the pupil has to lay out in alphabetical order in an arc, tracing over their shape and saying the letter and saying the alphabet in the correct order up to the point where an error is made. Each teaching session begins with five or ten minutes of this alphabet work starting from the letter preceding the one where the first error was made until the whole of it has been learnt. A range of games is included in alphabet work.

More advanced work centres upon dictionary use and the four quartiles with an explanation of how the pupil should be helped uncover them using a problem solving strategy.

In Section Two the Reading and Spelling packs are introduced (Prince-Bruce 1984). The purposes of the two packs is to establish a secure relationship between symbol and sound beginning with single letters, progressing through blends and vowel combinations to complex letter groupings such as *-igh* and *-ough*. Every sound is presented through the three major senses so that associations between visual, auditory and kinaesthetic areas can be established. The practice with the packs ensures that the visual stimulus 'a' must immediately evoke the sound (a) or the automatic writing of 'a' when required. The articulatory feel of the letter is also used as the bridge between these. This systematic and multisensory approach ensures that the pupil has the opportunity to learn any missed at an earlier stage.

The Reading pack is built up as the pupil learns the letters and blends for reading. The letters are printed by the pupil on the blank cards, playing card size and on the reverse a drawing or picture is made of the clue word which the pupil has selected to unlock the sound e.g. *a – apple*. On presentation of the letter or blend on the front of the card the pupil says the key word and sound(s) the letter(s) make.

The Spelling pack is built up in a similar fashion. The teacher articulates the sound, the pupil repeats it, noting the articulatory 'feel', writes the appropriate grapheme down from memory, reads what has been written and then checks by looking at the card whether this is correct. 'The use and practice of the Spelling pack is the key to the programme' (p. 25). Over time other letters making the same sound are added and these appear on the back of the card in order of frequency of use. Vowels are noted in red and suffixes in green. If a key word is needed this is written on the back in pencil.

In the third section the Handwriting training system is described (Morse 1984) and has already been given in Chapter 6. The format for the introduction of each letter is similar to that presented in Chapter 6 but a round and upright cursive is used. In section four Morse also provides guidance for those pupils who have wider difficulties in the motor coordination area.

Section five contains some records of written progress through the scheme of three pupils and the final section (Montgomery 1984) describes Multisensory mouth training.

The third book in the series is *The Early Stages of the Programme* (Prince-Bruce, Morse and Cowdery 1985). It gives an overview of the whole programme, the structure, the terms used in the first part of the programme and gives example lessons of particular aspects. The rest of the book explains the linguistics of the early stages and sound pictures, Simultaneous Oral Spelling, the l-f-s rule and then a range of games to reinforce the teaching points made.

What becomes apparent is the tightly structured nature of a teaching session which is highly intensive and demanding of both pupil and teacher. One hour sessions are conducted with pairs of pupils matched for sociability and in terms of skills and needs. A typical teaching session has the following work order pattern:

• alphabet work;
• reading pack;

- spelling pack;
- words for reading;
- words for spelling;
- dictation;
- pupil uses new words in own open-ended writing;
- games and activities to reinforce learning.

The Programme: The Later Stages, D Part One (Prince-Bruce, Cowdery, Morse and Low (1986) give an overview of the whole programme and the purpose of its structure. The full set of diacritical marks are explained but only the breve and macron are suggested for the pupil's use. There then follows the full teaching order of the programme in a chart cross referenced to rules, packs and pages. There are seventeen detailed pages of this and then pages 23–75 contain the phonemes still to be introduced, the rules and generalisations associated with them, related vocabulary, dictations and games.

The Programme: The Later Stages D Part Two (Morse, Low, Prince-Bruce, and Cowdery 1986) introduces the higher order end of linguistics teaching with more on open and closed syllable, vowel digraphs and diphthongs. Silent letters, word families and stable final syllables appear with example lesson plans, alternative approaches to suffixing work, prefixes, possessive rules and finishes the programme element with accented syllables, accents in English. There are then a series of related games pp. 57–80. The complete reading and spelling pack cards are then shown in full.

There are three final books in the series – *The Handwriting Copy Book* (Morse 1986), the *Infant Handwriting Copy Book* (Morse 1988) and *The Spelling Notebook* (Cowdery 1987). This is a reference work and contains a summary of all the linguistic rules and teaching points governing English spelling which a teacher and pupil might conceivably need. It is an indispensable companion to the series but also useful as reference and source book for anyone interested in spelling in general.

Figure 7.3 shows the results of some remedial work with Steven based upon TRTS. He received six twenty-minute tutorials over a period of six weeks from a student in initial training in a setting where he was not permitted to learn cursive writing. He can clearly be seen to have cracked the alphabetic code and now has some chance of making progress.

A remedial spelling/writing correction strategy: Simultaneous Oral Spelling – S.O.S.

This system was first introduced into a remedial programme by Bessie Stillman in 1940 and it became part of the Gillingham, Stillman and Orton Dyslexia teaching Programme. Hickey made it a basic constituent of her remedial programme. S.O.S. is a powerful strategy which should only be used to overcome errors which do not respond to any other treatment. For most developing learners it is not necessary for teaching them a spelling.

It is a rote learning strategy and as such must be used sparingly otherwise it annihilates a pupil's powers to generalise and use analogies, making them become dependent rather than independent spellers. Look – cover – write – check (Peters 1967) is not the same strategy.

S.O.S. protocol

- Look up the word in the dictionary with help if necessary.
- Write down its spelling from the dictionary *naming* the letters.
- Check that the spelling is correct. Here the teacher should also check so that the word is correct from the outset.
- Cover the spelling and then the pupil should write it from memory saying the *name* of each letter as he or she does so.

- Now they check with the original spelling.
- They should repeat this S.O.S. procedure three times.
- The criterion is three correct spellings in a row.
- Next day it should be checked to see if it has been retained.
- If it has not, identify the area of error and this time use lower case wooden or plastic letters to build the word correctly three times saying the names of each in the process.
- Repeat the S.O.S. procedure and check again.

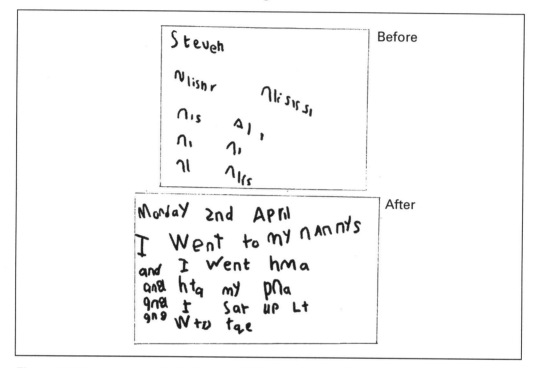

Figure 7.3 Progress made by Steven (6½ years) after six lessons on TRTS (Reduced to ⅓ size

Summary

The identification of spelling errors and spelling difficulties is discussed in relation to the spelling task and examples are given of types of assessment which can be undertaken particularly in relation to performance based assessment.

Developmental, corrective and remedial spelling approaches are discussed and exemplified. What is clear is that any method which systematises and presents an orderly approach to the teaching of spelling during the course of reading and writing development will prove helpful to most spellers. Over reliance upon worksheets as a substitute for direct teaching will be unlikely to lead to good spelling development particularly in children with learning difficulties. Worksheets are very popular with Learning Support Assistants but may merely serve to occupy the pupil's time in a seemingly constructive manner without improving reading or spelling even when the activities are enjoyable.

Dyslexics are the three and four time failures of such systems and so to get them back up to grade level they need a specialist form of intensive teaching which works best in tutorial matched pairs according to the writers of the programmes.

Chapter 8

Reading

Introduction

In mediaeval times education was mainly provided by the church and religious orders except for private tuition for the sons of the rich and later the privately endowed merchant schools.

The earliest method of learning to read was by a system of alphabetic spelling using 'black letter' a gothic style of print which was difficult to decipher visually making the spelling method more appropriate. Putting the dot on i's was an innovation to help clarify particular letters from each other, as in Figure 8.1.

Figure 8.1 Gothic or black letter

The ABC spelling method of learning to read was only replaced in the 18th and 19th centuries when the sounds of the letters were taught together with syllables in the Sunday schools and Dame schools. Over this period the black letter had been replaced by print with the advent of the printing press. The method of teaching reading in the UK remained a form of alphabetic phonics up to the Second World War. Initially the reading material was that in the handwriting copy books which abounded at the time. Gradually these were superseded by children's story books associated with phonic schemes. One of the major schemes of the period was published by Ginn and was the Beacon Readers (Fassett 1927). This taught systematic phonics for reading and spelling as well as using Look and Say strategies when appropriate. The phonics approach is known as a *code emphasis* method.

After the war a new method of teaching was introduced from the USA which by the standards of the day was modern and up to date. Instead of the traditional stories and fables of the older schemes there were stories about children. It was written in the print script favoured then by educators for being easier to read and had 'modern' illustrations. The Janet and John scheme was the prime example of this new *meaning emphasis* or Look and Say method.

The advantages of the method were that words of interest to the pupils could be used. As soon as a few whole words from the scheme were recognised by sight the early reading books could be read and this could prove highly motivating. In a phonics scheme it might take six months before the mechanics had developed sufficiently to read anything of interest and the reading material was confined to such things as 'The pig with a wig did a jig in the bog'. From the earliest stages in Look and Say the books could be more pictorially interesting and attention could be directed to meaning.

However the advantages were found in the end to be outweighed by the disadvantages and so modern schemes and methods since the 1980s have incorporated mixed approaches. This was to avoid the heavy demands made upon the visual memory by Look and Say. There were equally artificially controlled vocabularies and meaningless repetitions and confusability arising from words with similar patterns – 'was' and 'saw'; 'monkey' and 'money' and so on. The most significant problem was that the pupil was given no skills with which to tackle new words until a basic sight vocabulary of 50 words was known. The pupil had to guess from the picture clue, the syntax or the general meaning of the flow of words, semantic content. There was no recognition developed that English is basically an alphabetical language with consistent patterns in words.

Although the recommendation in the Look and Say schemes was that the sounds of letters should only be introduced after the basic sight vocabulary had been established, what Francis (1982) found was that children with no reading problems quickly learned to infer the initial sounds of words whether these were taught or not and used these to help make better guesses in reading whereas the poorer readers at six had failed to do this. When they did learn the sounds of the letters they then tried to sound out all the words which led to further problems. Much earlier Chall (1967) in a major survey of reading methods had found that more pupils were disadvantaged by the meaning emphasis methods and failed to learn to read than by code emphasis ones. There were still a significant number who failed by either method, presumably those we now know as dyslexics.

Reading acquisition

What has become clear from such researches is that unless the letter sounds are *taught from the very beginning* of learning to read, especially within a Look and Say context, a significant number of children become confused. Thus it is that the principle of learning sounds to help in decoding the initial sound of words has now been incorporated into most schemes. However, good practice can take decades to percolate from research into practice for in 1981 Grundin found that the Look and Say method predominated in teaching reading in infant schools and this still obtained in 1993 (Hinson and Smith). Even so some teachers might not teach sounds for reading at all despite what the scheme recommended.

The Pictogram System (Wendon 1985) has also had a significant impact and has helped many teachers organise their reading provision on a more balanced basis because of its systematic way of introducing letter sounds with stories and games. Another significant force in the teaching of reading was Smith (1973, 1985). His analysis from a linguistic point of view was that reading should be taught as a *psycholinguistic guessing game,* as a top down activity with constructing meaning from text playing the most significant role. Meaning was best derived from sentences and so it was important that children had interesting stories to read.

Waterland's (1985) *apprenticeship approach* to reading also gained supporters. The method was based on the idea that we learn to ride a bicycle by getting on it and riding and that in reading children will learn best by reading. This was a view first propounded in 1936 by Witty and Kopel based upon their researches of what worked best. Waterland's classroom was given over to reading activities where adults and children could sit together like at home and share reading activities. The *real books approach* is also a top down method in which children select whatever book they think they might wish to read and take it to the teacher who reads it with them, for them, or listens to them, as appropriate. It takes a high degree of reading teaching skills to manage learners reading in such a highly open system but it can be done. Now in the literacy hour *group reading* takes a significant part (Southgate-Booth 1986). To introduce more structure some schools have *colour coded their library* of books so that the pupils can be guided towards books appropriate to their reading skills.

These are just a few of the main approaches to reading which have been adopted. There have been others such as *i.t.a.* (Pitman 1961) in which 44 symbols were created to represent speech sounds to supplement the phonics approach; diacritical marking systems were also proposed and even words in colour. None of these has prevailed for a variety of reasons not always educational. *Lloyds* (1993) *system of phonics* is based upon the i.t.a. principles but uses ordinary alphabet letters.

As has already been indicated in Chapter 7 there have been a number of reading and literacy surveys which find there is insufficient data collected on the same basis to demonstrate a real decline in reading standards over the decades. The SATs results have however provided data which shows that a significant number of pupils are not reaching level 4 in reading at eleven and are thus not equipped to cope with secondary school learning. The target has been set that 80 per cent of pupils must reach this standard by 2002. This does at least recognise that there is a continuum of ability and skills in which by any system some will take longer to achieve level 4 than others. However a number of schools have communicated to the LDRP that their literacy results at Key Stage 1 have been up to standard or above but with a significant decline at Key Stage 2 of the scores of the same pupils. This is unlikely to mean that the pupils have forgotten some of their literacy skills. It may mean that there needs to be a drive to give more attention to teaching literacy skills in the junior phase or that the targets which have been set are harder to achieve than at Key Stage 1 and may in fact be wrong.

There is insufficient research however to find what works quickly and well. A *combined approach* to the teaching of reading was found by Hatcher, Hulme and Ellis (1993) to be better than either method on its own. They found that 130 poorer readers in Cumbrian schools benefited significantly over controls from being taught the sounds of the letters, and letter combinations with regular reading practice. When the paper was presented at the British Psychological Society conference it was claimed to be the first study of its kind in Britain! This indicates not only the poverty of the country's research base but also that in different parts of the country and even within counties and boroughs, changes to more effective mixed methods still may not have taken place. It also suggests that newer approaches such as emergent writing and creative spelling which take account of the literacy knowledge children bring to school are not widespread amongst reading teachers.

Parents in partnership (Wolfendale 1987,1997) with schools is an increasingly important paradigm in reading provision. Parents learn how to listen to their children read with the support of the school and are encouraged to read stories to them on a regular basis. Illiterate and semiliterate parents in the best schemes are helped to learn to read with their children and in separate support provision in adult literacy projects.

There appears still to be wide variety in the effectiveness of early reading provision which new funding initiatives will seek to address by retraining teachers and introducing the Literacy Hour.

The substantial reforms introduced by the Government CATE committee (1983) and affecting ITT courses from 1987/9 have now come to fruition. As a result we now find that student preparation is not heavily biased in favour of one particular method of teaching reading, on the other hand it is cursory, (Gorman 1993). ITT has to be changed again.

Reading futures

It is perhaps surprising that at the end of the 20th century when we have voice-activated computers and word processors, we should be worrying quite so much about standards in reading. Perhaps the new millennium will introduce a new era in learning when it is no longer necessary for us to read and write and reading will become a pleasure pursuit with special classes such as for yoga.

Reading failures

In addition to the outlines already given on the basic approaches to teaching reading, what is a consistent factor across all of them is that reading teachers can make any scheme or system work in which they believe. This is as long as they are well organised in terms of the resources, they are systematic in their approach and that their method is structured and cumulative. All normal readers will learn to read by any such system. But each will have its different proportion of those whom it predisposes to fail. This seems to be 4 per cent (Rutter *et al.* 1970) in the Look and Say environment, and 1.5 (SED 1978, Clark 1970) in a phonic environment. Larger numbers of failures have been identified in inner city areas and because of social, cultural and second language problems (Rutter *et al.* 1979). Now a third substantial factor has come into play and that is the demands of the National Curriculum. Teachers are finding that their reading development activities are being constrained by the need to cover the syllabuses of the subject areas. Wragg (1997) found that 68 per cent of teachers gave this as the main constraint to reading teaching in primary schools.

The pupils who were identified as reluctant readers by Goodwin (1995) gave a variety of reasons for their reluctance such as, being forced to read in a big group; going on the reading scheme; reading aloud without having a chance to read the text in advance for themselves; and noting that other children were permitted to read to the teacher for longer or shorter times. What put them off reading were limited opportunities for choice of reading materials in the classroom; an inadequate range of books and a dislike of reading aloud. Another view from pupils was obtained by Duchein and Mealy (1993). Their pupils were only just functionally literate and they felt that if they had had more opportunities for sustained silent reading they might have continued to enjoy it and improve their skills.

It is important to know and understand the views of these pupils who are destined to be lower attainers if we are to help them retrieve this position. More investment in an attractive and interesting range of reading books is necessary and the careful choice of several reading schemes which have a high interest factor and plenty of supplemental materials from which to build a personal approach for individuals. These materials need to be accompanied by opportunities for small group reading, individual reading to the teacher and silent reading opportunities on a daily basis. A number of primary schools already operate a silent reading period each day after the lunch time session when it can have a calming effect upon the children and gives the body a period of rest in which to relax and digest the lunch as well as giving time to become immersed in a book.

Readability

Readability is a significant factor for it is possible for young skilled readers to read adult texts but without grasping much of the meaning because the vocabulary in them is beyond their experience. Technical texts also pose difficulties for many school age and college readers because they contain several concepts in the sentences and specialist terminology which needs to be understood first. Mathematics is a good example of using a specialist language to which children need a carefully graded introduction.

There are various measures of readability which can be used to check the level of reading a text requires. One such is the Simple Measure of Gobbledygook or SMOG Index (McLaughlin 1963) also recommended for use by the Basic Skills Unit. A literate person is one whose comprehension is equal when reading to his or her comprehension of the spoken language. Functional literacy is the ability to cope with reading material such as signs and simple forms with a reading age of about eight years.

SMOG is probably a more effective measure of readability when used on higher-level reading material. Unlike the Fry and Spache readability measures which allow for the artificial frequency of polysyllabic words by excluding all proper nouns, McLaughlin's measure counts all the repetitions and tends to give spuriously high scores in story book materials for younger children which may include words like grandfather, Jennifer, elephant, helicopter and caterpillar. The lowest reading age calculable with SMOG is eight years. The procedure is as follows:

- Count 10 consecutive full sentences at the beginning, middle and end of the reading material to be assessed.
- In the 30 sentence sample count every word with 3 or more syllables. Each repetition is counted.
- An estimate is made of the square root of the polysyllabic words counted to the nearest perfect square. For example if 61 polysyllabic words are found then the nearest perfect square is 64 and the square root is 8. (Select the lower of the two squares when the scores falls exactly between them.)
- Add 3 to the approximate square root. This gives the SMOG grade, that is the reading grade the individual must attain if she/he is fully to comprehend the text.
- Now add 5 to arrive at a *reading age*.

Reading testing and diagnostic identification of reading difficulties

The text, *Reading: Test and Assessments* by Pumfrey (1985) contains a summary of a wide range of tests. Those produced since are mainly updates and revisions of these or new products covering niches and new strategies e.g. phonological approaches.

What is needed by the teacher is a well standardised test with which the results of a school can be compared in relation to age and area. A test of word recognition is quick to administer individually and the Schonell test is still useful and widely used. Although first published in 1946 it has been checked at intervals since for reliability and validity. The original manual contained a wider range of reading, spelling and number tests which have not become so popular.

On its own a word recognition test is insufficient and needs to be supplemented by a sentence or paragraph reading test to check other skills. Examples of this might be the updated Neale Reading Analysis which also gives a comprehension test and a test of speed and takes about 15 minutes to administer individually. It also contains a miscues analysis and other items. It is particularly useful in that if the comprehension test scores are higher than the fluency scores it is an indication that the pupil is of higher ability and is reading below mental age level indicating specific problems rather than a general slowness in learning. Low comprehension scores in the presence of average or good fluency indicate the reverse and that an increase in language based work is necessary as described in Chapter 5.

Tests such as the Salford Sentence reading test can be useful indicators and have like Neale three equivalent forms so that six months does not have to elapse before retesting. The Daniels and Diack Reading test 12 is a group reading test with multiple choice answers to insert. Handwriting difficulties can depress the performance somewhat and able pupils can make good guesses at answers without being able to read the words properly but this is true of most group tests. It is therefore important that any test result is used as supplementary information not as a 'truth'.

If the errors of any reading test are recorded even when this is not part of the format, a useful diagnostic inventory can be drawn up for developing later interventions.

When a pupil has difficulties in reading at the projected age group level signified by the test it is essential to do a further exploration of the word attack skills. This can usefully be started by checking if the pupils know the sounds and names of any letters and if so do they then know any blends. There are a number of tests of phonics available such as Carver's and a full review of these and phonic resources is given in Hinson and Smith (1993). The Aston Index includes a letter test which can be used diagnostically equally well with five year olds as for the seven year olds for whom it is recommended. It also contains the Schonell Reading and Spelling tests and a vocabulary test all available for use by teachers. The NFER publishes a wide range of both old and new tests which can be administered on application under licence by teachers including their own series of standardised tests for schools.

Reading development: formative interventions

Spelling and handwriting approaches

These have already been described in Chapters 6 and 7 and the crucial thing for reading is to incorporate over time the 200 basic words for reading and spelling which are found in most children's books. As pupils learn these at different rates, class spelling tests based upon them can prove demotivating, unless a good measure of success can be ensured for all with sections of the list over time. Best is to enable the pupils to chart their own progress on these words preferably using the computer which can check them and give the teacher a print out on a regular basis.

If a pupil is having problems learning some key words one of the strategies which might be tried is precision teaching.

Precision teaching

Strategies such as Precision Teaching for reading or for spelling are always worth trying to see if they can overcome a learning barrier but must be carefully monitored so that if there is a lack of immediate success it can be discontinued and substituted with a tuition programme.

Precision teaching is not really a method of teaching but a structured system of assessment. The pupil is merely asked to look at the words and try to learn them for the assessment.

Precision teaching is used to kick start a pupil's reading when there is difficulty in learning a few particular common words. Used as a remedial strategy it can empower the pupil, for success when it comes, is easily seen and may be quickly achieved. It is not a procedure to be used for every new word as it merely reinforces rote learning rather than generalising and problem solving strategies. The pupil might be encouraged to try a *visualisation* strategy to aid the memory e.g. imagine the letters especially in the tricky area are written in a coloured, woolly substance and try to project this vision on the classroom wall before writing them down. The PT procedure is as follows:

- Decide what the pupil will learn e.g. to read *come, said* and *their* correctly.
- Decide the form of the response e.g. the pupil will read the three words aloud.
- Decide on the conditions e.g. the task will be presented visually.
- The criterion for success will be that the pupil has mastered the skill when the words can be read 100 per cent correctly to the teacher (or into the tape) at a rate of 1 word per second for 20 seconds.
- The probes. A reading probe will be given every day for 20 seconds. The order of the words in the probe will be randomised.
- When implementing the programme:
  the pupil will be given one minute's study time;
  the probe will be given at the same time each day;
  the format will be see to say;
  the number of correct and incorrect responses will be counted and recorded on a chart by the pupil;
  the procedure will be timed and controlled by the pupil.
- The PT will be discontinued after the pupil has met the criterion on three successive days.
- If the task proves too difficult it will be sliced (made easier) and two words will be given. If it still proves too difficult a different method of learning will be used.

Shared reading

In the early stages of reading pupils cannot know enough at the outset to help them decode text by sounding out unknown words even if they were to know some sounds. The pictures in the books tell a story and the text beside or beneath the pictures tells the same story in words. Thus it is possible for the child to turn the pages and 'read' the pictures. Shared story reading such as this with adults will teach the basic concepts about print and that it can be followed from left to right. Large books to read to the class with multiple copies of the same story are used to enable beginning readers to pick up these books and read them again and together. In the process of shared reading pupils will learn particular words and this is why schemes are constructed to try to give the right amount of repetition without being boring and to provide a carefully controlled introductory vocabulary.

It is at this same time that children need to be learning some of the most frequent initial sounds because this will help them reduce the number of words they could choose from to make sense of their reading of a sentence e.g. 'The big dog b-.' The options after **b** are fairly limited to a verb beginning with **b**-. Probably 'barked' would be a good guess and the picture would confirm 'big dog' and 'barking'. Thus it can be seen that sentences, pictures and initial sounds are important to the beginning reader in constructing meaning from text. Likewise the non-attainer at seven or eleven will respond to such an approach but the text needs to meet their older reading needs and they may have to be very specifically taught to use an initial sound to start to decode a word. They may need to be shown how it can narrow down the options in a reasonable way. If they do have some reading skills they will often have developed the habit of reading and filling in with words which sometimes make sense and sometimes do not. It is necessary temporarily to slow down their reading to give them a little more time to enable their brains to do this form of processing. Asking them to read a paragraph to themselves first before reading it aloud to the teacher can help understanding as can asking them to read each section twice before discussing it. Discussion of what is read is also important for it reminds the reader that text has a meaning and that the full task is to gather this meaning as they read.

Tizard *et al.* (1982) found that pupils who were heard read at home showed more significant reading gains than those given extra tuition by teachers at school, with the poorest readers making the most significant gains. Thus it is that current policies on reading are directed to gaining the full involvement of parents and extending tuition to them where necessary and feasible in education for parenthood projects and parent involvement plans of schools.

Onset and rime

Good readers have been found to operate on text in different ways from poor readers (Clay 1979, 1989, Bradley and Bryant 1985). The better readers adopted a more top down approach to reading and tended to use just the initial sounds of words to help them without sounding out the rest of the word. They would tend to use analogies with other word endings which they did know to help them (Goswami 1992, 1994) as in *-and, b-and, s-and, st-and, gr-and, br-and.* The initial sounds might be single sounds or digraphs and blends which are called the *onsets.* The *rime* is the end section of the word and some schemes have onset and rime games built into them as a variant of 'snap' or as in 'fishing for sounds' where the sounds might be onsets or rimes.

Phonological Awareness Training

Goswami (1992, 1994) rejected the notion that the ability to identify and use analogies appears in later reading development and showed that young readers could identify rimes in words and will also make word play with them as in doggy, moggy, froggy, poggy especially if encouraged to do so. Failure to be able to do this is an indicant of likely reading problems. Wilson (1994) developed a Phonological Awareness Training (PAT) training programme based upon this research for older pupils, seven years and above, having difficulty with reading. Her method was to teach them how to split onset from rime, segment the initial sound, and then for about 10–15 minutes a day spend time generating words. They are given the onsets and a set of rimes to work with. Thus a worksheet might consist of all the letters of the alphabet as onsets and four columns headed by different rimes with which to generate words.

The PAT approach is used to supplement a reading scheme or reading approach and is meant to be used every day. The first three days are given over to worksheet completion; on day four they do reading and 10 spellings; on day five they are given five sentence dictations. There are five placement sheets in which the pupils read lists of words. If longer than 60 seconds is taken then the placement begins at the next level down. The pupil needs to get at least 14 out of 20 words correct before a new worksheet is given. As the programme is so carefully constructed it needs to be followed systematically. Although the worksheets may look dull and uninteresting the children enjoy them and 'one cannot fail to notice the excitement as the children improve' (Thomas 1996, p. 17). In an experimental trial in which all subjects had reading difficulties and with 24 matched controls, aged 8–11, working on the programme for 20 weeks, the experimental group made significant gains in reading and spelling.

Phonics

Phonics teaching is often represented as learning the separate sounds of letters and then blending them together as in *c-a-t.* What must be avoided is the intrusive schwa sound or 'uh' noise with each letter sound e.g. cuh - ah - tuh – says 'cat' because of course it does not! Thus the pupil should learn to mouth sounds quietly for blending or encoding as this helps avoid the schwa sound. Next there are some ways of teaching phonics which are more helpful than others. For example in learning to sound out the word *stand* it is better *not* to teach the pupil to do successive or cumulative blending e.g. *s - st - sta - stan - stand.* Instead the strategy should be to teach initial single sounds and initial blends such as *s-*

and *st* -; basic syllable structure cvc so that pupils know that every syllable must have a medial or middle vowel which has either a short sound which should be tried first and a long sound when the vowel says its own name. They should also be taught end blends e.g. *-nd, -st, -ld, -lt* and so on in order of frequency or need from the texts being read. The word *stand* would thus be decoded in the following way: *st - a - nd*.

As only about forty per cent of words are phonically regular in this way pupils will need further linguistic knowledge added to the phonics programme. This avoids the meaningless letter strings approach where words with common patterns are lumped together but have little possibility of being any value in generalising to a range of other words e.g. the 'string' *ree* is contained in *tree, three* and *street* but it is more powerful for children to learn the blend *tr-* and double vowel *e*'s sound and then *thr* as the digraph blend *th* and *r* with double *e* and finally the three letter blend *str - ee - t.* This is a *logical form of phonics* and can lead on to more complex and irregular word structure governed by linguistics. In all of this phonics teaching it is important for development that the pupils learn the meaning of the key vocabulary such as letters, blends, consonants, vowels and syllables.

Pattern recognition approaches

Reading is undertaken by the visual pattern analysers in the retina of the eyes and then further analyses take place at the cortex (Dröscher 1975, Deutsch and Springer 1992). They can quickly enable a pupil beginning reading to identify the printer's 'a', the child's reading book 'a' and cursive 'a' as all the same letter and making the same sound. The walls of the classroom should have examples of each type so that they can have plenty of experience with these different forms. It is only in handwriting that one form, the cursive, should be taught because here we are concerned with learning a fluid movement. Some early studies of tank recognition (Allen 1965) showed that when novices were given simple jigsaws of Conqueror tanks to construct and then were shown pictures of a variety of tanks they could always identify the Conqueror in whatever view it was shown although they were unable to describe it in a way that would distinguish it from the other tanks. This principle when applied to teaching beginning readers in reception also worked (Montgomery 1977, 1979). The pattern of the ball and stick print in children's books was analysed and it was found that it was mainly composed of circles, short lines, long lines and short loops, just the sort of structures our visual system is set up to analyse.

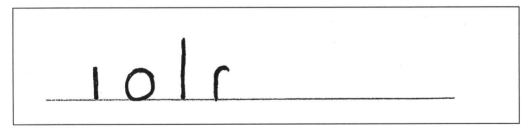

Figure 8.2 Patterns in letters

From these simple shapes 23 of the 26 letters of the alphabet can be constructed. From the circle and the short and long 'sticks' 15 can be made i.e. a b d i k l o p q t v w x y z. Reception class groups were trained to copy such ball and stick patterns from left to right and to put together jigsaws of nonsense words. The experimental groups after eight training sessions, twice a week for fifteen minutes were found to be more than two reading books ahead of matched controls as recorded by the teachers. Non-readers in the programme began to read (Montgomery 1977). When the jigsaws and ball and stick patterns are based on words in the reading scheme or the sight word list then more progress can be expected.

Pause, prompt, praise

This strategy is in every teacher's repertoire. Novices and parents may, however, need to be encouraged to refrain from correcting a child too quickly, and being punitive and over critical when helping decode the text. They may not even think of praising their children at regular points and generally encouraging and motivating them. Some in extreme cases have been known to adopt a very harsh stance and beat their children for stumbling over reading, others may have the need to show off their own abilities and are hypercritical of the young reader which is very demotivating. Some parents are barely literate themselves and may be frightened to try to help their child and will avoid it and in some cases act against it.

When hearing children read the teacher listens carefully and when there is a hesitation does not jump in immediately so that there is time for a second attempt at decoding to take place. The first attempt may be to look and say in reading the sentence, however this word may not be recognised and so the next strategy should be for the pupil to reflect on the sentence and predict the word using the initial sound. The picture clue would then be used to confirm this if necessary. If the pupil cannot do this then the initial sound, single sound or blend as appropriate, should be given as a *prompt*. When the correct word is achieved the teacher quietly says, 'Good' without interrupting the reading. When that section or sentence has been completed further encouragement can be given by asking for rereading and questions may be asked about the text to check for comprehension. Any onsets not known can be recorded afterwards and made the subject of direct teaching.

Hearing reading, an informal reading inventory (IRI)

Figure 8.3 (p. 109) is an example of an IRI for hearing reading (Montgomery 1990). It covers a broad range of behaviours which can contribute to difficulty or success and enables the teacher to intervene or arrange for an IEP (Individual Education Plan) to be drawn up.

An example might be that a pupil reads haltingly in a monotone. Ask the pupil to read the piece again and this time stop at the full stops and commas and take a quiet breath whilst the teacher taps the table twice slowly before reading is continued. This gives the eyes time to scan ahead and decode as well as absorb some meaning from the text. It will also begin to help with audience effects. The next step may be to practice dropping the voice at a full stop and taking a slow breath. Pupils may only segment part of an onset e.g. 's' in *stop* rather than 'st' the initial blend. The strategy would be to do some direct teaching of this blend on the reading task and then reinforce it later with work on syllable structures and onsets and rimes.

Supported reading

For beginning readers reading for extended periods can be tiring and so sharing reading is an important aspect of reading time. It begins, or should begin, with parents reading to and with their children. Older siblings might also be encouraged where appropriate to read to the younger ones but not in place of parents. It can also be particularly enjoyable to obtain 'talking books/audio books' from the library to listen to, both adults and children. Reading along with the tape, or following it can also encourage reading skills to develop and reinforce others.

In the classroom teacher and pupil may read together in *supported reading* sessions or the teacher may have a big copy of a book and the pupils shared copies and they might read along with some sections together and then discuss them. It is helpful if an easy chair or two can be placed in the classroom which can hold an adult sitting by a child or two children sitting together sharing a book. The most important aspect is to set up the ethos of a reading environment where people read to each other and together and where older

Categories	Examples	Month
TEXT	Book and page no. Criticism, if any e.g. gender, race, class or moral issues.	
WORD ATTACK SKILLS	Guesses from initial sound, tries blend, self corrects, syllabifies uses onset and rime, articulates clearly.	
COMPREHENSION SKILLS	Can answer factual recall questions, can predict from pictures, sentence or story, can answer inferential questions.	
AUDIENCE EFFECTS	Pauses and drops voice at a full stop. Read in units of meaning not word by word. Speed right.	
BEHAVIOURAL SIGNS	Check reading position, body posture. Does she/he use bookmark or finger above or below the words?	
EMOTIONAL SIGNS	Tenseness? Lack of fluency. Jigging. Monotone. Breathlessness. Fixed smiling.	

Select one key item on which to intervene._____

Figure 8.3 Monthly Progress Chart

pupils may come in and read or share a story. They may also bring in books they themselves have written to try them out on their target audience. It is extremely important that men and older boys are seen reading books too so that it is not seen by some as a girls' occupation and to be avoided.

Another strategy under the umbrella of supported reading is *group reading*. In group reading the technique to be avoided is single pupils reading out loud to the whole class. For although they may volunteer they may find it is far more difficult than they thought and they can perform poorly in their own eyes and develop anxiety about the process. Instead it can be much more helpful to encourage small groups of threes to sit round together and read their reading book together.

Language experience approach

This method was originally developed (Olson 1977) to help readers with difficulties learn to read. The main principle is that it uses oral skills as a bridge between utterance and text.

First the teacher establishes a partnership with the pupil and starts from the point the pupil has reached in literacy skills. Second the pupil is helped to understand the necessary separation of the writing process into two parts requiring two roles. These are the role of author and the role of secretary both of which are essential to work of quality (Peters and Smith 1986). The teacher then works with the pupil to find out the context of the subject and what the pupil wants to say. The pupil dictates the account or story to a scribe, a tape or the teacher and it is written down verbatim. This is then read so that what is read are the words daily used to describe events for often the words in the reading schemes are outside their register. This first draft is then studied and discussed, edited and new sections may be added to develop or improve it. When the pupil is satisfied the story is printed and suitably illustrated with pictures or photographs.

It was also found to be more motivating to the pupils when their own accounts and stories were written down in this way for them to use as reading material later. It is a technique frequently used in remedial settings to encourage reading. When this was coupled with their own pictures and photographs and title page with the author's name upon it, motivation to practice reading it was significantly enhanced (Fisher 1982). She found however that it was still necessary to add to this a programme of phonics and word attack skills in order to keep their development moving forward. Older pupils and skilled readers frequently enjoy story writing for a wider audience and it is a strategy which under the aegis of writing and publishing can encourage older poorer readers and writers to commit themselves to print and then they may be encouraged to read them to the younger children so gaining good practice at a number of levels.

Technology and reading

Now that word processors and personal computers are widely available in schools writing and publishing for reading can be more easily practised. There are also a large number of teaching programmes available for promoting reading skills. These are however mainly limited at present to phonic drills and word association. Even some of the phonics are inappropriately scaled in their order of introduction and some are wrong in confusing vowel digraphs and diphthongs, consonant digraphs and blends. Nor do they always use appropriate techniques in their 'teaching' presenting 'letter strings' that have no meaning or linguistic validity and so have no power to generalise to a wider range of words. These reservations are also true of some phonics schemes (Montgomery 1997b). They are probably best used to reinforce particular teaching points already identified by the teacher.

CD-ROMs as data sources are extensively used in secondary schools and need to be more used in primary schools. They can serve two functions, the first as a source of information and the second as reading material in association with sound and pictures. If poorer readers are allowed to work on the information in pairs they can support each other's reading and can find the strategy highly motivating giving them wider reading practice.

The *ARROW technique* (Lane 1990) refers to Aural, Read, Respond, Oral Written in which self-voice is used. The technique is flexible, a typical reading example might be: the pupil hears the teacher reading a piece of text; the pupil follows the text; the pupil responds by reading the text live and is recorded; the pupil listens to self reading the text following it at the same time; some of the key words may be written down or sentences used for dictation.

According to Lane's researches the technique can be motivating by offering endless repetition without criticism, there is increased attention to self-voice inputs and it increases subvocalisations which are supportive of both reading and spelling. '*Language Masters*' are more simple devices which replay several words for reading and spelling. The teacher can record appropriate words geared to pupils' changing needs.

Tape recorders are still very useful forms of technology especially where poorer readers record themselves reading a passage and can then play it back listening and reading and self correcting as necessary. At a simpler level an adult may be present to help in the corrective and developmental feedback.

Paired reading

This technique was first developed by Morgan and Lyon (1979) and is a system in which the child and parent or child and teacher read along together. When the reading is going well the child can raise his or her hand as a signal and the adult stops reading. As soon as the child begins to falter the adult picks up the reading again at the child's pace. The technique provides instant reinforcement and an immediate correct model of fluent reading. Meaning is established in the usual way by discussion of the book and the pictures in the conversation afterwards. Shephard (1986) in a teacher research project found that paired reading was more effective with 6–7 year olds with reading difficulties in the earlier stages whilst pause, prompt, praise was more effective in the later stages and with more able readers.

Miscues analysis

In the 1940s Spache analysed errors in reading into a number of categories – substitutions, additions, omissions, reversals, inversions, and refusals. These categories were used by Goodman (1969) to undertake miscues analyses and develop strategies for intervention. They also form the diagnostic basis of the original Neale (1958) Reading Analysis recently revised. Chambers (1987) illustrates the miscues technique and how the errors may be recorded in a quick code. The errors are regrouped into positive and negative and from these it is possible to decide whether with prompting the pupil can decode the word using onsets, syllabification or by using syntax and meaning. The negative errors would be ones which bear little relation to the word to be read and these are then provided by the teacher to help preserve the meaning for the pupil.

The categories of miscues are however too global to be really useful for developmental intervention. For example it is more important for the teacher to know what the substitutions are or which letters and syllables have been omitted, reversed, added and so on than to name the category. This is illustrated in the next section.

Formative miscues analysis

When hearing reading it is important to use all the strategies possible to encourage and motivate the novice reader. In association with this it is important to listen very carefully to note the actual error which the pupil makes. Thus if the pupil reads, 'The train is going under the (pupil refers to picture) - tunnel', instead of, 'The train is going under the bridge,' it is a fair bet that the five year old has never travelled on a train and this is a best guess. She might have been on the underground and it would be a good idea to find out later whether she has any real experience of what is being read. It could be helpful to discuss this with the parent and try to arrange a trip or arrange an I-Spy railway outing for all the class so that the relevant vocabulary of a scheme book can be underpinned. In the rest of the reading it can be noted whether the pupil is using or can use onsets to decode words in context. If not it may just need a little encouragement or prompting and example to get the strategy going. If it does not prove possible then it may well be that the pupil's knowledge of initial sounds and blends should be checked to identify which if any are known. It can then be expected that those known should be used in decoding. Pupils may need permission to guess a word from its onset before they begin to develop the strategy.

If pupils are not reading the correct endings and miss -*d, -ed, -es, -ts, -er* and so on, then they need to be encouraged to read the phrase again. If these key letters are still omitted when the brain has had a second chance to scan the words then these past tenses and plurals need to be pointed out to encourage them to let their eyes scan fully through the word. Next they should be asked to read more slowly for a little while to see if this enables them to gather them up in the general reading. In addition these endings need to be taught for spelling and reading and any difficulties noted in distinguishing them. Pupils who have suffered from mild hearing difficulties, or are suffering from glue ear may find these endings difficult to identify in speech and so have not incorporated them into their vocabulary skills. A careful articulatory training strategy is needed to support the learning.

Reading *was* for *saw* and *on* for *no* may well be classified as reversal errors or sequencing problems but they are really neither in a diagnostic sense. They are a very good cue or indicant that the pupil is using a Look and Say strategy to recognise a word. The eyes fixate on groups of letters at a time and all or any may be used as key indicants or critical features for identification. If the pupil during reading learns to focus on the front end of words and tries to mouth the letters, the onsets or blends, it is then not possible for them to read *was* for *saw* or *on* for *no*. The eyes can then be allowed to sweep across the rime to try to say the whole word using context clues and analogy to aid the process. If this still does not result in the correct word in context then syllabification can help and some further prompts.

Poor readers often become so distressed by their slow and laboured reading that they try to hasten and then make many errors and can lose the sense of what they are reading. Rereading and slowing down the pace of reading can prove helpful as well as teaching more onsets through reading games and spelling teaching.

Higher order reading skills

The higher order reading skills are also often referred to as higher order cognitive skills such as reading for deeper as opposed to surface meaning, reading for the main point, skimming and scanning and so on. These will be given more detailed treatment in Chapter 10 on *study skills*. What is important is that once pupils have begun to learn to read – *reading acquisition*, they should begin to use their reading skills to learn other material from secondary sources – *reading development*. This however should continue well into secondary school and beyond if the necessary higher reading skills are to be developed. It is often the case that reading teaching in a systematic fashion ends at the end of infant schooling to the detriment of learning and creating substantial difficulties for those who have not acquired the necessary skills by that stage.

Reading for an audience

Reading round the class should not be a strategy employed to develop reading. It is rarely successful and can induce a great deal of anxiety and stress. Many pupils wait in trepidation for their turn, losing the sense of the piece whilst they calculate then practice their sentence. Having volunteer pupils read aloud to the rest can also induce feelings of inadequacy in the listeners. A better strategy is to encourage pairs and small group reading so that they can practice audience effects. This means that they need to have some training in this form of reading. They need help with breathing, phrasing, units of meaning, pacing; using full stops to drop the voice and pause, using commas to pause and let the eyes run ahead to capture the meaning, reading a passage silently before reading it aloud; reading sentences and passages as though they are public announcements, learning a part and then reading the play aloud and so on; making up role plays and then writing down sections of it to read aloud and discuss.

Older pupils some of whom may be less good readers may gain a lot of confidence and motivation practising and then reading story books to very young children. It is a useful strategy for giving them text at their own reading level even though the content is below their interest age.

Summary

Reading skills are still crucial if pupils are to have access to the current school curriculum. Failure to become literate can also have a severe disadvantaging effect in career terms. There is sufficient applied research from across the decades to show how to be effective in reading teaching. Most teachers will say that they use mixed methods but it is often not a judicious mix but an arbitrary one.

In this chapter a range of developmental and formative methods are described, all of which teachers should be using as pupils' skills change and develop.

Formal testing is described and is suggested to be of most use for looking at class and teacher progress. Performance based assessment is recommended alongside diagnostic testing in order to identify needs and teach to these more precisely.

Chapter 9

Study skills

Introduction

Study skills is an umbrella term for what were once called Library Skills and now Information Skills, such as how to look things up in alphabetical order; using an index and a catalogue; reading titles, side headings and summaries to find out what books are about and so on. The study skills approach includes not only finding the information from libraries and other sources such as the 'web' and CD-ROMs but also linking this use to the wider skills of reading, asking questions, and making notes as tools in self-directed learning (Wray 1989).

The typical content of study skills programmes is illustrated by Pascal (1998) in his One Day courses for NASEN. The programme covers *Active Classroom Revision; Examination Skills* such as question analysis, answer planning and proof reading; *Specific Skills –* organisation of notes and study time, note taking, note making, essay planning; and finally *Learning Techniques*. These activities are directed to organising memory for better recall and are useful end strategies. But it would be better if we did not start from there. If we can make the original learning more effective revision would not be required.

The title study skills is used here because of its practical value in directing attention to the *process* in which the learner is engaged rather than the content which is being studied. This is becoming an important distinction in what has been termed 'the Information Age' when information is so readily available that key words can summon it up from disk and no search skills are necessary. What is becoming increasingly important however is to know how and where to find information when it is needed and then how to manage, organise, use and communicate it effectively to meet specific purposes such as in decision making and problem solving.

Study skills are a form of self-directed learning and are used whenever material is read or viewed in order to use in a communication. Reading is still one of the major areas in which study skills are applied and so study skills are sometimes referred to as 'higher order reading skills'. This distinguishes them from the reading skills used in reading a novel or a newspaper.

In the Schools Council Project (1980) to promote literacy in the secondary school, reading was defined in two ways – *receptive reading*, a running read such as we use when reading a novel, and *reflective reading*, a more complex activity in which we use study skills to glean information and ideas from the text. In fact it is equally possible to apply the same terms, receptive or reflective, to viewing of video and screen data or real life events.

One of the major concerns of the project was that pupils did not distinguish between the two forms and tended to apply the same strategy, receptive reading, to all their study tasks. A series of activities was devised called Directed Activities Related to Texts (DARTs) in order to encourage pupils to slow down and engage in more reflective reading. The activities illustrated different ways in which pupils could be obliged to give detailed attention to text and the results could be discussed with them to show the value of adopting different study strategies. Reflection helps them gain metacognitive control over their mental processes of which they may initially be unaware but then can promote and control them better in subsequent activities. Watson (1996) showed the value of such reflection to her groups with moderate learning difficulties.

Different types and levels of study skills are needed for different tasks from simple note taking to writing a report or doing research. The first thing which should be done is to *survey* the information by *scanning* the title, subtitles, looking at the pictures, reading the summaries, flipping through each page, using the index to locate specific information.

Most pupils are unaware of these skills and they need to be specifically taught. They may even feel they are cheating if they do not start at the beginning and read through. Thomas and Harri-Augstein (1984) found that 50 per cent of University undergraduates used inappropriate reading strategies when asked to study text. They frequently used receptive reading strategies, straight reading through repeated several times. This was found to be inappropriate for successful completion of a short answer paper or making a summary of the text. Those who used a mixture of rapid reads and a slow note taking run were successful on the short answer paper and those who included pauses for reflection and reorganisation of notes, or worked backwards and forwards through the text were successful on both.

In addition to scanning a text Anderson (1979) found that there were other activities going on. He found that nearly all his students were trying to answer three additional 'how' questions. These were:

- How much do I already know about this topic and text? If anything is already known it can act as *advance organisers* (Ausubel *et al.* 1978) to make later acquisition more effective.
- How interested am I in it?
- How difficult or time consuming will it be for me to learn what I need to know from it?

If by scanning they could not answer all these questions they went on to read sections in more detail or the surveying would break down and they turned to another book or another activity.

Some cognitive activities used in studying

In reading for information surveying, locational and reference skills may be used. In reading for the main idea or to understand the logic of a piece, interpretive skills are needed to understand structure and sequence, to find meaning and to understand tables, graphs, illustrations and ideas. If it is necessary to understand the overall structure of something then information has to be organised, summarised, outlined and perhaps labelled. Critical comprehension will involve the use of thinking strategies at literal, interpretive, critical and creative levels. In the process we may reflect on ideas presented, tap into the writer's organisational plan, relate new ideas to old using mental imagery. All of these activities are potentially at work together and as can be seen it is essentially a constructive learning activity: constructive in the sense of the learner or reader being actively engaged in *making meaning*.

Post study activities

Study in schools and colleges is usually undertaken in order to learn information and understand ideas of others. Thus it is that a number of post-study activities have been designed to help reinforce the strength of the learning and aid later recall. Examples are: note taking, essay writing, diagramming, charting, sketching, concept mapping, mnemonics, and SQ3R (*Survey* the information, raise *Questions* about each part, then *Read, Recite and Review* – 3R). Each of these when first introduced can be interesting to the learner but as time wears on most of them will be given up as they are essentially too tedious – all except sketching which can have an impact in its own right. Even so it may be better to sit and paint the real thing rather than to vivify it from sketches. Most of them involve rote learning activities after the event whereas if the initial learning task was involving and constructive, directed to some real purpose the learner wanted to achieve then there would be little chance of forgetting. When indeed cognitive study skills activities were undertaken by students then they found they forgot very little (Montgomery 1994) and their examination results improved accordingly.

The average adult reading rate for recreational/receptive reading is about 350 words per minute. After rapid reading courses readers have achieved speeds of more than 1,600 words without loss of comprehension. For pupils in schools the rate builds as they become more fluent from about 75 in Year One to about 230 in Year 6 and so on. Fluency in reading is important in studying textual material for it is a handicap if the pupil's attention has to be divided between decoding the text and thinking about its deeper meaning. The tendency will be for poorer readers to remain at a literal and surface understanding of the material. This can be counteracted by allowing pupils to work together on all study skills activities so gaining reading support without the need for the intervention of the teacher or learning support assistant. It is cost effective as a method.

Study skills and the curriculum

Study skills have for decades been found to be inadequate. Perry (1959) first reported that his Harvard students were unable to use books flexibly to answer the different questions set and tended to read the text straight through wherever the information they needed was to be found. Thomas and Harri-Augstein (1984) found similar results in the UK.

Osborn's (1963) studies of primary children showed similar results and secondary pupils fared little better according to Maxwell (1977) and Sayer (1979). It was for this and similar reasons that the researches on the Effective Use of Reading (Lunzer and Gardner 1979) and Extending Beginning Reading (Southgate-Booth *et al.* 1982) and Study Skills in the Secondary School (Schools Council 1980) were established. Colleges, LEAs and schools across the country picked up the problem and tried to do something about it with varying degrees of success.

Even though pupils might know how to survey text there was no guarantee that they would use the skills and save themselves time (Neville and Pugh 1977). They needed systematic teaching in primary and then again in secondary school. There was also little correlation between reading ability and the ability to use effectively a range of study skills. As a result of all this one major teaching issue began to emerge. In the earlier studies where library skills had been taught these were separate from the curriculum and few teachers knew about it (Winkworth 1977) and there was little transfer to the curriculum (Bullock 1975). The new approach was to integrate the teaching of study skills into the curriculum and let them arise naturally in the course of study. However the danger was found (Patterson 1981) that many of the needed skills would not be taught. The development of a whole-school approach to this (Winkworth 1977) was seen as an answer to this criticism and many training programmes were developed with schools to try to achieve this. However this was not always found to be effective (Montgomery 1984; Meek and Thomson 1987). Wray (1989) recommended a judicious mixture of both approaches to ensure that the skills are taught and then used. Winkworth (1977) divided the study process into six stages:

- Definition of subject and purpose;
- Location of the information;
- Selection of the information;
- Organisation of the information;
- Evaluation of the information;
- Communication of the results.

In the last ten years partly because of the information revolution and more particularly because of a concern to ensure that students at all levels really *learn how to learn* and can become *self organised learners*, the conception of study skills has been significantly developed beyond a consideration of the narrow confines of information skills (Weinstein *et al.* 1988). Examples of these strategies follow.

Teaching for learning using cognitive study skills

Reading for the main point or main idea

Prose: The following extract and main point exercise was taken from Royce-Adams (1977).

> With a food surplus, the Pueblos were able to turn their attention to other activities besides locating or growing food. In one particular area – pottery making – the Pueblos developed a high degree of artistry. Potters became artists and developed individualised techniques, painting fine-lined geometric designs as well as reproductions or life forms on their vessels. Paints were improved and pottery has been found that contains three or four different colours. (*From Columbus to Aquarius,* Dryden Press 1975).

Identify the main point of this extract: _____.

Although this was originally designed as a paper and pencil activity for individuals it has much a more powerful use as a teaching and learning strategy if the pupils in pairs read the passage and discuss the answer they are going to offer and its justification first. Next in a whole-class interactive teaching session their responses can be presented and argued through. After this they can do similar activities on other material in the subject area in which they might learn that most simple texts contain the main point in the first sentence, very useful knowledge for scanning activities. Later they could be introduced to paragraph writing patterns. For example they can be asked to decide which of the following writing patterns is exemplified in the Pueblo passage:

a. illustration – example
b. definition
c. comparison – contrast
d. sequence of events

e. cause and effect
f. description
g. a mixture – state which

Again this should begin as a pairs exercise followed by class discussion. Further activities on the same theme may then be undertaken to reinforce the ideas and then at some point the pairs can try to reformulate the passage in each of the different patterns to get the feel of the different options available in writing about any subject. Pupils might be asked to read a poem and find its main point or central idea. They should first of all be allowed to discuss their ideas of the main point with their partners. This ensures that each has read through it and can clarify some of the meaning with a peer as well as permitting every pupil to frame an answer and discuss it. If the teacher first asks the whole class (interactive teaching) only one or two are really required to think and put their ideas into words, the rest may remain passive listeners. The pairs strategy also has the ability to involve pupils who may not at first think from the content that there is any relevance in exerting themselves to think. Listening to and helping a partner can overcome this hurdle and make the activity enjoyable for its own sake. All the cognitive skills activities require 'brain engage' or thinking work and this can also be made explicit.

What is our life? a play of passion;
Our mirth, the music of division;
Our mother's wombs the tiring houses be
Where we are dressed for this short comedy
Heaven the judicious sharp spectator,
That sits and marks still doth act amiss
Our graves that hide us from the searing sun
Are the drawn curtains when the play is done.
Thus march we playing to our latest rest;
Only we die in earnest – that's no jest.

(Walter Raleigh)

The main point is of course 'life is a play' and it is an interesting way of using metaphor. After feedback to the whole class on the main idea and the introduction of the term metaphor they can be asked to identify the six ways in which he supports his assertion or exemplifies his main theme. Stating that there are six ways provides that little bit of problem solving challenge again for the pairs. When they have worked on this for a while a whole class feedback session can be given. If they are finding the task too hard the noise level will rise above the quiet buzz and the feedback session can begin early so that all understand the first example and try to find the rest.

In order for the pupils to understand fully the nature and use of metaphor in this context it is necessary for them to apply what they have learnt to a new situation. For example they might next be given a metaphor on which to construct as a class a similarly structured poem or piece of writing, this time using interactive teaching – 'Life is like an apple'. This is a difficult concept and so cannot be solved easily without using all their brains and some teacher guidance on how to structure the approach so giving them a schema to follow. They will need to dissect the apple, quite helpful here if there is a real one to cut to list the 'hooks'. These will be the spherical/ball shape, the 'dimples' at each end, the peel, the flesh, the juice, the sweet/acid taste, the core, the seed, the stalk. Now pairs can take each one in turn and think how it resembles some aspect of life, perhaps noting down their ideas for the discussion and a group 'poem' may be constructed from their efforts. If they then go on to research and collect other metaphors the collection might well reveal some which will encourage pairs or individuals to try to construct their own poems.

As can be seen, the main point strategy can be used as an introduction which gives a rest from reading a poem, working through the difficult vocabulary to establish comprehension and then discussing what it is about. Vocabulary can always be clarified as the pupils work through the poem but only after they have had a chance to puzzle it out between them.

Pictures. It is equally possible to apply the main point strategy to a painting, a video extract, a play, events happening naturally and advertisements.

Concept mapping comparisons

Concept mapping is related to the notion of identifying main points. Now the mapping links them and also includes related ideas in the net attached to each main idea. The essence of the map is that it represents one's own ideas about a subject and by representing these on paper they can be inspected, compared with those of others and discussed. As new knowledge is accumulated it can be incorporated into the map and a new map may need to be drawn showing a complete change in the whole structure so that developments in learning can be seen.

It is a useful strategy for finding out what pupils bring to a topic and getting this recorded. Subjects might be: castles, settlements, rivers, weather, flowers, fish, food, tools. In addition any subject in the school curriculum can be begun with a '*brainstorm*'. After several teaching inputs, readings and so on the pupils can be asked to draw another concept map to show their current thinking. From this the teacher can see conceptual developments without having to read large volumes of notes which may or may not reflect knowledge or understanding. To help the pupils reflect upon what they know and have learned, ten differences between the pre- and post-teaching maps may be asked for together with their reflections upon these. Again pairs work can help focus the attention as each discusses the work with the other and tries to explain it.

The rationale behind all this is that we so often do not know what we think until we try to explain it to someone else. Brainstorming and drawing the concept maps enables the pupils to bring to the forefront of the mind the previous knowledge and experience and inspect it to try to establish connecting links. Having heightened awareness in this way there is a better chance that the information in the new learning will be integrated into the past structures.

Concept completion

A completion exercise: partial extract.

UNDER GROUND by James Reeves

In the deep kingdom under ground
There is no light and little ____

Down below the earth's green ____
The rabbit and the mole explore.

The quarrying ants run to and fro
To make their populous empires ____

Do they, as I pass ____
Stop in their work to hear my tread?

In pairs the pupils should fill in the gaps trying to reconstruct the author's meaning. On completion they can be asked for *three* reasons why they produced words which rhymed. Those who finish quickly can try the exercise again but find another word to put in the gap which may or may not rhyme but preserves the sense.

Assessment

If learners take on an assessment role then their learning of the material is likely to be as high as 95 per cent (Race 1991) and is able to reach deep levels so that it is available for transforming and using in various creative ways. ITT students were asked to evaluate one of the tests of reading set out in a workshop and to use the criteria described in a lecture on 'What makes a good test'. Inservice students on a distance programme were asked to write a short answer paper on Dyslexia worth 100 marks. It must consist of True or False, multiple choice and sentence completion items. The main bulk of the questions had to be based upon three recent research papers and their own knowledge of the subject.

In general science and biology teaching pupils were asked to work in small groups to produce an end of year exam paper. They then had to draw up answer plans and assign marks to model answers to each question. Younger pupils did similar activities but in relation to two questions. They were all given previous exam papers to base their ideas upon and all their text and notebooks.

Editing and marking

Pupils' writing from previous years can be used as edit material. Good and poor examples can be used for comparison to discuss what makes quality writing. The subject can be a story or a narrative such as one about the Wars of the Roses. The original can be used as a *scaffold* for producing a good account and pupils can learn from assigning grades based upon subject criteria.

Older pupils working for public exams can be given the task in pairs to mark an exam essay using a criterion referenced grading system given. They then have to justify the mark they have given and write some positive points of guidance on how the writer could have improved the essay. Again content is learned incidentally in this process as well as exam technique.

Summarising

There are many summarising strategies which can be used as part of study skills to enhance learning.

Most study material contains information of various kinds such as facts, opinions, methods, steps, ideas and so on. A quick assessment by the teacher can enable such questions to be asked as:

Identify the five (ten etc) *main points* in the chapter about e.g. the role of the church/ monarchy/peasantry. Extra marks and special praise can always be given for finding more points.

Ask the pupils to write a summary of a book/chapter they have just read in exactly 50 words, a *minisaga*. This really causes them to focus on the essentials of the text and to consider each word of their sentences carefully.

A book or a section of work can be recorded as a *summary*. Pupils often do not know how to summarise something and so the introductory techniques of stating how many main points there might be or how many words they are to use can be helpful training exercises. They have to stop copying out sections verbatim and think over the sections of the content. Discussing how they approached their task will give helpful clues on how to develop their techniques further. Many careers such as police investigation work, travel agency, travel guiding, advertising, teaching, research, journalism, medical practice and so on require summarising skills. The value of the technique should be emphasised.

Writing summaries for different *audiences* can help pupils understand the deeper structure of learning contents. For example a section of historical information might be written up in the style of a modern day newspaper such as *The Sun*. Pupils can have a lot of fun with this a well as secure their knowledge of an historical topic. They might be encouraged to put all their work together as an historical newspaper, or present it as a version of the 'Today' Programme on radio or a news broadcast on TV. The National Curriculum is still so full that much of the development work on such projects would need to be done independently outside lessons but the enthusiasm which can be generated is usually sufficient for this to happen. Writing the same information for different audiences can also help it to be learned in a pleasurable way rather than by rote. The audiences may be real, historical, or in different registers for different cultures and sub cultures.

Critical reviews of topics will include a brief description of the key aspects with some appropriate evaluation. Examples of the structure of such reviews can be used as models for the pupils to follow. They have to gain more than a knowledge of the content in order to do any summarising task such as this. It is also important to identify the overall structure of the ideas and their relations to each other. Different review perspectives can also be adopted such as in relation to gender, ethnicity and class not only in English classes but also in technology, science, art, geography, mathematics and history.

Comparing and contrasting information is another approach to identifying main points and summarising the key issues in many subjects. Sometimes it can be helpful to tabulate such data. At other times the differences can be represented diagrammatically.

Organising, tabulating, classifying, ordering, diagramming, categorising are all strategies for reducing information into smaller manageable and more meaningful chunks. The process of doing so is also very useful for assisting learning at deeper levels to take place especially where the learners have done the work for themselves.

Time lines, lists, critical incident analyses, and *chronologies* are in their own ways summaries which can be useful processes to aid learning.

Teaching. In order to help pupils to learn it is sometimes helpful and interesting to provide them with learning materials and set them to design a short teaching session on some aspect. This can be prepared in small groups and then the mini teaching session can be given to the group. Some might be encouraged to give their presentation to the class. Nothing concentrates the mind more on getting down to the essentials of a subject than when it has to be taught to someone else, as every teacher knows. After assessment it is one of the best methods for ensuring something is learned. Teaching sessions need careful structuring so that the same material is not repeated and the class do not have to listen for long periods to topics which the teacher could present better. This is where group work is an important substage and all presentations must have a time limit. An alternative may be for the presentations on what they have learned to be offered at parents evenings as a change from wall displays and neat books. Both parents and pupils gain an enormous amount from these teaching sessions.

Exhibitions and posters also summarise achievements and can be accompanied by pupils giving mini presentations on their work and what they were trying to achieve. Even the youngest of pupils can do this.

Other types of summary might be to make 2 *overhead transparencies* to illustrate the main points of a topic. Only seven words to a line are permitted and only ten lines to be used so that it is large enough for all the class to see easily and compare summaries. They can learn from this that the best method is to put as little as possible on the OHT and then the presenter uses these key points to elaborate upon.

On another occasion they might be asked to produce their summary notes as an A5 *four page leaflet* for visitors or as a *cartoon sequence.* Pin men drawing needs to be taught for those who would rather not exercise or exhibit their artistic repertoire. Personal computers can be used to support this if pupils prefer.

Preparing *annotated bibliographies* can be challenging activities for older pupils undertaking small topics or research projects. A list of about five works is sufficient.

Critical comprehension

There are many different higher order reading activities associated with critical comprehension which can be used in study skills activities across subject areas. There is not space to do more than identify them here as follows:

Drawing inferences and abstractions; recognising intent, bias and propaganda; evaluating or developing criteria for use in evaluation; distinguishing fact from fiction and opinion; judging truth or falseness; identifying relevance; interpreting and forming opinion and argument; making models and drawing analogies, predicting ends of stories, consequences and events; drawing conclusions and so on.

Designing and making study skills games

A constructive way of summarising and reinforcing study skills is for pupils to share projects on designing a study skills game. In English they might base the game upon a younger child's story book or a novel for older players. In subject areas key topics and chapters can be the information base. The purpose is to design a board game based on the text. The board should illustrate aspects of the text and the players move round the board by throwing a dice. Different squares can represent different levels or events and every few squares the players land on a 'special' when to move on they have to take a card from the pack and answer the question. Penalties can be built in and correctness of answers can be by agreement of players and if necessary reference to the text. The study skills questions should demand a range of different study activities and content knowledge.

Sequencing

Pupils can read a research paper/story/chapter or piece of poetry or prose to identify its main and subordinate points, separate these out and then put them in an order which reflects the meaning of the text. They can then be asked to make this into a *flow chart*. Alternatively the teacher can take a flow chart designed by another class, empty it of its contents and give it to the new class to puzzle out what goes in the empty boxes. In each case a puzzle or problem is given for the pupils to resolve. In the process they will have to give the content their most detailed attention and they learn it very well without any apparent effort, enjoying themselves in the process especially if they are allowed to work in pairs and are not made to feel it is some kind of test.

Any process or procedure in a subject area can be made into a sequencing activity. For example there is a *set sequence or procedure* to lighting a Bunsen burner in science or following a routine or recipe in technology, geography and maths. Once the procedure has been demonstrated and practised it can be useful to say, instead of 'Now write down that procedure', 'Now look at this work sheet with your partner and you will see that someone does not know how to do it at all. Write down the number of the sentences showing the order in which they should be'. This means that the poorer writers are not handicapped and can focus on the real issues. Scissors can be provided if they need to cut the text up and move it about physically. If there is a fear that scissors would be too big a distraction then prepared cut slips can be given out in envelopes which adds to the little bit of mystery.

The same technique can be applied to paragraphs or short stories. What sometimes results is that the pupils may produce a better order than the original author. Very young pupils enjoy being given puzzle envelopes in which the lines of a nursery rhyme have been cut up and jumbled. In pairs they can then practice their reading skills whilst they try to reconstruct the nursery rhyme correctly. Self correction can be built into the task by having a picture on the reverse of the card lines which is only complete when all the lines are in the correct order.

Cooperative learning strategies

Dansereau (1988) gave dyads scientific content to master. He broke the cooperative learning strategy down into six stages which he found facilitated cooperation and learning and labelled them MURDER e.g. establishing the positive Mood for studying; Understanding while studying, Recall – summarising what is read; Detect errors and omissions; Elaborate to facilitate learning and Review.

Summary

Study skills are a form of self directed learning and frequently involve active work on textual material. Although reading skills are taught in primary school it is not usual to teach higher order reading and cognitive skills there or in secondary school although they are considered to be essential to the educated person and a requirement for success in higher education.

Cognitive study skills were defined as those which 'engaged brain' and caused the reader, viewer or listener to interact with the material and grapple with its ideas and deeper meaning and structure. In reading they would break the reading process up and cause interaction with the text bringing about reflective reading which is so often necessary for text other than novels and newspapers because it is concept dense.

These sorts of study skills are different from those which involve lower order activities such as using a dictionary or an index and finding one's way about a book and what its main contents are, or recovering factual information from text and making notes. They are different in that the user is obliged to interact with the material and work on it mentally getting from surface to deeper levels. If teachers also ask pupils to reflect on their thought process and strategies for completing the task this can help to bring it into the realm of metacognition and make the learning even more secure.

It was concluded that it is important to incorporate cognitive study skills into all curriculum subject areas rather than try to teach them as a separate skills course.

Chapter 10

Writing

Introduction

It was reported in the THES 1981 (p. 5) that 25 per cent of first year students at university in Arts, Sciences and Social Sciences needed help with basic writing skills. Barrass (1982) reported that the reasons for this were lack of planning; failure to answer the question; failure to capture and hold the interest of the audience; lack of precision in the use of words and using long words where short ones would do. He also made an analysis of how people are judged by their writing. Thus if the writing was clear, with correct spelling, had good punctuation and grammar, and the arguments were well presented then the writer was regarded as considerate, well-educated, competent and forceful. If on the other hand the reverse was the case then the writer was regarded as inconsiderate, lazy, careless, uneducated and incompetent. Teachers in schools and employers at large appear to be little different in attitude.

In the 1990s Higher Education has seen a massive expansion in student numbers from about 8 per cent of the school leaving population to 30 per cent. With this has come complaints of a lowering of entrance and academic standards. Presumably those needing help with basic skills have increased at least in proportion to this wider access so perhaps things have not changed so much. At the least, 25 per cent of this enlarged group of students in HE need support and they have come through the school system without finding it.

However cognitively able students of any age are, at some point they must at present still commit their thoughts to paper and the paper evidence provides a substantial weighting in the final award in most courses apart from Art, Design and Technology and the Performing Arts. The lower attainers make up 40 per cent of the school population, many semiliterate, who leave without any formal qualifications and so it is surprising that the subject of how to write is not given more detailed treatment. The main vehicle for learning to write appears to be the practice of writing without direct tuition in the techniques of authorship.

In this chapter writing will be temporarily disconnected from transcribing which involves spelling and handwriting skills or word processing. It will also be separated from vocabulary and grammar for on these subjects there are many school textbooks and manuals for guidance and these aspects are usually taught in schools. This leaves the techniques of authorship and developing writing which involve not only reasons, goals and motivation, but also thinking, planning and organising.

The main technique which nearly all teachers use for composition, the story schema is that the writing must have a beginning, middle and end, but there the lesson seems to end. The following sections are therefore about a *grammar of writing*, that is an understanding of the way different forms of writing are organised and how the pupil learns the relevant schemata for producing it.

Skilful writing

A skilful writer is able to select and organise the content of the writing to fit the purpose and in line with an overall plan. There are various strategies for developing this plan and one basic method is to use text structure or story schemata to do this (Rumelhart 1977). Only if the pupil or student is aware of the structure of a text does it appear to have an improving effect on their own writing (Hiebert *et al.* 1983).

Lower attainers and writing

It would appear that whereas good writers and successful pupils in school learn about the internal organisation of texts spontaneously from reading others do not. These others tend to be the slower learners, the learning disabled such as dyslexics and those with subtle language difficulties with verbal CATs scores being 15 points lower than nonverbal scores (Mellanby *et al.* 1996). Palinscar and Brown (1986) attributed these differences to a difference in learning style and Torgeson (1982) suggested that it was because they were inactive learners. The inactivity was attributed to a problem in *metacognition*.

The deficits in metacognition were a lack of awareness and use of organisational strategies. This lack of awareness prevented them from using the schemata for writing. Hence dyslexia teachers find that with very much older pupils they are still having to remind them to use the basic story schema – beginnings, middles and ends whereas very much younger good readers will already have absorbed this.

It could be argued in the case of all these pupils with learning difficulties and lower attainments that they are so effortfully preoccupied with the mechanics of reading they fail to grasp the overview of the organisation of what they read. This then has implications for their writing and they are doubly handicapped for they are struggling with the mechanics of spelling and handwriting as well as content so that they have little cognitive time and space for higher order aspects of processing.

Many lower attaining pupils including beginning writers start writing without any general plan and produce phrases and sentences in a semi-linked form more as a serial production of random thoughts than a composition to communicate.

Culturally different writers

Culturally different pupils frequently lack the standard text knowledge of the school. The closer the match of the language of the home to the formal language of the school then the closer will be the match to school texts making it easier for this group of pupils to acquire writing grammars.

Conversely the oral language of pupils from another culture and lower socioeconomic groups is more distant from that of the school and so does not map easily onto its structures. Their language is frequently abbreviated and content bound. For example a pupil looking at a series of stimulus pictures sees first a boy and girl playing football and then a broken window. The third picture shows an angry adult gesticulating at them. When asked to explain what the story is about the pupils with distant language usage might say: 'They broke it 'n 'e's angry'. There is nothing wrong with the comprehension but the form does not help them with school work since it is too closely dependent on having the pictures present. Lack of practice in listening to and using extended oral language gives them little opportunity to discover writing schemata and implicitly make use of them in their writing.

If we can teach lower attainers what other pupils pick up from their ordinary reading and apply in their writing then this could be a significant support to them. The following sections will consider this problem of what can be taught.

The writing task

The writing task appears to involve three stages of planning, in the first of which ideas are developed, information is gathered and the content is organised. These are the higher order skills. Next these ideas and contents have to be written down, the translation stage. In this the intellectual skills of spelling, punctuation and grammar are needed to get it down on paper. The final stage is the review when the author edits and revises the plan and the content as necessary. Less skilful and beginning writers often omit this stage altogether.

In less skilful writing the author may gather ideas and information but may not have an overall plan and so writes up the notes as they appear in the notebook trying to make connections in the process. In student essays this is frequently transparent and every new paragraph begins with the same form – 'Norton *et al.* 1993 found', based on the notes. Several radical edits of such material can convert it into a readable form but it is best when this is done to fit with an overall plan.

In an APU survey a range of writing tasks were identified for study (Gorman 1986) and these provide a useful checklist for forms which pupils' writing might take. They were: Description / observation, record / report, plan / speculation, narration, instruction / direction, argument / persuasion, evaluation / review of evidence, correspondence / request, explanation / reflection, imaginative response / expression of feelings, reasoning, editing, extended pieces of writing. They were marked for content, organisation, grammar, spelling and style.

Planning for writing: writing grammar

Story schemata

It is usually suggested in story writing that the beginning introduces the character and the setting, the middle is where something happens to the character or she/he does something and the end gives the result or consequences of the action (Applebee 1978). Teachers often give introductions to story lessons on the use and nature of describing words, the adjectives. They then find only the good writers transfer this knowledge to their actual stories.

Beginnings

The teacher can select the first sentence or paragraph from one of a range of books suitable for the age group. The extract is read with the pupils and then they should be asked what type of beginning is illustrated by it. They can make up a category and it can be noted on the board. A further set of extracts can be given out for pairs to discuss and to note down their ideas on types of beginning to share with the rest of the class. Some examples follow from the bookshelf:

1. My dear wife Carrie and I have just been a week in our new home, 'The Laurels', Brickfield Terrace, Holloway – a nice six-roomed residence, not counting basement, with a front breakfast parlour. We have a little front garden: and there is a flight of ten steps up to the front door. . . From *The Diary of a Nobody* by George and Weedon Grossmith.

2. We set off in an open cart drawn by four whip-scarred little oxen and piled high with equipment and provisions. No mediaeval knight could have been more closely armoured than Tilly and I, against the rays of the sun. . . From *The Flame Trees of Thika* by Elspeth Huxley.

3. LONDON. Michaelmas Term lately over, and the Lord Chancellor sitting in Lincoln's Inn Hall. Implacable November weather. As much mud in the streets, as if the waters had but newly retired from the face of the earth, and it would not be wonderful to meet a Megalosaurus, forty feet long or so, waddling like an elephantine lizard up Holborn Hill . . . From *Bleak House* by Charles Dickens.

4. For the most wild, yet most homely narrative which I am about to pen, I neither expect nor solicit belief. Mad indeed would I be to expect it, in a case where my very senses reject their own evidence. . . From *The Black Cat* by Edgar Allan Poe.

These extracts illustrate ways in which the authors introduce character, set the scene, place the events in time, create atmosphere, imply mystery or suspense, and indicate humour and sometimes do several of these.

Some examples from childrens' stories follow – these were harder to find:

1. It was halfpast nine on a dark April night that all the excitement began. The village of Peterswood was perfectly quiet and peaceful, except for a dog barking somewhere. Then suddenly, to the west of the village a great light flared up. . . From *The Mystery of the Burning Cottage* by Enid Blyton (Mammoth Press).

2. Slithering snail slime! said Gert. 'Look at this, Lil, in The Daily Spellegraph.' Mmmmm.......Warm spells........ She read. What's that, a new kind of curse? No. That's the weather forecast, you angel, replied Gert. . . From *The Twitches* by Roy Apps (Simon and Shuster).

3. Omri emerged cautiously from the station into Hove Road. Someone with a sense of humour and a black spray-can had recently added an 'l' to the word Hove on the street sign on the corner making it Hovel Road. Omri thought grimly that this was much more appropriate than Hove which sounded pleasantly like somewhere by the sea. . . From *Return of the Indian* by Lynne Reid Banks (Chivers Press).

4. Franklyn could slide down the river bank all by himself. He could count forwards and backwards. He could zip zippers and button buttons. He could even sleep alone in his small dark shell. But Franklyn was slow even for a turtle. . . From *Franklyn* by Pamela Bourgeois (Macmillan).

It is possible to predict to some extent the nature of the book which will follow from the tone of these opening words. When the pupils come to write their next composition they can select a type of beginning which they will explore in their writing.

Editing beginnings
The 'Haunted House' example can be given to pairs to discuss and mark:

> 1. It was foggy. I went up to the haunted house. I pushed the door and it creaked. An owl hooted. I was scared. I ran home.

> 2. It was a cold, dark night and the fog sucked and floated round me and dripped from the ends of large leaves close by. The old house loomed out of the fog, black and sinister, its door ajar, yawning open. etc.

Pupils can easily see how in the second story extract the writer tries to set the scene and the atmosphere using particular words both verbs and adjectives to create a bit of mystery and fear e.g, sucked, loomed, yawning and cold, dark, large, black, sinister.

Pupils can collect and categorise interesting examples of beginnings from books and put them on disk for reference and use with other classes.

Middles
Studying middles is more difficult for extracts are not feasible and pupils have to rely on memory of the story line. However the main events can usually be recalled and these frequently in books for younger pupils appear as a sequence of events such as what the great green hairy caterpillar eats or what happens to Peter Rabbit as a result of eating Mr McGregor's carrots. In fact well-known fairy tales and fables can be used initially as they are short.

As sophistication increases there may be several parallel boxes in the middle instead of a chain of them representing events an so on. It can be helpful to pupils to have differently coloured B, M and E cards on which the outline plot is cast. If pupils are given a topic such as 'The Bank Robbery' they can work in pairs and map out the story they want to tell. It is not always necessary to go on and actually write it. It can be a more helpful stage for pupils with writing difficulties if they first of all learn to tell some of their stories from the cards to each other and sometimes to a larger group or the rest of the class with the plan on the board or OHP.

The reverse of this strategy can also be used as a pairs exercise. They can learn to map out stories with boxes to them to help them focus upon overall planning as both a learning and organising strategy.

Ends
Pupils often find it difficult to think of ways in which their stories might end and so they give them a standard treatment e.g. 'Then I woke up', 'Then he ran off'. It is particularly useful for lower attainers, according to Bereiter and Scardamalia (1982), if the pupils focus upon endings first and then they know what they are working towards. Their pupils said they found this strategy particularly helpful and it improved the overall quality of their writing.

Fairy tale schema

Simple schemata and direct instruction of writing should be introduced gradually in order from simple to complex. *Narrative* text is usually the simplest to begin with as the schema follows a sequential order. This is typical of fairy tales and folk stories. The stories contain a setting and one or more episodes. Each episode consists of three parts which are causally related (Rumelhart 1980). The pattern followed is: the *setting* in which characters are introduced in time and place (Goldilocks and the three bears); the *problem* – sets the story in motion and presents a dilemma or some adversity confronting the main character (Goldilocks enters the house of the three bears and finds three of everything); the *response* – the main character responds and expresses some thoughts and feelings, there is also an attempt to solve the problem (Goldilocks looks into and tries all sets of three things); this is followed by the *outcome* – what happens as a result of the response (she is caught and she discovers who owns the house, both at once).

Most teachers use *prediction* during story telling to discover if the pupils are comprehending the general development of the story and to encourage creative and reflective responses. What they might not be aware of is that it is also an important means of encouraging the understanding of the implicit story schema. It can be followed up with explicit teaching about schemata.

Prose writing for older pupils

Prose often has a 'pyramid' structure in which the main ideas are stated first followed by the supporting facts and details. The separate paragraphs contain the topic or main idea statement then the facts moving through to the summary or conclusion at the end. Poor writers find all of these organisational aspects difficult but especially the summaries and conclusions which give the reader the review. As the poor writer does not have the plan and the overview it is not possible to share it in the review. There will also be a failure to identify main and subordinate points and a lack of recognition that texts need to have an order.

Expository text structure

Cook (1982) identified five types of expository structure in scientific texts. These are *generalisation* in which a main idea is presented along with other sentences that support, clarify, or extend that idea; *enumeration*: a list of facts is presented; *sequence*: a description of a series of events or steps in a process; *classification*: a procedure for separating items into given categories; and *compare/contrast*: the similarities and differences between two or more things are discussed.

College students were trained in the recognition and then the use of these structures in a strategy training programme. The results in scientific tests and exams were compared with control groups. On a recall of important information test the trained group showed an 11 per cent gain and controls no gain. On problem solving tests the trained group showed a 24 per cent gain and the controls a 3 per cent loss. It was concluded that text structure was an important tool in helping students build connections needed for making inferences.

If we do not teach all pupils in schools about text structure we can speculate that we commit them to underfunctioning, especially the lower attainers. Examples follow of the sort of text structures to be found across texts in general and then some strategy training examples.

In expository text the main point is usually contained in the first sentence. The rest of the paragraph is an expansion upon that particular point. The expansion may take at least six different forms. These forms are:

> illustration – example; cause and effect; comparison – contrast;
> sequence of events; description; enumeration.

An extract from Royce-Adams (1977) demonstrates the structure of a typical expository text.

Illustration – example

> Simply put, comprehension is an act of understanding or the capacity to understand. It can be divided into three levels: literal, critical and affective. Literal comprehension is the basic level. . .

Cause and effect

Some material such as the Pueblo paragraph given in full in Chapter 9 can, as an exercise, be written up in each of these six different ways. It is a example of the cause and effect structure: 'With a food surplus, the Pueblos were able to turn their attention to other activities besides growing or locating food. In one particular area . . .' Knowing about schemata may not result in the perfectly modelled paragraph or account. It is possible to review a great deal of material before finding examples which fit the models.

Comparison – contrast

To help organise for these structures Thomas *et al.* (1984) recommend the use of attribute grids which can be filled in to record similarities and differences. Topic categories are listed on one axis of the grid and the dimensions of interest on the other. This enables a comprehensive comparison/contrast report to be written in which successive points on each are discussed in sequence across the grid. Too often pupils make incomplete lists of similarities and differences between subjects but fail to compare and contrast them as they go. Compare and contrast is really a two stage planning process and is treated as one in which the pupil writes out instantly from memory as points occur.

Sequence of events

In science, geography and technology diagrams and tables are frequently used to represent events and processes such as the water cycle, titration, distillation, the formation of rift valleys and so on. More could be made of these as *graphic organisers* and models of the way information can be represented. Pupils frequently can draw the diagram of the water cycle but do not know the strategy of following the process in sequence using the diagram when they have to describe it or discuss some aspect of it. Cartoons and pictures can also be used as organisers for writing as well as for telling the 'story' in subjects such as history and English. The sequences might then be historical and chronological, or critical incident pathways.

Description

In descriptive text there is an initial topic presented followed by a series of points that relate to it e.g.

> The swallowtail is one of the rarest and most beautiful of our native butterflies. Nowadays they are usually only found in the region of the Norfolk Broads. They live in colonies and the caterpillars feed almost exclusively on milk parsley. The adults are large and yellow with . . .

In descriptive writing in a subject area the pupils can be given the the topic or item statement. They should then jot down the list of attributes as they are recalled in note form. They can then mark the attributes as main and subordinate points and then write up their descriptions.

Enumeration

In an enumerated text there is a statement of the main idea and then the rest of the 'statement pie' follows (Palinscar and Brown 1986). The pie includes proofs, information and examples e.g.

Camels are important animals for desert regions. They can go without food and water for days because of their ability to store fat and liquid in their humps. Their feet are wide and have spongy pads that prevent them from sinking into the sand. They can close their nostrils to keep out grit in the sand storms.

Note taking

One of the significant problems in organising for writing is the assembly of information for use. It may, in story writing, be reliant upon the pupil's memory. The main problem according to the studies of Bereiter and Scardamalia (1982) with lower attainers was of getting access to what they did know and then giving order to it. Bereiter and Scardamalia produced a series of strategies which the teacher could use which moved the pupils from conversation to composition. Without this intermediate stage the writing was limited in content and of poor quality. It is a general awareness of this that encourages almost all teachers introducing written work to begin with a discussion of some kind to excite and extend recall of relevant information. Bereiter and Scardamalia went further than this and identified specific techniques which improved the pupils' writing. These were *prompting, brainstorming* and *listing of ideas*. These strategies opened up the memory. They then entered into planning discussions which gave ending sentences and using structures. They then finished the sessions with reviewing and editing activities. They also used on other occasions a modelling procedure in which the teacher wrote jointly with the pupils.

Note taking from textual and verbal sources has an array of techniques associated with it which are discussed in most books on study skills. They consist of *underlining, outlining, concept mapping, using side headings, writing key words and concepts* and so on. To assist in organising students are schooled in the use of loose leaf files and card and computer indices, in a sense the peripherals of writing. In addition to strategy training the important attributes of attention and motivation during collecting and organising frequently remain unaddressed. Studies by Reynolds and Shirey (1988) on attention, and McCombs (1988) on motivational skills training, both show that learning during reading and subsequent writing can be facilitated by improving these aspects of learners' behaviour.

For example, in a training visit to a Year One summer classroom with a student on ITT it became apparent that the lesson aims were not being achieved. The student intended the pupils to make notes upon a fish or sea dweller of their choice and write these in their books and learn about it in the process. As I moved round the class it was noticeable that most of them were copying notes but were talking to their neighbours on and off about something else. When I asked them to describe their sea animal without looking at the picture in the book or their notebooks they had no more than the haziest of ideas about it. One announced he was dyslexic and so did not have to do anything. A quiet discussion with the student and a check by her on what had been observed enabled us to draw up a plan. She would call them together mid-session and ask volunteers to describe their animal in thirty seconds without giving the name of it to see if the rest could recognise it from the pictures on the chart.

This was done and without exception after a hesitating sentence or two no fish that was recognisable was described although many pupils volunteered to share their descriptions. The student said she would let them continue their studies until the end of the lesson and in the thirty minutes 'talk time' at the beginning of the afternoon she would let them try again to see if they could do better. The pupils went back to their places and there was hardly a sound until the lunch bell. Came the afternoon and the student walked in to find all the pupils at their desks totally silent. As she crossed to her desk they all stood up in unison and waited in silence until she addressed them. She called the register and asked them to come and sit on the mat ready to describe their sea animals. Again they moved quickly into place without a sound. None of this had ever happened before even with the class teacher. They then had an enjoyable half hour of describing and guessing and returned to their places glowing with pride at her pleasure and their achievements. (The dyslexic pupil was told that even if he could not read the words yet he could study the picture carefully and would be able to do just as well as the others in the presentations. Which he did.)

The pupils were able for once to see the relevance of the study task to the aims of the lesson. They therefore gave what they did a significant amount of attention. Ross and DiVesta (1976) have in fact shown in research samples that the expectation of oral presentation facilitates acquisition by inducing awareness of objectives and of appropriate learning strategies by which these objectives can be achieved.

Specialist report writing

Most specialist disciplines will have formats for their reports. In science there is the classic one which is: having done an experiment the pupils are asked to write it up for homework. Later they may even be asked to produce elements of it or design a similar experiment in an exam or SATs task. However many experiments pupils write up in class using the experiment format it seems to have little impact on what they do when left to their own devices and their memories, especially the lower attainers. The 'A' streamed class always produced reports worth 8 to 10 points out of 12 whereas the rest averaged 3 to 4 marks although on questioning they knew the work.

Before any tests a standard homework was devised which was, 'Design an experiment you could do to discover if a pig can fly.' They were then asked in the following lesson to read out some of their designs. Results with the lower attainers followed a predicted pattern – 'You get a pig and stick a pin in it. It did not fly.' Their efforts were marked, e.g. marks out of 12 consisting of, half a mark for each bit of apparatus and one mark (generous) for the result which had not really been put to a 'fair' test. After some more examples and assignment of grades and much mirth the class was asked to construct a reasonable experiment. This was put on the board and the marks were assigned e.g. half a mark for a reasonable title, 2 marks for the diagram with half a mark for each label, 4 half marks for the procedure, 2 marks for the results and 1 for the conclusion plus two marks for a reasoned discussion. On the next test the lower attainers' performance was in the 7–10 range.

Teachers and many other employees have to produce a wide range of reports for many different audiences so it is worthwhile spending time on teaching the format of such reports to teachers and for them to pass this on to their pupils. The report writer frequently forgets that there is an audience to whom the report is directed and that it should therefore be self-contained and understandable. Here many students/pupils are so wrapped up in the process of obtaining the information and presenting it in readable form that they often forget to give it a title or an introduction. They sometimes give their inferences and evaluations before presenting evidence or instead of evidence, and do not discuss the several implications which might follow, only giving their own preferred response. They have to be taught that there are schemata for report writing which they should follow even if this is not made explicit in the problem or question presented. In its simplest form the schema would be:

Title; Introduction; Evidence/consideration of options; Summary and conclusions; References; Appendices.

Reports are easier to follow if the above are used as side headings under which the material is organised. Readers can then select which section interests them.

Essay writing

Essays are written in many subjects and each will have a similar schema to the report with an introduction, the main body of the essay presented in paragraphs of the selected type and a summary and conclusion.

Education essays based in the psychological discipline can be profitably written to a specific schema which helps the students draw out more information than if they write around the question or from a concept map of associations. Strategy training has been shown to improve students' grades (Montgomery 1993).

The first and most important part of essay writing is to examine the question and underline all the separate key parts. There are frequently three to five of these and they should be numbered.

Next about half a page of notes needs to be compiled associated with the numbered points as a map or lists. This is a private brainstorm session.

The writing of the essay can then begin with half a page to one page of introduction in which the key concepts in the question are examined. This is followed by a discussion of the theoretical frames of reference which apply in half a page and then the presentation of four pieces of research evidence, about half a page for each. An alternative can be two main pieces discussed at some length and a half dozen or more given passing reference. Most questions require some application. These can be drawn out at this point or discussed alongside each piece of research evidence. There then follows the summary and conclusions paragraph.

At the end of all this it is essential to proof read the essay, the review. In an exam references are not expected but in course work essays they should be presented at the end and document every name quoted in the essay.

Different questions will alter this balance of elements, some may require only a discussion of concepts and theory, even so some reference in the conclusions might well refer to the implications for research and/or practice.

Proposition and argument in writing

A proposition is a statement of what the writer wishes to 'prove' and the argument is the overall case which is made including the proposition and is also the separate points made in support of the proposition (Inglis and Lewis 1980).

'An argument is a more or less complicated set of premises supporting a conclusion' (Blair 1988 p. 16). According to Blair the most widely used argument displaying device or schema is the tree diagram with lines of argument shown as the main trunk, and the internal reasoning supporting main and auxiliary premises shown as further branching.

Assertions are flat statements presented without evidence stating that this or that is so. In pupils' writing there tend to be more assertions than argument and this point can be usefully made without going too far into a study of informal logic.

An example of an assertion is: Improving public transport will cut down on air pollution. We may wish to do both but there is no necessary logical connection between the two. For example we may improve public transport but no more people will use it.

Inglis and Lewis (1980) gave a list of *suspect types of argument* (p. 52) and how they could be identified by finding:

- persuader words;
- emotive language;
- generalisations;
- analogies;
- familiar appeals;
- conflation;
- rhetorical questions;
- syllogisms.

Having discussed the meanings of these terms and how they may be used to conceal an abuse of logic the pupils can be set to work in small groups to prepare a short argument for the school having, for example, access to the internet. Their report should not take up more than one side of paper. When they have completed their report they are then asked to rewrite it using as many of the ploys of suspect arguments as they possibly can. Older pupils and adults may easily do this directly without the first stage report. The following is an example of abuse of logic: For example:

> We request that all members of staff should be given places on the internet course so that they can be given an opportunity of keeping up with modern technology.

> Surely it is vitally important that all progressive and dedicated teachers equip themselves for this new industrial revolution which is on our doorsteps. A recent Government statement made it clear that all schools will be linked to the internet within a year.

> Who can deny that such inservice training is both desirable and logical? Teachers unfamiliar with the new technology will find themselves stranded like dinosaurs in this new world.

Actively using these forms gives them a higher profile in the mind so that they are quickly able to identify them when they see them in print or hear them in speeches. It is also fun to try to construct these passages together.

Summary

This chapter has concentrated almost exclusively upon organisation in writing, the grammar of writing. This is because lower attainers bring to reading and writing disadvantages which prevent them responding to the implicit organisation of text. They then fail to use schemata in planning and organising for writing and this places further handicaps upon them for they cannot reveal what they do know in a reasoned way.

Story and expository paragraph schemata were illustrated together with those of fairy tales, scientific experiments, reports and formal essays. Writers of all ages could benefit from some introduction to writing schemata.

Chapter 11

Thinking and problem solving

Introduction

Currently there is a wide range of approaches available from which to develop curriculum problem solving but it is the subject experts who need to modify their methods to incorporate the knowledge about thinking which had not been available earlier. The task is easier now and does not have to be invented from first principles. A good example is of Cognitive Acceleration through Science (CASE) developed by Adey and Shayer (1991) at King's College and now 'CAME', the mathematics project. Through cooperative learning and reflective thinking evoked by a series of specific teacher questioning strategies pupils' performance in science has been enhanced.

Philosophy for Children (Lipman 1991) is pursued through the analysis of specific stories. In fact many English and PSE teachers do use a range of curriculum texts through which they pursue some aspects of philosophical enquiry and this should be given more encouragement.

Gagné (1975) identified five major categories of learned capabilities. These were verbal information, intellectual skills, cognitive strategies, attitudes and motor skills. *Verbal information* consists of facts, names, principles and generalisations. It consists of the organised bodies of information such as in the National Curriculum and the learning of meanings (concepts). *Concepts* are the building blocks of learning (Anderson 1980). The interaction with the environment from the early years enables us to build up mental representations of the external world which are termed 'concepts'. Concrete concepts refer to objects and events in the real world which can be seen and touched such as tables and chairs. A category concept or classification table can be derived from these perceptual referents using various key attributes of the group. Thus chairs, tables and settees make up a group, category or class which is termed 'furniture'.

Event concepts can also be linked together and give concepts such as to 'chair a meeting' implying a whole set of related procedural concrete activities associated with the chairing schema. A range of concrete concepts and schemas can be linked together to form a constellation or abstract concept such as 'love', 'justice' and 'education'. Individuals contribute their own idiosyncratic pattern of experiences to concept formation. Sets of concepts and hierarchies of abstract concepts are referred to as *constructs*. Hierarchies of constructs are referred to as *attitudes* or conceptual hierarchies within which emotions and feelings may also be bound. Thus it is that learning is often intimately bound up with feelings of anxiety or pleasure and can provoke intense feelings.

When engaging in thinking at the simpler levels new concepts may be being constructed and this is the process of concept development. This is particularly evident when learning new subject contents and skills. Programmes overloaded with content may occupy all of student learning time in the area of concept development so that on entering employment there is little competency and capability to do the work for which they are employed. Organised bodies of knowledge are believed to provide the vehicle for thought. In problem solving a person thinks of many things and searches the stores of knowledge and information.

Intellectual skills are about 'knowing that' and 'knowing how'. They include converting printed words into meaning; fractions into decimals; knowing about classes, groups and categories; the laws of genetics; how to form sentences, adverbs and adjectives and so on. Concepts are the substance of intellectual operations from which we derive rules and principles and higher order rules.

Cognitive strategies are internally organised capabilities (Gagné 1975 p. 64) which the learner makes use of in guiding his or her attending, learning and remembering. These capabilities make possible the executive control processes that activate other learning processes. He thus distinguishes between cognitive skills and intellectual skills in that intellectual skills enable us to deal with the numbers, words and symbols of the world 'out there'. Cognitive strategies are directed to internal operations. The learner uses intellectual strategies in attending to what is being learned or read; in thinking about what has been learned we use cognitive strategies (Gagné 1975 p. 66).

Sophisticated thinking involves the manipulation of various levels of concepts by what we call *cognitive processes*. These may involve searching through concepts and constructs in sequential order, ranging through hierarchies of concepts for critical features, probing deeply into a construct, focusing on 'key' concepts with similar tags of reference, reordering and reconstructing to develop new constructs, scanning data and schema, missing key attributes and using personal or idiosyncratic attributes. It may also include retrieving old well tried strategies to solve a new problem or using part of an old strategy to help in the process. On appropriate occasions analogies may be used to solve old problems in an entirely different context in an imaginative and new way. Broad reading and broadening experiences can facilitate creative modelling and analogous thinking where there is flexibility in thinking and time for reflection. Many processes occurring simultaneously, drawing on many conceptual hierarchies is typical of multilogical thinking.

The different hemispheres of the brain are set up to engage in different forms of data processing. The sequential ordering processes are thought to be typical of the left or language orientated hemisphere. Imaginative, inductive and appositional thought processes (Gazzaniga 1967, and Bogen and Bogen 1969) are found to be characteristic of right hemisphere activities. The most creative of our scientists and artists appear to have had great facility in the use of both hemispheres. Regrettably western education has been accused of only valuing and educating the left hemisphere linguistic functions (Ornstein 1982). To this can be added that there is a world-wide tendency to develop monological, single track, context defined thinking through didactics.

Some cognitive abilities tests by Gagné's definition consist mainly of tests of intellectual skills. Teachers of science, maths and technology frequently claim to be developing problem solving abilities but now it would appear that this may not be so; instead they are posing problems to be solved mainly by using intellectual skills. Examples might be, to separate a mixture of sand and salt, to plan a party menu for four people with £10 to spend, and to design a bridge from straws and paper to carry the weight of a can of coke.

The essentials of *real problem solving* (RPS) and *problem based learning* (PBL) are that the initial problem is 'fuzzy'. According to Gallagher (1997) PBL has been around for more than two decades and its evolution has resulted in four elements: an ill structured problem; substantial content; student apprenticeship; and self-directed learning. He confirms that research supports the view that PBL is better than traditional instructional methods for:

- long term retention of information;
- conceptual understanding;
- self-directed learning.

The research of Dods (1997) showed that the didactics tended to widen the content coverage whilst understanding and retention were promoted by PBL. However because of their previous training it was found that students frequently demanded more information. Teachers and pupils on our courses behaved in a similar fashion.

Critical thinking theory and multilogical thinking

Critical thinking is: 'the art of thinking about your thinking while you are thinking so as to make it more precise, accurate, relevant, consistent and fair' (Paul 1990 p. 32).

The skills of accomplished critical thinkers are sophisticated and they are in command of the elements of thought which include an ability to formulate, analyse and assess those elements.

Self monitoring and self regulatory activities, according to Wang and Lindvall (1984) not only contributed to improved acquisition in their researches with students but also to improved generalisation and transfer of knowledge and skills as well as a sense of personal agency. Self regulatory activities have been defined by Brown *et al.* (1983) as including planning, predicting outcomes and scheduling time and resources. Monitoring included testing, revising and rescheduling, with checking to evaluate outcomes. Using criteria developed by the individual and those which were externally defined also formed part of a matrix of self regulatory activities. In a previous decade Flavell (1979) had established that *metacognition* was a highly important contribution to higher order learning. Metacognition was defined by Flavell as the process by which we think about our cognitive machinery and processing mechanisms. These metacognitive activities underpinned the development of the self regulatory and self management skills already referred to as well as the sense of personal agency. Failure to develop learning conversations inside the head, or metacognitions, left the learner in 'robot mode' according to Thomas (1976). This was a state of learned helplessness where the response to problems was to use old well-worn strategies even if they had little hope of success and to profit little from experience. He estimated that some 80 per cent of the population might be in robot mode.

Failure to develop higher order cognitive skills in schools and colleges was according to Resnick (1989) not surprising, for it had never been the goal of mass education to do more than develop basic skills of literacy and numeracy and core subject knowledge.

Teaching for critical and creative thinking by infusion

One of the most useful texts giving examples of teaching for critical thinking by a process of infusion is by Swartz and Parks (1994). They identify three different approaches to teaching thinking – the *Teaching of Thinking* in which pupils are given direct instruction in thinking in non-curriculum contexts. The *Teaching for Thinking* in which methods are used to promote thinking in curriculum contexts such as encouraging reflection through questioning, and *Infusion* which is their preferred method because they have found evidence that it is the one which does improve student thinking and enhances content learning. The infusion method involves the explicit teaching of a thinking skill then applying it to a particular content lesson. The whole procedure has one major disadvantage in that two lessons are taught in sequence, the thinking skill and then the application lesson. In both extensive use is made of graphic organisers to make sure all factors are considered. This could mean that more than a double lesson is required each time a new thinking skill is introduced. However, there are strategies by which such initial concerns can be overcome.

A typical example outline of one of Swartz and Parks lessons follows. The infusion lesson begins with an introduction to the thinking skill, it is encouraged and developed by explicit prompts and reflective questioning to encourage active thinking, the pupils then think about their thinking and then it is reinforced by application. The mode of working is Think – Pair – Share (p. 23). This has already been recommended as a powerful strategy for learning in the study skills and language chapters.

Asking pupils to think about a topic does not teach them to become skilful thinkers. The first task would be to discuss with the pupils the nature, for example, of skilful decision making and a graphic organiser is provided to show where they should arrive but it can be in their own words.

Skilful decision making

1. What makes a decision necessary?
2. What are my options?
3. What are the likely consequences?
4. How important are the consequences?
5. Which option is best in the light of the consequences.

(Swartz and Parks 1994 p. 39)

An example science lesson is about renewable energy sources and what a country should rely upon for the future. They have developed their plan for taking good decisions and are asked to review their previous knowledge on energy sources in the thinking actively section. Here the teacher uses reflective questioning techniques and explicit prompts such as asking why people today are concerned about energy; what are some of the optional sources available; what information might the pupils need to research; they make lists of known information with factors such as cost of production which might need to be taken into account. Groups then pick two sources of energy to research and fill in a data matrix with headings such as Options; Relevant Consequences; under these are placed the factors to consider e.g. ease of production; environment; cost; availability. From this each group decides which is the best source of energy and discusses why. They then have to prepare an oral or written recommendation giving the reasons for their choice.

In the next phase they are encouraged to think about their thinking, describe it and draw a flow chart to represent it. The flow charts should all contain the five key questions. They then discuss any difficulties experienced, the pros and cons of the procedure and compare it to the ways they ordinarily take decisions.

In the final phase they apply the strategy to a decision they are dealing with at the present, they consider other imaginary issues and later in the school year reinforcement activities are introduced and examples are given on pollution, endangered species, immigration and so on. Skill extension activities are also suggested such as work on determining the reliability of sources for decision making.

The final section of each chapter gives 30–50 examples across curriculum subjects for

Grade (year), topic and issue e.g.:

Grades 4–6: Mathematics: Fractions: What should be taken into account in choosing which operation to use to compare fractions? (p. 65)

Grades K–3: Literature: Three little pigs: What should the pigs consider in deciding how their houses should be built? (p. 64)

Skilful problem solving

In their approach to this Swartz and Parks make the argument that good problem solving can improve the quality of the lives it affects. Advances in science, medicine and technology have improved the standards of living of people today because problems were identified and solved. Everyday life as well as curriculum topics can present problems to be solved such as what to do when we get lost, cannot start the car, develop a rash, become too hot and so on. They then identify shortcomings in problem solving such as we do not recognise the situation as a problem; we make hasty choices or consider too narrow a band of solutions; we may fail to consider the consequences of our choices or the feasibility of them and the result is a poor solution. They show how the pupil can learn to be a skilful problem solver and by the same method as before go through the problem solving protocol beginning with the advance organiser:

1. Why is there a problem?
2. What is the problem?
3. What are the possible solutions to the problem?
4. What would happen if you solved the problem in each of these ways?
5. What is the best solution to the problem?

(Swartz and Parks 1994 p. 76)

The curriculum for infusion of critical and creative thinking which they identify and give detailed treatment is:

Skilfully managing thinking tasks

* decision making;
* problem solving.

Understanding and retention: clarifying ideas

a. Analysing ideas:
* comparing and contrasting;
* classification;
* determining parts-whole relationships;
* sequencing.

b. Analysing arguments:
* finding reasons and conclusions;
* uncovering assumptions.

Creative thinking: generating ideas

a. Alternative possibilities:
* generating possibilities.

b. Composition:
* creating metaphors.

Critical thinking: assessing the reasonableness of ideas

a. Assessing basic information:
• determining the reliability of sources.

b. Well-founded inference:
  i) Use of evidence
• causal explanation;
• prediction;
• generalisation;
• reasoning by analogy;
  ii) Deduction;
• conditional reasoning.

The book ends with chapters on teaching methods in infusion lessons; the role of metacognition, and how to select contents for infusion lessons.

Of special interest is the approach to creative thinking. They use the brainstorming technique first and then generate further possibilities by listing and considering aspects of the topic and recombining ideas to form new ones. They illustrate the use of concept maps as another way of generating possibilities and suggest that asking the question, 'Are any of these original ideas?' often promotes further and more original suggestions. The chapter on metaphors shows how they may be constructed by considering amongst other things the key characteristics which the object, person or event has in common with other things which might indeed make the metaphor e.g. 'All the world's a stage'. Throughout the pupil is helped to understand what are the errors or defaults in our thinking in order that they can be avoided.

If this sort of curriculum has been taught to all teachers in a school through inservice education it would be possible to build it into the whole-school policy on teaching and learning so that problem solving and thinking skills taught in one area could be guaranteed to be reinforced in other areas in a systematic way. It would share the curriculum time required for teaching thinking and might mean that there needed only to be a commitment to spending one period per subject per year on it.

Enrichment

Enrichment was first of all developed in gifted education programmes but it has come to be recognised that an enriched curriculum is the right of all pupils. Enrichment which merely teaches the subject contents of GCSEs to younger learners in the primary school should be discounted as should University projects in the secondary school. In the education of the highly able enrichment is coming to be regarded as more to do with process, with intellectual challenge and with the development of critical and creative skills. The sort of challenge is that which sets up a cognitive dissonance in which the learner reaches out to resolve the dissonance and in the process learns. This means that the problem should not be so distant or difficult that there is no way in which to approach it but in working to its resolution the pupils should experience intellectual challenge and cognitive stretch.

Some examples of programmes, materials and courses follow which are well established and which do offer these challenges.

Somerset thinking skills course (STSC)

This was developed by Blagg and his associates with Somerset Education Authority and is in its second edition (Blagg 1993). He distinguishes between cognitive resources and cognitive strategies basing this on the work of Nisbet and Shucksmith (1986). *Cognitive resources* are, for example, concepts of colour, shape, space and metaphor; skills include procedures for processing information, scanning, classifying, synthesising, making analogies and brainstorming; knowledge and experience made up of codes, symbols, conventions and rules, pairs experience, small group work and classwork; verbal tools consist of vocabulary, terminology, language register and forms. As can be seen, most of these are what are included as intellectual contents and skills by Gagné and will be the preferred terminology here. *Cognitive strategies* for Blagg's sources are the higher level control processes which select, control and manage the cognitive resources. This clearly matches the Gagné and Swartz and Parks' definitions.

STSC has a modular structure the roots of which it is argued are the foundations of problem solving. They focus upon reducing impulsivity, collecting relevant information and organising it, recognising the problem, scanning and focusing and defining the problem. They include a number of perceptual activities unrelated to the curriculum as with Feuerstein's (1980) IE (Instrumental Enrichment) on which it is based. The next level module is analysing and synthesising; followed by comparative thinking; position in time and space; understanding analogies; patterns in time and space all shown in sequence as the trunk of the tree arising from the roots. At the branches and foliage level come transforming and generalising; logical justification; critical evaluation; hypothesising; drawing analogies; and dealing in probabilities.

Within each module there are various modes of presentation such as numerical, tabular, verbal and pictorial with different levels of difficulty. The tasks are presented in order, first with a stimulus task then an artificial one and then a naturalistic one. In Foundations for Problem Solving, an example of a stimulus material is a picture of a living room in which a number of people are doing different activities and through the open door a patient in bed can be seen with someone in a turban taking his pulse and a woman carrying a hot water bottle towards the bed. The pupils are asked to scan the picture and the frame and then get into groups to discuss what they see, what it means and what is the relationship between the two. The frame underneath shows cartoon figures that give the key to understanding the nature and purpose of the activity (the five senses plus two extra ones, 'ESP and Metacognition', p. 39).

Artificial tasks are designed for pairs and group work and involve the development and use of 'cognitive resources' based on a range of activities including abstract search tasks. The naturalistic tasks include a consideration of a picture in which a woman has lost her key and pupils have to consider the options available and which are the most appropriate actions to take in relation to the four situations shown in the frame below the main picture. Pupils and teachers work for transfer and applications of strategies from one area to another. There are graded levels in each of the modules across all three types of task. A separate module represented as a watering can is the organising and memory module and emphasises the flexible use of strategies and revisits previous ideas and 'resources'.

Mediation by an adult is a key component as with IE and is integral to the learning experiences for this transforms the learning for the pupils and contributes to what they learn independently. In mediation critical experiences are emphasised and enable the pupil to make sense out of separate experiences and so build up their cognitive frameworks.

STSC is widely used in dyslexia programmes to build up the pupils' cognitive and learning skills. However as can be seen the programme is self contained and has to be bolted on to the mainstream curriculum.

What needs to be the next stage in development is for the best of these strategies and the most relevant to be absorbed into each curriculum subject.

Thinking action: the CoRT approach

An account of one of the de Bono (1983) CoRT lessons will illustrate the general themes and approaches in the programme as a whole. In each of the three levels of CoRT there are ten lessons each destined to occupy about 35 minutes. The lesson on *decision making* has the following design:

There are ten copies of each set of pupil lesson notes for each lesson. They are presented as an A5 folded leaflet in varying colours with different page 1 illustrations to carry the theme. Inside there is frequently the same format. An explanation of decision making and the issues it presents are summarised in a box. The teacher would first ask the pupils for information and ideas about everyday decisions we make such as what shoes to wear, what career to choose, whether to choose or decide to do this or that. Pupils are reminded to be clear about all the factors involved and referred to the other lessons they will have had on:

CAF – Consider All Factors
AGO – Aims Goals and Objectives
FIP – First Important Principles
APL – Alternatives, Possibilities and Choices.

The five practice items include such problems as: A police officer notices a strange light in a warehouse at night but is on the way home without a radio phone. A quick decision needs to be made about what to do. . .

After the practice items there are Process Notes. These indicate what the pupils should discuss after the practice items such as why some decisions are easier than others; what are the most important things to think about; how to judge whether the right decision has been taken.

Principles are then outlined in another box and the pupils are asked to identify the things it is important to do and know in decision making such as the real reasons behind the decision, the degree of reversibility of any decision, the consequences of not deciding and the importance of CAF etc.

In the final section three 'Projects' are suggested from which the pupils can choose. These are on the issues surrounding a kidnapping; the problems of a housing officer in housing the homeless; and how people decide to spend their money.

The advance organisers such as CAF and FIP make useful tags to help the pupils remember their thinking tasks and are less elaborate than the graphic organisers of Swartz and Parks but can serve much of the same purpose and can be alternated with them. In the CoRT programme there is plenty of scope for pairs and group discussion as well as whole-class debate and open questioning. Thus the development of communication, social and negotiation skills will be part of the process.

There is a lesson which directly addresses Other Points of View (OPV) and EBS – Examine Both Sides, which cover similar ground to the Infusion programme. However, the examples remain outside most curriculum areas and in the realm of general education. Being wrong in an argument or not thinking skilfully is introduced by work in one lesson on exaggeration and missing things out and in another by looking at making mistakes and being prejudiced.

In developing a whole-school policy based upon this programme it would be possible to share out the ten copies of the pupils' notes to departmental or subject representatives so that they could be scrutinised for their applications within subject teaching over a three year span. From the topics identified a thinking curriculum could be built into all the subjects so that they supported and reinforced each other and critical and creative thinking.

An example would be to reset the police officer's decision in the context of the Gunpowder Plot. It could be applied to the Watchman of the Guard or to Guido Fawkes himself. In looking at the options (CAF, EBS etc) a detailed scrutiny of the story and relevant pictures of artifacts, maps and plans could bring the event into sharp focus for the learners. This also brings it into the realm of PBL.

Maidenhead group of teachers' enrichment materials

There are three sets of materials published by LDA for the group. They are the Motorway Project, Townscapes and the Village of Eddington, all developed by a group of teachers in Maidenhead in the 1980s for highly able pupils in Middle Schools from 8 to 13 years old. The group was chaired by Johanna Raffan and included Deborah Eyre, these being past and current chairs of NACE (National Association for Able Children in Education). The Village of Eddington will be used to exemplify their approach which is similar in all three projects and which with a little teacher intervention can be used as class material for mixed ability groups in primary or secondary school. It can also be use as a model for developing other topics inside the curriculum.

The subject is life in the Village of Eddington circa 1787–1830. The pupils are given 12 tasks to do and each is accompanied by information sheets but they also benefit from access to a library or to a study box although the materials are self contained. Although teacher input is not required a mixed ability class will need some teacher support especially in getting started and perhaps in selecting easier tasks to begin with.

In task one the pupils are given a description of the village and are asked to represent what they have read as a map which could be one of several kinds of pictorial representation.

In task two the daughter of the manor falls off her horse in escaping from lessons and meets the gamekeeper's daughter. They compare notes about their different styles of education in the village school and with a German governess. The pupils are asked to prepare a tape of their role play of this situation. Their study materials are a three page extract from the village school log and two pages on life at the manor.

Task three continues with the subject of education describing the fine needlework the daughter of the manor has to learn and the pupils are asked to design their own sampler from the details and illustrations given and then embroider it.

A diphtheria epidemic threatens the village in task four and pupils have to take on the role of the doctor who has to try to prevent it taking hold. The data is information about the epidemic and extracts from the parish records of 1787 written in copperplate and they have to work out which families to contact and what questions to ask.

In task five Mrs Pike at the farm entertains the Parson and Mrs Ellis to tea. There is her account of her preparations and recipes which the pupils have to read and then recount the visit using the same style, language and spelling. They then have to prepare and cook her special cake recipes.

Subsequent tasks deal with the MOP hiring fairs, in which, with some library research as well they have to produce a poster advertising the event and sideshows. In the Workhouse topic they have to take on the role of the new overseer and his wife and make a log of the first weeks' activities and take an inventory of the furniture to be compiled from a copy of the poorhouse list of the time.

Other topics cover the Graveyard; the Hungerford Riots of 1830; insurance cover for the Doctor's cottage; designing a Boot Polishing Machine for the boot boy; and finally 'Below Stairs'.

As can be imagined it is a powerful vehicle for studying a period of history in depth and in breadth. The tasks require a range of cognitive skills in planning and managing one's own learning plus the exercise of a range of cognitive study skills and communication skills. There are no attempts to make explicit the thinking skills involved but this is where the mediation of the teacher can prove useful and can direct pupils to reflect upon their thinking in the process of undertaking each of the tasks.

LEA projects and other sources

The DES/HMI initiative in 1981 was to link Institutions of HE and teams in the Local Authorities to develop inservice training courses and materials for the able pupil. A significant number of projects were set up helped also by funding from the Schools Council Programme Four directed by Ralph Callow and many useful materials were developed across the country in Essex, Cornwall, Manchester, Croydon, Surrey and so on. More than 15 years on it would be useful to revisit some of these and to bring them up to date in terms of cognitive skills, find where they matched the National Curriculum and redevelop them for whole-class learning. *NACE journal* regularly contains reports of new projects in its section on Able Pupils Thinking. One such was the *CAPSOC project* (Bentley 1995). It addresses the thinking skill of decision making.

In *Teaching Children to Think* Fisher (1994) has produced a range of suggestions for developing thinking skills approaches in the primary curriculum by suggesting 'fuzzy' problems such as the following in music:

• Sound pictures – what pictures does a piece of music evoke in the mind's eye? Try drawing and painting this.
• What creative movements best express the mood of a particular piece of music?
• Design an instrument from a collection of junk.
• Experiment with pitch using glasses containing water.
• Invent a sound accompaniment to a story.

(Fisher 1994 p. 238)

These are indeed typical examples of what teachers might do in developing pupils' perceptions and creative problem solving.

Fisher has also developed a useful protocol for creative problem solving based upon the questions of Osborn (1963). This is the *SCAMPER* checklist for creating ideas:

• **S**ubstitute – Who or what else instead? Other time or place? etc.
• **C**ombine – Unite, recombine? Combine purposes or ideas?
• **A**dapt – What else is like this? What ideas does it suggest? etc.
• **M**odify – Magnify? Minify? Multiply? What to alter, add or change? etc.
• **P**ut to other uses – New ways to use? Modified fits other uses?
• **E**liminate – What to remove, omit, get rid of? Part or whole?
• **R**earrange – Try a different layout, pattern or scheme? Turn it round? Opposites?

(Fisher 1994 p. 49)

Problem based learning

Settlement: The traditional approach to this National Curriculum topic might be as follows:

An information section in a text; some information from the teacher; some questions and answers about the topic to be studied. Then there will be worksheets given out and maps and things to do. This will be followed by a review session at the end to check answers and key information.

1. On the work sheet the period under study is circa 350 AD when Roman power was declining and there was an influx of Saxons into the south and east of England from

Germany. There is a map of the area including a river and potential sites for settlement.

2. The pupils are given a list of things the settlers must consider and the reasons why, e.g. defence and the need for a wooden stockade and a ditch. Pictures illustrate this and the dwellings built.

3. The pupils must now consider the sites and choose the best by allocating them marks out of ten for the following five attributes:

(a) good defensive position;
(b) supply of timber;
(c) nearness of farming land;
(d) nearness of water;
(e) avoidance of marshes.

Apart from allocating ten marks on the basis of no other criteria the only intellectual requirement is for the pupil to be able to read and add up. No cognitive challenge or effort is involved. The pupils can happily chat about other things and also copy each other's results down avoiding any cognitive effort at all. Later in tests pupils may be asked to give dates, reasons, or discuss why the settlers came and where from, and to give details of the nature of their settlements. If they do not revise and rote learn the notes made in their books they will recall very little of such an experience.

The PBL approach to this might be to start with the fuzzy problem. In pairs the pupils should look at the map to note where the settlements occurred and in pairs put themselves in the position of the settlers and try to hypothesise why they might choose those spots. They should try to form a description of each from the map details and find any common factors. This task should occupy 5–10 minutes and then they should share their ideas with the rest of the class and agree a best fit hypothesis.

In phase two new information should be presented and this can consist of a page or two of information so they can employ some study skills. Pictures of artifacts, and drawings of the life of the Saxons could now be presented. The pupils are asked to consider the following questions working in pairs or small groups of three. First they should raise a hypothetical answer to each question before looking at the study materials.

(a) How did they come?
(b) Why did they come?
(c) Why were they permitted to settle?
(d) Given the tools and materials available what sort of settlement could they build?

At intervals, for a change of activity, the pupils can share their findings and hypotheses with the rest of the class.

The key topic of what sort of site they will need to find can then be addressed now that they have the background. They should identify in their groups five or six essentials which a site they choose should fulfil and then apply these to their study of the map to decide on the best site. In the final session groups should explain which site they have chosen and give reasons for their choice. This procedure will take slightly longer but the final section could be set for individual homework.

As a follow up they might focus on a particular aspect of Saxon life such as boats, tools, clothes, food, for research. Thus not every lesson must be problem based but it is helpful to begin a series with such a lesson to excite interest and motivation treating it all perhaps like a big detective story. There are a wide range of resource which can be used to reinforce the learning once they know something and they can learn more from a video tape with such advance organisers than if it is used as the primary and initial source of information. Preparing the mind for the new information is important if deep learning is to take place. Ensuring there is pupil discussion before more public sharing of ideas will help them to be clarified and expressed more succinctly.

Comparisons of real settlement sites with modern maps can bring it into the present and careers in archeology, history and geography can be mentioned as well as using such knowledge as a backcloth to novels. A useful example here is Ellis Peter's Brother Cadfael detective stories set several centuries later and available as audio tapes as well as in book form. The idea of introducing these things is to extend the pupils' interests and experiences beyond the school walls.

Other PBL example topics

1. When the subject of Homes in different environments, in history and in different cultures is being studied Homes on Stilts may be one topic. In PBL instead of being given the title the pupils are given details about climate, monsoons, terrain, general physical geography, flora and fauna and tools available. In groups of three they are asked to examine the resource materials and slides etc. and then discuss and design the sort of home which would take account of the setting. They usually come up with homes on boats and homes on stilts. They should then be asked to present their arguments for and against their chosen designs. At the conclusion of the session they can be shown pictures of how the locals solve the problems.

2. In a study of the local area pupils seldom have an overview or an understanding of how others may view it. Even in an historical study it can be important to start from the here and now before probing into the local past. A collection of holiday brochures can be brought in of pupils' ideal locations for a vacation. Pairs should then research the brochures to identify the types of information and the language register in which they are written. Using similar headings they should then apply these to a selected part of their home area and document it with Polaroid photographs and cut outs from local newspapers and magazines. At intervals the teacher can call them all together to share aspects and to develop points. They can paste up their four page leaflets and word processing for homework and then hold an exhibition in which they can offer to do verbal presentations of their holiday offers. Follow up work on other peoples' views and comparative studies of the photographs can lead into further work on the same area in the Victorian era, plus a new brochure and language register and interviews with their oldest relatives born in the area. It can also lead to the usual work on local survey and to visits to the local museums and libraries for research.

3. As a 20 minute problem based introduction pupils can be shown a pictorial map on which five or six sites are under consideration for building a castle – a hilly area; a high circular plateau; an island in the middle of the river; a plot of land near a village in the fork of the river; a plot near the forest and some quarries and so on.

In groups of five, pupils have to imagine that they are the site agent for the place designated for their group and then have to produce a marketing brief to try to persuade the teacher (now titled the Lord or Lady of the manor) in 1200 AD to purchase their particular site. After 10 to 15 minutes discussion (some may like to record a few notes) one of each group with the help of the rest has to make a presentation. When these are over the teacher can then help them to develop the criteria for a good castle site and then by comparing and contrasting the features of each site they can decide on the best one. The teacher can then factor in such things as cost and give details of the actual period labour charges for walls, slits, crenelations and so on plus the master mason's rates and those of the work people. As the work proceeds they can begin to compare their hypothetical site and castle with some of those in existence and then select one to study in further depth. This should preferably be one close by so that a visit can be arranged for more intensive study and some measurements. Pictures and ground plans of some of the more important castles of the period can be studied together with their owners and how and why they came to be where they were.

4. In science it is usual for pupils to study separation as a set of scientific processes culminating in pupils being given a mixture of sand and salt to separate. As they are frequently given the diagram to draw first and then get out the apparatus and set up the 'experiment' there is little experimentation or problem about it except the enjoyment of doing it all. It was found to be far more memorable as a learning experience when the pupils after studying various forms of separation entered the laboratory one day to be given little piles of an unknown mixture which they were asked to separate. There were two substances in it which someone had stirred up together.

In pairs the pupils are asked to hypothesise what the substances might be and to design some apparatus to finish up with two piles of dry clean substances. Ask them to consider what the dangers might be in not knowing what the substances are and how they would avoid them. When they have designed their apparatus and it has been checked to see if it is safe they should then set it up even if it is wrong and try it out. At the end of the session in the review a number will have modified their designs and now have semi-separated substances but know what they should have done to separate it completely. A few who went off on the wrong tack will want to set their apparatus up again in the lunch hour so that they can have the satisfaction of completing the task successfully. They remember this lesson very well.

5. Growing seeds is a popular activity. Pupils are asked to discuss what they think a seed needs in order to grow. When they have decided and shared their ideas and the teacher has filled in some details, they then know that they have to plant their seeds in a series of pots. Each pot must be deprived of just one of the different elements they think plants need in order to grow. No problem and not much of an experiment. However, some surprising things happen when in groups of five they are asked to design a series of experiments to find out what seeds need in order to grow. The most unlikely pupils demonstrate the ability to undertake negative induction and set up the correct design. All the groups should be allowed to set up their experiments right or wrong and the results can be scrutinised and the relevant thinking and experimental strategies can be explored.

6. A mathematical example of this sort of thinking is illustrated in the following: Three numbers, 3 6 and 9 represent a rule which I have in my head. In order to find out what my rule is you can generate some numbers too and each time I will tell you either – 'Yes, that is an example of my rule', or, 'No, that is not an example of it'. As soon as you feel you know what the rule is you can propose it and you will be told whether or not you are correct. If you are incorrect you can go on and propose more examples.

This can prove to be a useful exercise in examining metacognitive events in relation to number work.

Planning and managing one's learning and keeping it on task and on schedule

There are many activities which can be designed to help pupils learn and develop these skills. They need to start with small projects in which they have autonomy to try things out and to learn from their mistakes. Some of the activities already described can provide the initial training ground. An intermediate sized project might be to set small groups to design and develop a school handbook on study skills for Year 7 pupils. They can begin by discussing in their groups their first two weeks in their new school and how they felt and what they needed to know. They can review what they know of study skills across the subjects so far and draw up a checklist of skills crossmatched with subjects. This can form the basis of a small-scale research project using presentational skills of various kinds, including statistics. It can form the basis of a useful audit of the degree of permeation of study skills.

A newspaper project. Designing a class or year newspaper using PBL and modelling the processes and roles in a newspaper office can be undertaken with pupils across the age ranges. A full description of how to set this up has already appeared in Montgomery (1985, 1996) and illustrated with work of reception pupils and later years.

Summary

The basic components of intellectual activities have been outlined and a distinction drawn between these and cognitive strategies. It is suggested that neither of these are directly taught in most curriculum studies but arise and develop incidentally during learning.

Once again lower attainers need some direct teaching of critical thinking skills and these can be developed in problem based learning experiences with curriculum subjects.

A number of methods for teaching thinking were discussed and the infusion methods and materials and problem based learning were particularly recommended. These can be integrated into existing curriculum work simply by changing some of the teaching methods that we use.

Chapter 12

Number and mathematical difficulties

Introduction

The SATs assessment survey in mathematics by OFSTED (1996) showed that under two thirds of pupils achieved level 4 in the National Curriculum at the age of eleven. A new target of 75 per cent was set for this to be reached by the year 2002. There was an improvement in 1997 bringing the level up to 68 per cent. The strong initial improvement was probably accounted for by the tests bedding down and teachers learning to teach to them.

Comparisons of the results of 19 countries in the Third International Maths and Science Study (TIMSS) conducted in 1995 showed that English pupils had done relatively well in written science tests at nine and thirteen, but were below the international average in maths. The English pupils had, however, done much better in the applied maths and science (TIMSS 1997). The survey found that English 13 year olds were among the best in the world at applying maths and science skills in real life situations a 'cause for celebration' according to Harris, one of the NFER researchers contributing to the study. Only Singapore did better overall than England. Scotlands' 13 year olds were in sixth position tied with Rumania, behind Singapore, England, Switzerland, Australia and Sweden. Despite this feature of 'coming good in the end' these results created further anxiety about the standards of pupils' maths and mathematics teaching as the national proclivity for dwelling upon faults swung into operation.

Even the reported deficiencies in the general achievements of our pupils in numeracy in comparisons with pupils in other countries appeared to be equivocal and seemed to result from incomplete data and analysis. An analytical study of the TIMSS results undertaken by Edge and Stokes (1997) found that the results were affected by the amount of time devoted to the subject and the range of topics studied. They found that English and Welsh pupils spend more time on Science (2.5 to 5 hours per week) than many other countries such as France and Luxembourg (1.5 to 3.5 and 1 to 2) and studied a very wide range of topics in maths in comparison with all the other countries. The Science curriculum in England and Wales was also much broader than most other countries. The researchers suggested that the tests in the TIMSS study may also have been better matched to our science rather than our maths curriculum.

The fact that our pupils' abilities in problem solving are superior to those in other countries provides some endorsement of the progress which has been made since the Cockcroft report in 1982. This report analysed mathematics teaching and found little evidence that standards of numeracy were declining although comparisons between eras were difficult to achieve. There was also little dissatisfaction amongst employers with regard to mathematical capabilities of school leavers although media reports had suggested grave concerns as now. However the report found that many pupils left school with negative attitudes to maths and many adults had deep-rooted feelings of anxiety about it. A significant number of pupils did show difficulties with maths and some had severe problems. The report concluded that a 'back to basics' approach could not be recommended and instead more attention should be paid to applying maths skills to *real* situations for their failures were more in the area of problem solving than in basic skills after the age of 11.

Teachers, it was recommended, should not just teach skills but should help pupils achieve understanding of maths concepts and how they can be applied in different practical situations. To achieve this, much more discussion of maths problems needed to take place between teacher and pupils and between pupils themselves. The report found that pupils should be taught to use calculators for this in no way reduced mathematical thinking. However Straker (1998) reported from the National Numeracy project that pupils were still not being taught to use calculators properly.

The Lower Attainers in Mathematics Project (LAMP 1984) was set up to help teachers interpret the Cockcroft Committee's recommendations (para 458) and to encourage teachers to change their attitudes about the ways in which lower attainers learn mathematics. The main approach was to enable pupils to arrive at conventional methods and terminology through participation in problem solving activities and investigatory maths. It also suggested approaches to differentiation for the different rates of learning and for making links with other subjects. Books of example problem solving approaches developed with teachers and lower attainers were produced as part of the project by, for example, Ahmed (1987) at the West Sussex Institute of Education and in the Nottingham University Project on maths for lower attainers.

The HMI (1991) report recorded (p. 22) that following the implementation of Key Stages 1 and 3 of the National Curriculum many promising aspects were observed and even pupils finding learning difficult appeared to have benefited. The greater incorporation of problem solving and practical work had appeared to improve the performance of the pupils with learning difficulties. This was particularly the case where attempts had been made to forge cross curricular and home-school links. Thus in the intervening period since Cockcroft it would appear that good progress had been made and is being sustained even now despite reports to the contrary.

What must not happen is that teachers revert to a narrow basic skills focus. The HMI report recommended that many of the secondary school teachers working with lower attainers were in need of more help and support in the preparation of their teaching. Most schools in the survey relied too heavily on commercially produced schemes which they used in an undifferentiated way. This resulted in pupils adopting a step by step recipe approach to maths rather than engaging in mathematical thinking and understanding. The schools thought they had implemented the new maths system, but Williams (1990) found that the teachers were having difficulties with the more innovative aspects of the curriculum and it was these that were appropriate for pupils with learning difficulties i.e. using and applying maths, problem solving and investigative activities. The task analytic, step by step approaches so often adopted acted to prevent pupils exploring other strategies and algorithms which might have been shorter and more appropriate.

Studies by Peterson, Fennema and Carpenter (1989) developed the notion of *Positive Approaches to Maths*. Positive approaches involved the pupils constructing their own mathematical knowledge, and skills being taught in relation to understanding and problem solving. This approach was endorsed by Daniels (1993) whose studies emphasised that pupils should learn to reflect upon their mathematical thinking thus developing in them metacognitive strategies to facilitate their understanding of mathematical concepts and processes. To help in this Braten (1991) used the work of Vygotsky (1978) on Zones of Proximal and Distal development to underpin maths teaching strategies.

The internalisation of knowledge does not involve simple copying and rote learning, it involves active interpretation and transformation of instructions which may be mediated (Feuerstein 1995) by the teachers and other learners, otherwise the knowledge may remain inert or at superficial or surface levels.

Mathematical abilities

There appears to be general agreement that there are two levels of mathematical ability, *elementary mathematics* including basic skills and *advanced or creative mathematics*. Mathematical ability has a correlation with general intelligence as measured by IQ tests of + 0.6. This means that the predictive capacity from one to the other is 36 per cent. In addition to these abilities there also appears to be a specialist factor particularly associated with spatially related aspects of maths.

Mathematics is an hierarchical skill in which one step is dependent upon a complete grasp of earlier ones and thus it is not possible to skim over letters and words to get a general gist of the problem. Instead each segment has to be taken into account in order to carry out the correct operations. If early stages of learning are missed this can have severe consequences for subsequent learning. Thus one of the key problems causing mathematical difficulties can be factors surrounding teaching and the transmission of basic skills and concepts. Secondary to this are the pupils' abilities and needs.

Low WISC-R scores on either verbal or performance items will be reflected in later attainment. Low verbal processing ability in the early years in the presence of good spatial ability may undermine later maths attainment and pockets of talent could be seen in dealing with problems involving few computational skills. All the factors which contribute to poor language development may thus handicap mathematical development. Calculators may help overcome some of these problems but not the gaps in learning which inevitably arise from lack of vocabulary comprehension and other language skills. Low performance scores in the presence of very good verbal skills may give rise to a profile in which the pupil is good at following algorithms and using computational skills but has a limited grasp of spatial concepts and creative mathematics.

There are differences in the achievements of male and female pupils (Burton 1986) but it is not clear that these are due to sex differences in themselves. They may more probably arise from the way the sexes are differently treated (Burton 1986) or are perceived. Inuit children for example show no differences in spatial abilities, but boys from about the age of 13 in the UK move ahead of girls in maths as more problem solving and spatial skills are involved. Girls generally develop better in verbal skills than boys in the early years and tend to be better in arithmetic than boys at this stage.

Other individual differences which have a strong effect on mathematics are levels of anxiety which individuals can tolerate. Emotion and anxiety have a blocking effect on mental arithmetic for example and a lot of operations in maths require mental work especially in IQ and attainment tests. Some people operate at higher levels of anxiety than others and can easily become very tense and overanxious so that their performance rapidly declines. In the classroom, mathematics teaching very often seems to induce fear and this can lead to failure in learning and fear of failure. Of 50 teachers studying a module in mathematical difficulties for their MA SEN, 49 of them reported having fear of failure in any kind of number work and some of them were very anxious about it. The fear in many cases had generalised from their own teachers who were often seen as tempestuous and impatient (Montgomery 1996).

A specific disability such as dyscalculia (Kosc 1974) has not as yet been clearly identified except as a special problem with establishing and using phonological codes in which the saying of a known table, for example, may create confusion (Miles 1993). Such verbal processing problems can result in the pupil starting well and then faltering and becoming confused e.g. '1 times 6 is 6, 2 times 6 is – um, 12; 6 times 6 is 18, 7 times – er seven is 28. No that's wrong I've forgotten it'. But the pupil is often able to give the sums of the numbers such as 6, 12, 18, 24, 30, 36 and so on. Difficulties are particularly seen in the learning of the 7 and 8 times tables. This may or may not be accompanied by dyslexic problems. The presence of dyslexia, distinct from generally poor reading abilities due to slower learning, was identified in the 1970s by some psychologists as severe reading (and spelling) problems in the presence of good mathematical abilities. Now it is understood that dyslexia may well be accompanied by mathematical difficulties.

An investigation of effective teachers of numeracy in primary schools (Askew, *et al.* 1997) found that it was not necessarily those with A-levels or degrees in the subject who were effective teachers but those who were effective were more likely to have received inservice training. The study involved 90 teachers and 2,000 pupils over two terms and was funded by the TTA. The highly effective teachers were distinguished by the connections they made within the areas of the maths curriculum e.g. between fractions, decimals and percentages and by the ways in which they encouraged children as young as five to explain their thinking. The researchers found that almost all the teachers were using similar methods: mental test and written exercises to practise skills, whole class interactive sessions and individual and small group work. Setting across the age groups and the same published schemes were in use by both the effective and the less effective teachers. It was characteristic of the most effective teachers that they believed all pupils could become numerate and should be challenged by their work and they recognised the value of helping pupils develop mental strategies. The lowest gains in numeracy were achieved by teachers who dealt with different areas of maths separately, and who used assessment mainly as a check that taught methods had been learned rather than as a diagnostic method for informing subsequent practice.

The following of textbook programmes with all pupils proceeding at their own rate through the scheme, often inappropriately termed *individualised learning*, has seldom been shown to be effective in developing mathematical thinking. Pupils following such programmes may complete whole sections of textbook work without ever having grasped the mathematical understandings. Pupils can learn a recipe, a step by step formula for completing the examples, without needing to reflect upon their learning and they may copy the answers from peers.

There are a range of methods which effective teachers use in an appropriate mix, for example: drill and practice, 'interactive' teaching which may be used to reinforce or develop understanding, small group learning, task analysis, real problem solving, miscues analysis and intervention, computer aided learning, mediated learning, reciprocal teaching, and individualised work sheet or textbook based learning.

In their studies of *positive approaches to teaching mathematics* (Peterson, *et al.* 1989) found that learning was effective when mathematical instruction was organised to help pupils, in that pupils' development of mathematical ideas provided the basis for sequencing the topics for teaching. Schemes and textbook programmes must therefore be adapted or mediated by the teacher to reflect the pupils' needs. They emphasised that mathematical skills should be taught in relation to understanding and problem solving and that pupils should construct their own mathematical knowledge in the process.

Schoenfield's (1985) studies of mathematical problem solving showed that *small group work* was one of the most effective ways of promoting learning and he listed four ways in which it did so. Teachers had the opportunity to assess learners and provide support as they were actively engaged in the problem solving. The group decision making facilitated the articulation of knowledge and reasoning as the learners justified their reasons for choosing alternative solutions to other members of the group. Those who were unsure of their abilities had the chance to see others often more capable struggle over difficult problems. The learners gained practice in collaboration and negotiation skills required in real life situations. Thus it can be seen that what has been described as good differentiation in an earlier chapter, and as essential for reversing lower attainment, is an important teaching strategy in mathematics. Schoenfield described how one teacher thought aloud as he went through the steps to solving a problem. He illustrated problem solving procedures such as breaking the problem into component parts, drawing diagrams and hypothesising, each process was identified and labelled. This enabled the learners to see the range and flexibility of the strategies as they were applied to the problems.

Interactive teaching has become a popular term for the formal teaching session with the whole class when the teacher by *judicious questioning* in the Socratic style helps pupils to understand what has just been explained or read. Palinscar and Brown (1984) however describe a different conception of the term and refer to it as *reciprocal teaching*. The teachers assumed the role of learners and vice versa. The learner in the process of tutoring has access to the teacher's knowledge and understanding without necessarily being directly taught and they believe that this is what facilitates understanding. In the process of the tuition it is quite easy for the teacher following the instructions to identify learning gaps or misunderstandings and correct them. The learner in controlling the material and giving the tutoring has to interact closely with the mathematical concepts and processes. This is when individualised tuition for some of the time is important and plays a vital role in learning. Thus in a 35 minute teaching session in secondary or an hour of focused teaching in primary it can be seen that the larger the class the less opportunity there is for this individualised, diagnostic teaching. Class size in helping lower attainers is thus a crucial factor.

Social mediation in the learning of mathematics was described by Newman *et al.* (1989) when the responsibility for progress is transferred from teacher to learner and then back again in a series of cycles of increasing understanding and learner control. They describe dialogues between teachers and learners in which the problem is posed, followed by an estimation of the answer by the pupil and then questions from the teacher to confirm what the pupil knows. For instance, with a problem, 'How many times does 6 go into 14?' The pupil estimates 'twice'. They confirm 2 times 6 is 12 and 3 times 6 is 18 and so on. The initial step of estimating is one which pupils find particularly difficult. Mediation in learning was a concept introduced by Feuerstein (1980, 1995) in his work with severely low attaining pupils from the holocaust and then refugee children. He showed how non-attainers could come to achieve very high levels of learning and move from being learning disabled to highly able in a process of learning to learn through mediation in his Instrumental Enrichment programme.

Real problem solving is a description of the attempt to design mathematical questions and experiences which have some relevance to the daily life of pupils. For example, a session to reinforce estimation and addition skills might take the form of presenting pairs of pupils with maps of the London underground, and then asking them to work out together an estimate of the fastest route from a particular station to get to the shops in Oxford Street, or the computer centre in Tottenham Court Road, and from there to the Cutty Sark exhibition in

Greenwich etc. When they have been given several estimations they can then be given some numbers to work with. e.g. 'On average it takes three minutes to go between each underground station, therefore how long will you take to get to Oxford Street?' and so on. The problems can be made more interesting and complex by having to pick up parcels off the main route; meeting friends above ground and going on together; closing stations because of problems; closing particular lines because of bomb threats or signal failure so that the route has to be more circuitous; comparing different routes; having only a fixed time to catch a train at a mainline station; calculating how early they would have to leave home to catch such a train and so on. With the slowest of learners it would create a good learning experience to visit London and let them plan a trip on the underground which they undertake. In small groups they might take the adult to the various places of interest. The experience and the report back session(s) will enable an extensive vocabulary to be developed.

Analysing learning to identify problems

In order to help pupils to overcome their difficulties in mathematics it is not only necessary to use appropriate teaching strategies but it is also necessary to look at pupils' learning. Their past learning experiences may have created an anxiety about maths which has to be dispelled. There may be an inherent fear of maths teachers which has to be combated by the new teacher and there may be gaps in the knowledge hierarchy and errors in it as well as general delay developed over time. Tracing these problems with the pupils can be a first strategy and first stage to recovery. This cannot be achieved in interactive sessions but it can be analysed most closely in small group and individualised teaching during PC1 sessions (Chapter 13).

Tracking the origins and the processes can often also reveal to the teacher the most appropriate method and point of intervention. Taking an interest in this way in a pupil's past learning experience and the current progress can prove extremely supportive and generate a new interest in mathematics learning as well as giving confidence that the problems met are not insuperable. Tracking back through the mathematics work book with the pupil can indicate areas of success and areas where work needs to begin. Evidence can often be found there of the origin of the errors, the nature of errors or types of difficulty. This detailed and personal attention is most important to all learners but is essential to increase the *motivation* and so re-establish the *self-esteem* of lower attainers.

Identification of types of difficulties

There are a range of difficulties which may be observed. Pupils may make errors in *basic facts*. A basic fact is any two one-digit numbers and their sum such as 3+5=8 (addition) and any two one-digit numbers along with their missing addend e.g. 8-3=5 (subtraction). There are 100 basic facts of addition and 55 basic facts in subtraction. Giving the pupils a graded set of examples to work out will identify where the errors in basic facts are. There may also be errors in basic computational strategies called *systematic errors*. The basic strategy used to arrive at an answer may itself be incorrect but it is most often the sub-tasks of it which are faulty and give rise to the errors. For example, in an addition sum there may be difficulties in the sub tasks of grouping, counting, place value and so on.

In addition to these errors in basic facts and skills pupils may exhibit a range of other problems. They may have *developmental difficulties* such as problems in counting, conservation, numbering/naming, classification and discrimination, reversibility, set inclusion, sets and subsets. There may be *memory difficulties* observed in problems with the recall of basic facts, verbal associations, number sequences, and mathematical signs. At a more complex level problems with *algorithms* may be seen. For example, there may be difficulties in conceptualising what a particular algorithm is doing, consistently using a procedure, regrouping or renaming, dealing with calculations involving zero, dealing with remainders, sequencing the division algorithm, dealing with decimal point rules.

When spatial problems are involved a whole new set of problems may be identified as *geometric difficulties* in discriminating shapes and their properties, inclusion and membership relations, symbols for geometric ideas, numerical or algebraic representations of spatial problems. At the problem solving level there may be difficulties with *worded problems* involving reading and language difficulties, translation from words to symbols, selecting appropriate operations when these are not made explicit in the problem, selecting appropriate operations in an appropriate order to enable the problem to be solved, estimating the reasonableness of an answer.

A major study by Shuard et al. was begun in 1980 into the relationship between reading and mathematics. It was found that readability could significantly affect success in maths and that a problem presented verbally might go unsolved whereas if it was written in numbers it could be solved easily. Seven major reading factors were identified:

Vocabulary: some words such as hypotenuse and coefficient are only used in maths, others have a special maths and a general meaning e.g. product and field.

Symbolic language: x means times and x = 3 means x replaces 3; xy means x is multiplied by y.

Sentences and their structure: although the sentences follow the rules of English they often refer to other sentences such as 'Applying the above rule'.

Flow of meaning: not all the units of meaning are represented in the text but have to be inferred, or questions are asked about them e.g. If Jill has three apples and Jack has three more than her, how many have they together?

Special reading techniques required: not only do we have to learn the symbols and read them we also have to have the spatial awareness to appreciate the full meaning as in the case of the use of brackets, and lines representing fractions.

Appearance of the text: clear layout and pleasing appearance can increase readability and motivation to read.

Ambiguities of text: The text might ask, 'Do you know of another way to construct a right angle?' The response required is not clear.

Number vocabulary itself may be particularly problematic where pupils do not have well developed language. They can be disadvantaged from the outset by lack of the knowledge of fundamental number concepts which underlie any calculations they might be asked to undertake. They then have a double translation problem, first from word to concept and then from concept to mathematics task. The following are examples of the ten most common words in four important categories:

Quantity: big, some, light, lot, more, same, different, small, great, many. Length and space: long, line, fat, high, piece, half, across, square, corner, straight. Position: in, up, out, down, under, top, after, left, last, next. Time: time, day, night, morning, fast, quickly, speed, month, evening, age.

Preschool learning and early learning in Infant school therefore needs to be very much concerned with ensuring the language of maths is understood in its general everyday use before it can be applied to number problems. The pressure to return to whole class formal teaching which is currently being experienced must be responded to with care. It must not encourage a return to teacher led didactics. The term for formal class teaching which has been introduced to try to avoid didactics is 'interactive teaching'.

Miscues analysis

Just as reciprocal teaching and individualised tuition can identify learning gaps and learning difficulties so an analysis of the bookwork a pupil has completed can give insight into the problems. Miscues analysis is a strategy for analysing errors prior to intervention and is recommended by a range of mathematics experts (Hughes 1985, Chinn and Ashcroft 1993, Daniels 1993).

An example of a miscues analysis would be to study and identify the errors the pupil has made as in the following sums. Then the pupil would be asked to explain the workings and be helped to gain insight into the error and how it might be corrected. Reteaching of the algorithm may well be necessary.

1. a) 83 + 49 = 1212   b) 35 + 67 = 912   c) 43 + 72 = 115
(fails to regroup in a and b).

2. a) 46 − 39 = 13   b) 372 + 295 = 123   c) 154 − 86 = 132
(takes smaller number from the larger whether numerator or denominator).

3. a) 22 × 3 = 66   b) 43 × 5 = 255   c) 29 × 6 = 424
(in b and c multiplies correctly but also multiplies the carrying number by the same amount i.e. 5 × 3 =15 carries the one onto the tens column and also multiplies it by 5 adding it to 4 × 5 = 20 so getting 255).

There is a danger in having algorithms so firmly entrenched that this can prevent the solver from seeing or using short cuts. Strategies to encourage flexibility in problem solving also need to be developed with pupils.

An example might be to try to encourage them to look outside the terms of reference of the problem in order to seek a solution e.g. The problem is to join all the nine dots with one continuous line in only four movements:

```
    •   •   •

    •   •   •

    •   •   •
```

The Government established a Numeracy Task Force in 1997. According to Merttens (1997) the co-director of the Hamilton Maths project in Oxford, there are a number of things which the Task Force should do. Prime amongst them is that it should listen to teachers in its search for better teaching strategies. The Government want numeracy teaching to be more active; according to Merttens, so do teachers. She is concerned that a Government plea for a return to interactive teaching should not become a return to chalk and talk with telling being the predominant mode. She pointed to the need for high quality inservice training if teaching was to be improved and this has to demonstrate how differentiation is to be achieved. Her differentiation model is one of 'layering' in which the bulk of the class can engage in one type of follow up activity whilst the high flyers and the strugglers are offered activities which are related but appropriate to their needs.

Because of the nature of mathematics it may well be the case that a small group of pupils or one of them could be engaged in a *distance programme* on GCSE or A–level maths whilst the slower learners are still learning the algorithm for addition and the rest are on multiplication. Having sufficient flexibility in teachers' thinking about such different needs is very important. Having the physical resources available to meet high flyers' needs while dealing with the rest of the class is also important. To meet such needs some schools have introduced the notion of *mentoring* so they can meet and learn from students and staff in local colleges and higher education institutions.

Merttens reported that the National Numeracy Project calls for a minimum of four focused lessons a week with a substantial amount of up-front teaching. Numeracy is defined as including the application of number in measures, geometry and data handling. It includes some 'on-the-rug' teaching followed by differentiated tasks or activities and this is in line with OFSTED's model of good practice. What primary teachers want to know, according to Merttens, is what more active teaching looks like and how teachers are to be supported to do it well. What they are sure of is that it is not secondary teaching taken down a few years; it is a specialised skill. Her answer is to say that we can do no better than consult primary teachers themselves.

While it is important and useful to consult teachers and mathematics experts it is not all that needs to be done. Often what is taking place at a particular time in schools and is considered to be 'good practice' is not good enough. Wider frames of reference need to be consulted so that we apply what is known from research on children's learning and studies of cognition to the mathematics curriculum and mathematics teaching. When we do so we can see that there is a misunderstanding developing about the nature of interactive teaching and on-the-rug teaching. Small group work in maths is often no more than individual work done in groups (Bennett 1986) and being able to put a question at the end of a sentence about numbers does not convert it into a real world problem. Pupils find such approaches lacking in relevance and there is frequently a mismatch between their perceptions of relevance and their teachers' (HMI 1986). Listening to pupils is therefore particularly important.

Summary

The principles underlying good teaching and learning and differentiation have already been established in section one and the themes derived from this have been developed in relation to positive approaches to mathematics teaching in this chapter. Best practice uses a mixture of teaching and learning strategies and the focus of them is developing mathematical thinking, understanding and skills through real problem solving and reflection upon the process of learning.

Whatever the mode of transmission, lower attainers need to experience some individualised learning and teaching to address their problems. This should take place in the ordinary classroom as part of the teacher's general diagnostic teaching. Lower attainers particularly need to perceive the relevance of what they are learning by using it to solve real world problems.

Chapter 13

Behaviour and social skills management

Introduction

Children who are distressed for whatever reason may 'act out' their distress and perhaps become fidgety, noisy, attention-seeking or disruptive; they may lie, steal and bully other children or they may become withdrawn, passive, dreamy and isolated, disappearing into the background, hardly noticed as long as they produce a little work now and again. When such behaviour shows a persistent pattern across a range of subjects and activities and often with a range of teachers then the pattern is regarded as indicative of emotional and behavioural difficulties.

The tendency to 'act out' or externalise problems is said to result from believing that the source of reinforcement is beyond control due to some external factor such as chance. If such an *external locus of control* (Rotter 1954) is held there is little incentive to invest personal effort to strive for success. A common consequence of an external locus of control is poor social skills and poor adaptive behaviour (Gresham, *et al.* 1987, Knight 1992).

Lower attainers may regard their failure as a depressing consequence of low ability and their self-esteem and motivation to work is diminished (Cooper 1984). The more difficult and disruptive the behaviour the lower the sense of self-esteem has been found to be (Wilson and Evans 1980).

Although the tendency had been to regard the child as 'owning the problem', recently the focus has been to redirect attention to the disturbing or challenging behaviour (Galloway and Goodwin 1987) and to consider the problem from an ecological perspective (Mittler 1990). In this model the interaction of a range of factors contributes to and causes problems. This means that an ecosystemic approach to intervention (Molnar and Lindquist 1989) is required. According to Cooper and Upton (1991) the approach combines the following elements:

- a management function – it aims to control and change behaviour;
- a developmental function – it emphasises building cooperative relationships;
- a reflexive function – it depends upon self scrutiny by teachers.

(Cooper and Upton 1991 p. 23)

Associated with this there has been a move towards positive approaches to discipline (Wheldall and Merrett 1984; Cheeseman and Watts 1985; Chisholm *et al.* 1986; Luton *et al.* 1991).The Elton Report (1989), a major survey of discipline in schools, in fact found that 'punitive regimes were associated with worse rather than better standards of behaviour' (S 4.47).

Negative disciplining techniques can be a major contribution to disruption (Scott MacDonald 1971, Elton 1989). Negative responses to the pupil's behaviour and other children can mean the attention seeker can soon grow used to them so that the more the sanctions are used the less effective they become. Keeping children in after school or in detention and sending out of the room may have dangerous or legal consequences and should be avoided. Keeping a whole class in because one or two have misbehaved is particularly unfair and should not be used.

When the number of desists and negatives exceeds the number of positive statements and behaviours a failing teacher is being observed (Scott MacDonald 1971, Montgomery 1984, 1989). The only way to retrieve this is systematically to replace negatives by positive and supportive statements. Not infrequently a teacher feels that the overall balance of the responses being made are positive and so a careful record needs to be made to demonstrate the actual situation and the effect even single positive responses can have.

A few teachers have the sort of personality and attitude which make it impossible for them to praise pupils for their achievements. They always seem to be seeking to find weaknesses and misdeeds so that they are always catching pupils being bad and reinforcing their failures. This is the path to lower attainments of both teachers and pupils.

Observing and targeting problem behaviours

It is extremely important to identify precisely which behaviour it is that needs to be changed and what has precipitated it. This is often identified as the ABC of intervention i.e. Antecedents – Behaviours – Consequences. It is also important to describe the behaviour seen rather than one's inferences about it, for example: 'Sue hit Jamie' is a factual statement whereas 'Sue is aggressive' is an inference not necessarily true at all and certainly not a fact. When a pupil is being particularly problematic it is actually helpful to write down several observations of the problem behaviour as follows:

> James stood up, looked around the room, saw me watching him,
> sat down, picked up a piece of paper, turned round in chair then
> stood up and walked slowly to the sand tray. He dribbled sand
> through his fingers onto the floor, watched Emma filling pots and
> making pies. Moved over to the large boxes, saw empty trike,
> climbed onto it. Pedalled it round room and outside.

This small segment shows nothing unusual on its own but when it is repeated day in and day out and is precipitated each time by any activity which requires James to sit down and try to write his name and his news or read, then it has a significance. James' wandering behaviour is of concern. It enables him to avoid sitting down at a desk and preparing to read or write. As he wanders so he can disturb and annoy other children working but the wandering behaviour of itself is clearly not the problem. He most likely has a handwriting coordination problem and difficulties with reading and spelling which need directly to be addressed through an assessment through teaching strategy (Montgomery 1996). We might also decide to change his behaviour as well by giving him praise and support every time he sits at his desk and looks at a piece of paper or a book trying to extend his on-seat time each day rather than catching him out of seat and remonstrating with him. Systematic classroom observation is a powerful tool for teachers in the improvement of classroom performance (Montgomery 1985, Bailey 1991). Sometimes merely observing and recording a pupil's behaviour is enough to stop the problem behaviour.

Ecosystemic management functions: controlling and changing behaviour

Changing the learning climate and changing the behaviour using C.B.G.

The initials stand for *Catch them Being Good*. There is a considerable amount of research which has shown that teachers spend most of their time attending to pupils when they are off target, not working and being disruptive (Kounin 1970, Scott MacDonald 1971; Wheldall and Merrett 1986). When they are working and being constructive they receive little positive support and encouragement, the teacher accepting their good behaviour without question. Pupils who receive little attention, support and approval at home will tend to seek it at school from teachers or failing them, from peers. If they cannot gain this attention and recognition that they crave through their work they will find other means to satisfy their needs. Thus teachers must raise their praise but keep it quiet.

The strategy C.B.G. is one which all teachers think they use but when they are recorded the number of desist and and negative, unsupportive behaviours and comments outweighs the positive and supportive ones. The less successful the teacher the fewer the positive responses and failing teachers gave none (Scott MacDonald 1971).

The C.B.G. strategy requires that:

- The teacher positively reinforces any pupil's correct social and on-task responses with nods, smiles, and by paraphrasing correct responses and statements and supporting their on-task academic responses with such phrases as, 'Yes good', 'Well done'. Incorrect responses should not be negated but the pupil should be encouraged to have another try, or the response should be, 'Yes, nearly' and 'Yes, and what else. . .', 'Good so far, can anyone help him or her out?' and so on.
- It is very important to remember to praise C.B.G. behaviour as well as answers to questions. This needs to be done more discreetly. It consists of going to children when they are on task and working, and making quiet supportive statements and comments. They may not choose to respond immediately but over time they will be found to increase their time on task even if they laugh off any praise.
- When pupils are working and it is not a good idea to interrupt them at that moment simply standing near them, looking at their work and smiling is very supportive. Detailed looking at work as they are doing it and moving on shows them you are interested in it and them. They know or feel you will intervene if there is a problem even if you yourself are just looking.
- It makes them feel that you are actively involved with them and the work they are doing for you and that you consider it to be important enough to give it and them your attention. If a teacher sits at the front and marks the books of another class it demonstrates an 'us versus them' attitude with tasks handed down to the lower orders without them having any intrinsic worth. Even if the teacher is marking that class's work and is calling individuals up it is far better to be out and around the room doing the marking.

- At its simplest C.B.G. is one form of Behaviour Modification technique in which the teacher positively reinforces desirable behaviours emitted by the child gradually *shaping* them towards desirable ends determined by the teacher without the child being aware of the process or the goal (Blackham and Silberman 1971). In such an instance – behaviour shaping – there is no cognitive input.

In the original researches the teachers were told to ignore any undesirable behaviour and only support those directed towards the target ones. This of course has deleterious effects on the other pupils who see the target child getting away with misbehaviour and so the behaviour of the whole class can deteriorate. To avoid this situation it may be necessary to tell the pupil to stop talking, sit down, open book and start reading but then *immediately*, give attention, support and encouragement for the on-task behaviour.

Children learn vicariously how to behave in classrooms as much from what happens to other children as from what happens to them and thus it is important to stop unwanted behaviours at their outset and when they are in the earliest stage. This may be compared with the strategy of 'nipping things in the bud' described by Laslett *et al.* (1984). Where a child is very disturbed it is possible within these parameters to ignore a significant proportion of the unwanted behaviour and for the other children to identify him or her as a special case. In some circumstances it may be necessary to seek the support of the rest of the children in helping an individual gain mastery over unwanted behaviour.

General classroom management strategies, 3 Ms

3Ms represents a series of tactics which effective teachers have used to gain and maintain pupils' attention whatever teaching method or style they subsequently employed. When teachers with classroom management disciplining problems were taught to use these strategies in observation and feedback sessions they became effective teachers (Montgomery 1984, 1989, 1998).

Management – phase one

The teacher makes an *attention gaining noise* such as 'Right!', 'OK class 3', 'Good morning, everybody', 'Uhummm!' or bangs the door or desk, claps hands. Some teachers simply wait quietly until the noise subsides as the pupils notice she/he is present. Next the teacher gives a *short verbal instruction* such as: 'Everybody sit down', 'Get out your English folders', 'Come and sit on the mat', 'Sit down and listen carefully' and so on. At this point twenty of the pupils will do as requested while ten do not. The effective teacher pauses, looks round, spots those who are not doing as requested and quietly *names* these pupils and individually instructs them to stop what they are doing and to listen. This is usually quite sufficient if a *check back* look is given to bring the whole class to attention.

The mistake that the ineffective teachers make is to begin to shout 'Be quiet' and 'Sit down', as a general instruction to all pupils. The raising of the teacher's voice and the general command to those who are already behaving as requested begins to engender hostility in them. Some who were attending now begin to chat causing the instruction to be repeated louder still and thus contributing to the general level of classroom noise. This seems to transmit the information that the teacher is not quite in control and can surreptitiously be disobeyed by an even larger group. Thus in a short period of time the class has become out of control. The teacher at this point usually becomes very exasperated and red in the face and shouts the class into submission. These 'shock tactics' become less and less effective the more they are used and it takes a considerable amount of time and effort to reconstruct this teacher's behaviour to make it effective, allowing the opportunity actually to teach something (Montgomery and Hadfield 1989, 1990). Many give up the struggle and 'teach' over the noise so that the level of attention and achievement of all pupils is low.

The effective teacher, having gained the pupils' attention and silence will immediately launch into the introduction to the session or begin reading the story. During the teacher talk or story it is necessary for a range of attention gaining and maintaining tactics to be employed, for example:

- pausing in exposition to look at pupil talking until she/he stops;
- walking to pupil and gently removing tapping pencil or note;
- asking the talking or inattentive pupil a question;
- repeating the phrase just given;
- insert 'and Goldilocks said to the three bears!' in the middle of the story looking hard at the miscreant;
- use hand signal or finger on lips cue to quieten;
- use 'stink look'.

The main point about this phase of the lesson is that if a lot of controlling techniques need to be used then the material and the mode of delivery should be reconsidered and wound up as soon as possible.

Monitoring – phase two
As soon as there is an activity change from pupils listening to getting out books and writing or going back to places to work this is when disruption can and does arise. The monitoring strategy needs to be brief, perhaps lasting no more than 30 seconds. As soon as the pupils are at their places the teacher should move round the room to each group or table very quickly and quietly settling them down to work. It is essential not to linger to give detailed explanations at this point but to say that you will come back shortly to help, going to the noisiest group first but making sure that all are visited. If there is not a lot of space to move round then a vantage point should be selected and the monitoring directed from there by calming gestures and quiet naming.

In addition to activity change, monitoring should be used when pupils are engaged with tasks and the noise level seems to be rising and attention to be slipping. This can be noted at any time by the well attuned ear and usually only requires that the teacher looks up and round the room to the talker. A pointed look may well be all that is required, or very quiet naming. The important thing is not to nag and be noisy about criticism and having told a pupil to be quiet to look up and check back on the pupil within 3–5 seconds.

Maintenance – phase three
Once the pupils have been settled by the monitoring techniques to the task, it is then advisable for the teacher to move round the class to each individual to find out how the work is progressing. In the maintenance period all the requests and queries of individuals can be dealt with. During a lesson period or period of study within a curriculum area each pupil should expect to receive some form of individual constructive and developmental comment on the work – PCI. This has been called *Positive cognitive intervention* (Montgomery 1984, 1994, 1996). In this steady move round the room the teacher should look at the work with the pupil and offer *developmental* advice which makes a positive statement about progress thus far and then offers ideas and suggestions for extension, or through constructive questioning helps the pupils see how to make the work better or achieve the goals they have set themselves. When the work has been completed again there should be written or spoken comments as appropriate and further ideas, for example:

Jason, I enjoyed your story very much. The beginning section was very good, it set the murky scene very well. I think you should look at some of Roald Dahl's characters to help in writing about your people. If you look up one or two I will show you what I mean.

Chrissy, the colours in your picture are beautiful, next time I want you to explore the effect when you only use a palette of three.

At intervals during the maintenancing period the noise will fluctuate. As soon as the level goes above 'interested work' or an individual's voice is clearly audible and does not stop after a few moments then a quick monitoring session should ensue. This may only need to be the raising of the teacher's head to look in the direction of the noise to cue the pupil to silence or it may again involve 'stink look' and quiet naming. If this does not suffice then it may be necessary to go over and settle the problem.

Some individual behaviour management strategies

Behaviour modification strategies are most frequently advised upon by the School Psychological Services and they may also offer training courses to help the management of particularly difficult, often disruptive pupils. BATPACK courses (Wheldall and Merrett 1984, 1985) and their books on positive approaches to teaching are all based on the principles of reinforcement established by Skinner (1954) in his studies of Operant Conditioning and most books on classroom management and managing difficult behaviour include this (Cheeseman and Watts 1985; Chisholm *et al.* 1986; Luton *et al.* 1991). The pupil emits unwanted responses which the teacher learns to ignore but reinforces the closest opposite and desirable response. By a process of continuous positive reinforcement the behaviour is gradually *shaped* towards more 'desirable' ends.

In the case of a disruptive pupil close observation and identification of the target behaviour is needed together with the drawing up of a reinforcement schedule and school behaviour management plan. Even so it is impossible to reinforce each occurrence of the desirable behaviours and it may be better to put the pupil in a much smaller class – a group of 8–12 with a specially trained teacher whilst the main part of the programme is being implemented. Rogers (1994a) suggested withdrawing disruptives for regular 20 minute sessions to be given social skills and behaviour management training from trained teachers. Other colleagues, including playground and canteen helpers, need to be made aware of the main elements of the 'therapy' if all the work in the classroom is not to be undone.

Many of the studies in the USA used positive reinforcements which not only included giving merit points for good behaviour but also enabled them to be saved up to spend time on hobbies, games or to buy candy, paints and even make-up. As a rule it is not surprisingly found that when the novelty has worn off the pupil decides not to work for more credits. This is supported by the work of Deci and Ryan (1983) and Ryan *et al.* (1985) who found that extrinsic rewards such as these actually cause a decline in motivation over time whereas intrinsic motivation is raised by a *positive supportive learning environment*. It is thus the teacher who is the real source of motivation and it is the teacher's smile and genuine support and praise which is the all-pervading and prime motivator.

Modelling is another strategy the teacher may use (Blackham and Silberman 1971). At its simplest level it involves the teacher saying such things as 'Very well done, the Green table is ready', 'Show me who is ready', 'Michael was really listening so he is doing it well', 'Sharon has a good idea, watch how she does it', 'I like the way Gary helped him' and so on. Other children vicariously learn by watching the reinforced model (Bandura and Walters 1963). In more sophisticated versions the model is reinforced and then the pupil watching is reinforced for any approximation towards the good behaviour of the model. A range of different models need to be selected so that one child does not become a 'star' for the others to dislike and even bully.

Time out, when pupils have become overexcited, distressed, are upset or having a tantrum a 'time out' corner, cushion or seat can be very useful. Pupils can take themselves there to have 30 seconds peace and quiet to recover or they can be sent there knowing no other pupil must look at them or speak to them until they come out or it is agreed that they can come out when they are calm. It is not advisable to send them out of the classroom for they may run away and be involved in an incident outside. If the pupil is unmanageable it is wisest to send another responsible child to the head or deputy to summon help.

Disruption on this scale is serious and of course the parents would need to be consulted about underlying difficulties and joint efforts to help the child. For a period of time it may be essential to draw up a *behaviour contract* with the pupil and parents stating attainable goals (Rogers 1994a) and the ways in which the pupil will behave and this will be signed by all the parties. The class teacher and any specialist teachers will sign the record at the end of each session or write a comment on the pupil's conduct. At the end of the day the record is inspected by the head or deputy and commented upon. This should only need to be kept up for two or three weeks and then the pupil should be officially signed off for good behaviour and the record filed. Such periods can give an opportunity for attitude change and a review of the child's needs in more detail and may be enough to deal with the problem. The contract may have to be redrawn at a later stage as some new factor arises. It is so often found that the counselling relationship which is established between the pupil and the person to whom the daily report is made can develop strongly enough to make the pupil want to work for the good opinion of that person and she/he will seriously try to iron out what before may have seemed to be insuperable difficulties.

Coping with confrontations

These are most often explosive episodes involving an individual pupil and teacher or pairs of pupils in a fight. There may be little done to have provoked the outburst or it may be the end of an episode of noisy disruption ending in verbal abuse which the teacher in desperation seeks to stem and which causes the final outburst. The teacher may already have tried calming strategies and may have asked the pupil to stop the tirade or to sit still and get on with his or her work. The pupil has thrown down the gauntlet and challenged the teacher verbally or physically. The teacher has a range of options to select from – summon help if necessary; offer choices (Rogers 1994 a,b); recover the situation (Montgomery 1989) by:

Deflecting (the confrontation) – putting it on hold (give time for things to cool down and for brains to be engaged) – *normalising* (continue with the lesson as though nothing had happened and support the work effort using P.C.I.) – keep pupil behind at the end of the lesson and then *counsel.*

The ecosystemic developmental function

The Behavioural Support Teacher (BST)

In some schools there may be a BST or a coordinator may be responsible for developing team approaches to disruption within the education authority. It may be more economical to appoint behavioural support teachers than to establish units for children with EBD even though these may be attached to schools. The evidence is not yet available. The most important activities of the BST recorded by Rennie (1993) were:

- withdrawing 'problem' children;
- counselling them;
- supporting other staff in their classes;
- devising behaviour modification programmes;
- supporting individual children;
- advising other staff on class management.

Rennie 1993 (p. 9)

It can be seen once again that some training in counselling is an important requirement and in particular the Rogerian approach is favoured (Rogers 1980; Hall and Hall 1988; Knox 1992) and offers opportunities for *reframing* and personal insight.

Assertive Discipline (AD)

AD was developed by Lee and Marlene Cantor in the USA in 1976. It is a method of disciplining based on behaviour modification. It consists of a highly structured and administered system of rewards and punishments. Rewards may be stars, merit marks, play time, and even tangible rewards such as prizes and gifts earned by the collection of tokens or merit points. Gifts are less popular in this country than in the USA. The punishments or consequences are at no more than five levels of increasing severity: having one's name put on the board; keeping in for five minutes at playtime, isolation for a short period; reporting to the head, informing parents. At the first infringement a warning is given. Having the name put on the board five times leads inevitably to the next stage of punishment and the penalties are non-negotiable. It can ensure a quiet, calming discipline. Cantor insists that no child's name should be put on the board or the list until two other pupils have been praised. The system is graded according to individual school's policies and the staff team must agree to implement it systematically. Teachers learn to establish no more than five clear rules, for example: follow instructions the first time they are given; put your hands up to answer questions; keep noise level low; keep your hands, feet and objects to yourself; do not talk while the teacher or other pupils are talking.

Behaviour Management Products Ltd was set up in the UK in 1991 to carry out the AD training and claimed that over 2,000 schools were using the system. Makins (1991) reported that schools adopting the system were able to see the difference within a day. However, older pupils can come to see this system as a joke or it fails because all teachers do not keep to the rules.

Developing social and communication skills

It has already been noted that pupils with EBD often lack these skills so that programmes of learning which incorporate skills development, mediation and confrontation management for pupils can be particularly helpful (Bowers and Wells 1988; Curry and Bromfield 1994).

Developing personal controls and keeping the team informed and involved

A not infrequent experience is of emotionally disturbed children such as Lisa who at five years would scream and scream and bang the chairs and tables and throw things about whenever the teacher tried to call the class together on the mat for story or a teaching input. She made such a noise that the other children were frightened and could not hear what the teacher said. We agreed that the teacher would tell Lisa that she would not be given the teacher's attention in these episodes as in the past to try to calm or stop her – which had made it worse – but she would get the attention when she came and sat down and listened. The teacher explained to the other children what would happen and that they would all work together in this way to help Lisa regain her place in the class and that it would be difficult for a little while. The strategy was also explained to colleagues and agreed with the head. There would be no intervention except to stop the child harming herself or others. The story session began, Lisa sat at a distance quietly then opened the music cupboard, got out the drum and chime bars and banged and screamed for a full 15 minutes. She was given no response, the teacher quietly keeping the others on the mat. Suddenly Lisa put down the instruments and said 'Oh you!' and then went and sat on the mat with the others. The story was continued and she was welcomed with a smile and involved in it.

Parents as partners and team members

Parents should wherever possible be regarded as part of the discipline management team. Most will agree to support the school's strategy at home although some may need help to change their own disciplining techniques or extend the quality time they spend with their child. The BHT may be able to offer this counselling and support as a form of family therapy (Hoffman 1981, de Shazer 1985).

Ecosystemics and Reflective Teaching

This depends upon self scrutiny by teachers and within it *reframing* can be a powerful strategy. It means:

> to change the conceptual/emotional setting or viewpoint in relation to which a situation is experienced and to place it in another frame which fits the 'facts' of the same concrete situation equally well or even better, and thereby changes its entire meaning.
>
> (Watzlawick and Weakland *et al.* p75)

Reframing disruptive behaviour by a teacher may be to see it as a result of a learning difficulty; reframing by a pupil may mean, for instance, that a bully is helped to see the actions from the victim's point of view and is enabled to stop (Knox 1992).

There is a range of ways in which *reflective teaching* can be promoted. It may be through the processes of reflection on professional issues which arise from peer discussion, attendance at inservice courses, reading about and viewing practice issues, or from appraisal and review. According to Pollard and Tann (1994) reflective teaching implies an active concern with the aims and consequences as well as the means and practical consequences. It is cyclical and involves competencies in classroom enquiry, an open-minded attitude, a quality of judgment informed by the educational disciplines, all informed by the collaboration and dialogue with colleagues.

Physical organisation and professional activities

Looking again at the organisation of a room, the space for movement around it and changing the positions from which to teach all can contribute to easier classroom management (Montgomery 1990). Seating in rows instead of groups fits some learning activities better (Hastings 1995). There are more than a dozen ways of reorganising the seating for different types of learning.

Tactical lesson planning

This involves focusing directly upon what the pupils are doing at any point and is a major support to learning and teaching. A tactical plan simply means that each phase of the lesson has been constructed and timed to create an activity change for the pupils, from listening to writing to reading to speaking to practical activity to writing (recording) to speaking (reporting) and so on. Changing the tactics can cause marked changes in pupils' responses which can feed into the reflective process (Montgomery 1984, 1998).

Critical thinking about teaching and learning

It will be found that a move from more didactic methods towards *cognitive process pedagogies* or teaching methods which facilitate a greater amount of learning will also reduce the amount of time available for misbehaviour and inattention and these methods in themselves induce intrinsic motivation so that the pupils want to work rather than having to be made to. However, changes or improvments in teaching methods only arise where teachers have time to reflect upon their own teaching and the pupils' learning. The cognitive process techniques are also those which embrace the needs of those lower attainers who are resistant to and do not respond to praise (Hanko 1994). For them to change and become motivated and responsive they must experience genuine success and feel they have experienced real cognitive challenge, as Mark did with handwriting. He analysed his own writing and evaluated the effect of the cursive training. In the process he was empowered. He gained cognitive and then motor control as he tapped into his metacognitions.

Summary

Learning to cope with children with emotional and behavioural difficulties in classrooms faces all teachers at some time. The methods required are not punitive and harsh but calming, firm, fair, supportive and constructive. Too often pupils with such difficulties have been exposed to an excess of poor and inconsistent disciplining techniques and to inappropriate models for behaviour in environments in which their sense of self-worth has been diminished.

An ecological model of the difficulties was used as the context for the discussion and an ecosystemic approach to intervention was outlined. The role of learning difficulties in disaffection from schooling was stressed. Positive classroom management practices which gain and maintain control were described followed by individual and team behaviour management procedures which can enable teachers to cope.

Positive behaviour management strategies on their own will set up an appropriate climate and ethos but if the positive and constructive pupil behaviours are to be maintained then they must be combined with *positive cognitive interventions* to ensure that development in learning in content areas takes place.

Epilogue

It is my view that the current direction in which education is being propelled is the antithesis of that which would meet the needs of lower attaining pupils and achieve quality in teaching and learning in general.

In order to achieve progress standards appear to have been identified which fit a particular but inappropriate ideology and which hark back to an imagined golden era. On to this have been tacked a number of new initiatives to patch up this system. The volume of paper work has increased to the detriment of teachers' ability to prepare for pupils' learning. The conflict between these demands has induced teacher stress, making them vulnerable to illness and less fit to cope with the challenges of teaching and learners. It also hampers them from engaging in relaxed reflection upon practice and from undertaking teacher research into quality in teaching and learning.

To help redress the balance a number of cross curriculum skills have been identified in which core themes of development and cognition have been pursued to show how modest changes in class teaching methods can improve pupil attainment in general and produce marked changes in motivation and skills of lower attainers in particular. Their success alongside their peers enables them to gain in esteem so that they can become achievers and no longer be disaffected and troublesome.

The methods of teaching proposed are intimately connected with the needs of learners and the nature of effective learning. The methods have been tried and tested in classrooms with the full range of pupils and they include the lately fashionable 'interactive' teaching but in small doses.

References

Adams, M.J. (1990) *Beginning to Read: Thinking and Learning About Print.* Cambridge MA. MIT Press.

Adey, P.S., Shayer, M. (1991) *The Cognitive Acceleration Through Science Programme: CASE.* London, Kings College.

Ahmed, A. (1987) *Lower Attainment in Mathematics Project Handbook.* Bogner Regis: West Sussex Institute of Higher Education.

AHTACA (1985) *The Special Curricular Needs of Autistic Children.* London: National Autistic Society.

Ainscow, M. (1994) *Special Needs in the Classroom: A Teacher Education Guide London*: Jessica Kingsley/UNESCO.

Allen, M.D. (1965) 'Training in perceptual skills', *Science* **4**.

Alston, J. (1993) *Assessing and Promoting Writing Skills.* Stafford: NASEN.

Alston, J. and Taylor, J. (1987) *Handwriting Theory and Practice.* London: Croom Helm.

Anderson, T.H. (1979) 'Study strategies and adjunct aids' pp. 483–502. In R.C. Anderson, J. Osborn and R.J. Tierney (eds) *Learning to Read in American Schools.* Hillsdale, N.J.: Erlbaum.

Anderson, J.R. (1980) *Cognitive Psychology and its Implications.* San Francisco: Freeman.

Applebee, A.N. (1978) *The Child's Concept of Story.* Chicago Illinois: Chicago Univ. Press.

APU (Assessment of Performance Unit) (1991) *Assessment of Writing Skills.* London: Further Education Unit.

Ashman, S. and Creme, P. (1990) *How to Write Essays.* London: Polytechnic of North London Press.

Ashworth, J. (1996) 'Universities in, and for the world', *Royal Society of Arts Journal* **CXCIV**, (5466), Jan/Feb. pp. 36–45.

Askew, M., Brown, M. and Rhodes, S. (1997) 'Report on the nature of effective teaching strategies in mathematics in a small group of primary schools', *The Times Educational Supplement,* November p. 12.

Asquith, D. (1996) *Geography Themes, Curriculum Bank.* Leamington Spa: Scholastic.

Aston Index (1980) refer to Newton and Thomson op. cit.

Augur, J and Briggs, S. (Eds) (1991) *The Hickey Multisensory language Course: 2nd Edition.* London: Whurr.

Ausubel, D.P., Novak, J.D. and Hanesian, H. (1978) *Educational Psychology: A Cognitive View,* 2nd edn. New York: Holt Rinehart and Winston.

Bailey, T. (1991) 'Classroom observation: A powerful tool for teachers?' *Support for Learning* **6**, (1), pp. 32–36.

Bandura, A. and Walters, R. H. (1963) *Social Learning and Personality Development.* London: Holt Rinehart and Winston.

Barnard, H.C. (1961) *A History of English Education from 1760.* London: University of London Press.

Barrass, A. (1982) *Writing.* London: Longmans.

Basic Skills Agency (1997) *Survey of Basic Skills of Adults 16–60.* London: Basic Skills Agency.

Beard, R. (1984) *Children's Writing in Primary School.* Sevenoaks: Hodder and Stoughton.

Bennett, N (1986) 'Cooperative Learning. Children do it in groups or do they?' Paper presented at the DECP Conference London/*Educational Child Psychology* 1987, **4** pp. 7–18.

Bennett, N. and Kastor, T. (1988) *Analysing Childrens' Language.* Oxford: Blackwell.

Bentley, R. (1995) 'Able thinkers learning (CAPSOC)' *Flying High,* Issue 2, Spring pp. 10–18.

Bereiter, C and Engelmann, S. (1966) *Teaching Disadvantaged Children in the Preschool.* Englewood Cliffs, N.J.: Prentice-Hall.

Bereiter, C. and Scardamalia, M. (1982) 'From conversation to composition: the role of instruction in the developmental process' pp. 113–119. In R. Glaser (ed.) *Advances in Instructional Psychology* **2**. London: Erlbaum.

Blackham, G.J. and Silberman, A. (1971) *Modification of Child Behaviour.* Belmont: CA Wadsworth.

Blagg, N. (1993) *Somerset Thinking Skills Course Handbook.* Taunton: N. Blagg Associates.

Blair, A.J. (1988) 'Current issues in informal logic and critical thinking' pp. 15–29 and 'Teaching informal logic using "Logical self defense" pp. 60–64. In A. Fisher (ed.) *Critical Thinking,* Proceedings of the First British Conference on Informal logic and Critical Thinking, Norwich: University of East Anglia.

Bloom, B.S. (1956) *Taxonomy of Educational Objectives Vol 1.* London: Longmans.

Bogen, J.E. and Bogen G, M. (1969) 'The other side of the brain, III. The corpus callosum and creativity'. *Bulletin of the Los Angeles Neurological Society* **34** (4), pp. 191–220.

Bowers, S. and Wells, L. (1988) *Ways and Means: A Problem Solving Approach.* Kingston upon Thames: Kingston Friends Workshop Group.

Bradley, L. and Bryant, P. (1985) *Children's Reading Problems.* Oxford: Blackwell.

Braten, I. (1991) 'Vygotsky as a precursor to metacognitive theory 1: The concept of metacognition and its roots'. *Scandinavian Journal of Educational Research* **35** (3), pp. 23–30

Brooks, G., Latham, J. and Rex, A. (1987) *Developing Oral Skills.* London: Heinemann.

Brown, A. L., Brandsford, J. D., Ferrara, R. A. and Campione, J. C. (1983) 'Learning, Remembering and Understanding', In J. H. Flavell and E. Markham (eds) *Carmichael's Manual of Child Psychology* **1**. New York: Wiley.

Brown, M. (1982) *Low Attainers: Mathematics 5–16* London: Schools Council Working Party, Paper 72.

Brown, W. and Taylor, G. (1985) 'Impaired relationships and self image', pp. 7–13 In *The Special Curricular Needs of Autistic Children.* London: AHTACA/NAS.

Bullock Report (1975) *A Language for Life.* London: HMSO.

Burnhill, P., Hartley, J., Fraser, L. and Young, D. (1975) 'Writing lines:\an exploratory study.' *Programmed Learning and Educational Technology* **12** (2), pp. 25–30.

Burton, L. (Ed) (1986) *Girls into Maths Can Go.* London: Holt Rinehart and Winston.

Butler-Por, N. 1987 *Underachievers in School: Issues and Interventions.* Chichester: Wiley.

Cantell, M., Smyth, M.M. and Ahonen, T.P. (1994) 'Clumsiness in adolescence: Education, motor and social outcomes of motor delay detected at five years'. In S.E. Henderson (ed.) *Developmental Co-ordination Disorder: Special Issue of Adapted Physical Activity Quarterly,* Human Kinetics.

Cantor, L. and Cantor, M. (1991) *Assertive Discipline.* Revised edition. Bristol: Behaviour Mangement Limited.

Carnine, D.W. and Silbert, J. (1979) *Direct Instruction Reading.* Ohio: Charles E. Merrill.

Carr, J. (1970) 'Mental and motor development in young mongol children', *Journal of Mental Deficiency Research* **14**, pp. 205–211.

Cashdan, A. (1976) 'Problems of adjustment and learning' *Personality and Learning: Block 9.* Milton Keynes: Open University.

CATE 1983 CATENOTE 1. London: DES.

Chall, J. (1967) *Learning to Read: The Great Debate.* New York: McGraw Hill.

Chall, J. (1983) *Stages in Reading Development.* New York: McGraw Hill.

Chalmers, G.S. (1976) *Reading Easy 1800–50.* London: The Broadsheet King.

Chambers, P. (1987) *Reading.* Leamington Spa: Scholastic.

Cheeseman, P. and Watts, P. (1985) *Positive Behaviour Management: A Manual for Teachers.* Beckenham: Croom Helm.

Chesson, R., McKay, C. and Stephenson, E. (1991) 'The consequences of motor/learning difficulties for school-age children and their teachers: Some parental views'. *Support for Learning* **6** (4), pp. 172–177.

Chinn, S.J. and Ashcroft, J.R. (1993) *Mathematics for Dyslexics: A Teaching Handbook.* London: Whurr.

Chisholm, B., Kearney, D., Knight G., Little, H., Morris, S., Tweddle, D. (1986) *Preventive Approaches to Disruption: Developing Teaching Skills.* London: MacMillan.

Clark, M.M. (1970) *Reading Difficulties in Schools.* Harmondsworth: Penguin.

Clarke, A.D.B. and Clarke, A.M. (1973) *Mental Retardation and Behavioural Research.* Edinburgh: Churchill and Livingstone.

Clay, M.M. (1979) *The Early Detection of Reading Difficulties.* London: Heinemann.

Clay, M.M. (1989) 'Observing young children reading texts'. *Support for Learning* **4** (1), pp. 7–11.

Cockcroft Report (1982) *Mathematics Counts.* London: HMSO.

Code of Practice (1994) *The Code of Practice for Special Educational Needs,* Welsh Office, DfEE.

Cooper, M. (1984) 'Self identity and adolescent school refusers and truants'. *Education Review* **30**, pp. 229–237.

Cooper, P. and Upton, G. (1991) 'Controlling the urge to control: An ecosystemic approach to problem behaviour in schools'. *Support for Learning* **6** (1), pp. 22–26.

Cotterell, G. (1985) *Teaching the Non-Reading Dyslexic Child.* Wisbech: Learning Development Aids.

Cowdery, L.L. (1987) *Teaching Reading Through Spelling (TRTS): The Spelling Notebook.* Kingston Polytechnic, Learning Difficulties Research Project.

Cowdery, L.L., McMahon, J., Montgomery, D. (ed.), Morse, P., and Prince-Bruce, M. (1983) *Teaching Reading Through Spelling (TRTS): Diagnosis Book 2A.* Kingston Polytechnic, Learning Difficulties Research Project.

Cowdery, L.L., Montgomery, D. (ed.), Morse, P. and Prince-Bruce, M. (1984) *Teaching Reading Through Spelling (TRTS): The Foundations of the Programme Book 2B.* Kingston Polytechnic, Learning Difficulties Research Project.

Cowdery, L.L., Morse, P., Prince-Bruce, M. (1985) *Teaching Reading Through Spelling (TRTS): The Early Stages of the Programme Book 2C.* Kingston Polytechnic, Learning Difficulties Research Project.

Cripps, C. (1988) *A Hand for Spelling.* Wisbech: Learning Development Aids.

Cripps, C. (1995) 'Teaching spelling and handwriting', European Council of International Schools Conference, Nice, November.

Croll, P. and Moses, D. (1985) *One in Five.* London: Routledge and Kegan Paul.

Cropley, A. J. (1994) 'Creative intelligence. A concept of true giftedness', *European Journal of High Ability* **5** (1), pp. 16–23.

Curry, M. and Bromfield, C. (1994) *Circle Time.* Stafford: NASEN.

Daniels, H. (1993) 'Coping with mathematics in the National Curriculum. Pupils' strategies and teacher responses' *Support for Learning* **8** (2), pp. 65–69.

Daniels, J.C. and Diack, H. (1958) *The Standard Spelling Test.* London: Chatto and Windus. (Reprinted by Hart Davis Educational, 1979.)

Dansereau, D.F. (1988) 'Co-operative learning strategies' Chapter 7, pp. 103–120. In C.E. Weinstein, E.T. Goetz and P.A. Alexander (eds) *Learning and Study Strategies.* New York: Academic Press.

Davie, R., Butler, N. and Goldstein, H. (1972) *From Birth to Seven.* London: Longmans/NCB.

Dearing, Sir R. (1994) *National Curriculum, Revised.* York: National Curriculum Council.

de Bono, E. (1970) *Lateral Thinking.* London: Ward Lock.

de Bono, E. (1976) *Teaching Thinking.* London: Maurice Temple Smith.

de Bono, E. (1983) *CoRT Thinking Materials.* Oxford: Pergamon.

Deci, E.L. and Ryan, R.M. (1983) *Intrinsic Motivation and Human Behaviour.* New York: Plenum Press.

De Mink, F. (1995) 'High ability students in higher education', pp. 177–183. In M.W. Katzko and F.J. Monks *Nurturing Talent: Individual Needs and Social Abilities.* Assen, The Netherlands: Van Gorcum.

de Shazer, S. (1985) *Keys to Solution.* New York: Norton.

Denton C and Postlethwaite K. (1985) *Able Children: Identifying Them in the Classroom.* Windsor: NFER-Nelson.

DES (1977) *Gifted Children in Middle and Secondary Schools: A Report by HMI.* London: HMSO.

DES (1979) *Aspects of Secondary Education. A report by HMI.* London: HMSO.

Deutsch, G. and Springer, S. (1992) *Left Brain, Right Brain.* San Francisco: W.H. Freeman.

DfEE (1997) *Excellence for All: Meeting Special Educational Needs.* London: HMSO.

DILP (1993) *Dyslexia Institute Language Programme.* Staines: Dyslexia Institute.

Dods, R.F. (1997) 'An action research study of the effectiveness of PBL in promoting the acquisition and retention of knowledge' *Journal of the Education of the Gifted* **21** (1) Fall, pp. 18–25.

Dröscher, V.B. (1975) *The Magic of the Senses.* London: Panther Books.

Duchein, M. and Mealey, D. (1993) 'Remembrance of books past. Long past glimpses into alliteracy', *Reading Research and Instruction* **33** (1), pp.13–28.

Edge, A and Stokes, E. (1997) *Quality and Assessment in Secondary Education: An Exploration of Curricula and Examinations, Year 1.* London: LSE Centre for Educational Research.

Education Act (1981) *Children with Special Educational Needs.* London: HMSO.

Edwards, J. (1994) *Scars of Dyslexia.* London: Cassell.

Ehlers, S. and Gillberg, C. (1993) 'The epidemiology of Asperger Syndrome: a total population study', *Journal of Child Psychology and Psychiatry* **34,** pp. 1327–1350.

Elton Report (1989) *Discipline in Schools.* London: HMSO.

Englemann, S. and Carnine, D.W. (1982) *Theory of Instruction: Principles and Practice.* New York: Irvington.

Farringdon, D. (1994) ' The early prevention of juvenile delinquency' *Journal of the Royal Society of Arts* **142** (5454), Nov., pp. 22–31.

Fassett, J.H. (1927) *The New Beacon Readers: Teachers' Manual.* London: Ginn.

Feller, M. (1994) 'Open book testing and education for the future', *Studies in Educational Evaluation* **20** (2), pp. 235–238.

Fernald, G.M (1943) *Remedial Techniques in basic School Subjects.* New York: McGraw-Hill.

Feuerstein, R. (1980) *Instrumental Enrichment.* Baltimore MD: University Park Press.

Feuerstein, R. (1995) 'Mediated learning Experience' London Conference on MLE July, Regents College, London.

Fisher, J. (1982) 'Case studies in intervention'. Unpublished Inservice B.Ed dissertation, Kingston: Kingston Polytechnic.

Fisher, R. (1994) *Teaching Children to Think.* Hemel Hempstead: Simon and Shuster.

Flanders, N. (1970) *Analysing Teacher Behaviour.* Reading, Mass: Addison-Wesley.

Flavell J.H. (1979) 'Metacognition and cognitive monitoring', *American Psychologist* **34**, pp. 906–911.

Francis, H. (1982) *Learning to Read: Literate Behaviour and Orthographic Knowledge.* London: Allen and Unwin.

Freeman, J. (1991) *Gifted Children Growing Up.* London: Cassell.

French, J.D. (1957) 'The Reticular formation', pp. 232–238 In *Psychobiology: The Biological Basis of Behaviour*, Readings from *Scientific American.* San Francisco: Freeman.

Frith, U. (ed.) (1980) *Cognitive Processes in Spelling.* London: Academic Press.

Frith, U. (1985) 'Beneath the surface of developmental dyslexia' In K. Patterson and M. Coltheart (eds) *Surface Dyslexia.* London: Routledge and Kegan Paul.

Frith, U. (1991) *Autism and Asperger Syndrome.* Cambridge: Cambridge University Press.

Fry, E. (1964) 'A frequency approach to phonics', *Elementary English* **41**, pp. 759–765.

Gagné, R. M. (1975) *Essentials of Learning for Instruction.* Hinsdale Ill.: Dryden Press.

Galaburda, A.M., Signoret, J.C. and Ronthal, M. (1985) 'Left posterior angiomatous anomaly and developmental dyslexia. Report of five cases', *Neurology* **35**, Supplement 198.

Galaburda, A.M. (1995) *Dyslexia and Development.* Cambridge, M.A.: Cambridge University Press.

Gallagher, J.J. (1985) *Teaching the Able.* New York: Allen and Boston.

Gallagher, J.J. and Gallagher, S. (1994) *Teaching the Able: 2nd Edition.* New York: Allen and Boston.

Gallagher, S.A. (1997) 'PBL: Where did it come from? What does it do and where is it going?' *Journal for the Education of the Gifted* **21** (1), pp. 3–18.

Galloway, D. and Goodwin, C. (1987) *The Education of Disturbing Children.* London: Longmans.

Galton, M., Simon, R. and Croll, P. (1980) *Inside the Primary Classroom*. London: Routledge and Kegan Paul.

Gardner, H. (1990) *Frames of Mind. The Theory of Multiple Intelligences*. New York: Basic Books.

Gazzaniga, R. (1967) 'Split brain in man' *Scientific American* **217**, pp. 24–29.

Geschwind, N. (1979) 'Specialisation of the human brain' *Scientific American* **241** (3), pp. 158–167.

Gibbs, G. (1990) *Learning Through Action*. London: Further Education Unit.

Gillbery, C., Perrson, E., Grufman, M. and Themner, U. (1986) 'Psychiatric disorders in mildly and severely mentally retarded urban children and adolescents: epidemiological aspects', *British Journal of Psychiatry* **149**, pp. 68–74.

Gillham, B. (ed.) (1989) *Handicapping Conditions in Children*. London: Routledge.

Gillingham, A.M., Stillman, B.U. and Orton, S.T. (1940) *Remedial Training for Children with Specific Disability in Reading, Spelling and Penmanship*. New York: Sackett and Williams.

Goldstein, S. and Goldstein M. (1992) Cited in B. Ingersoll and S. Goldstein (1993) *Attention Deficit Disorder and Learning Disabilities: Realities, Myths and Controversial Treatments*. New York: Doubleday.

Good, T.L. and Brophy, J.E. (1985) *Educational Psychology. A Realistic Approach*. London: Holt Rinehart and Winston.

Goodman, K.S. (1969) 'Analysis of oral reading miscues: applied psycholinguistics', *Reading Research Quarterly* **5**, pp. 8–30.

Gorman, T. (1986) *The Framework for the Assessment of Language: APU*. Windsor: NFER-Nelson.

Gorman, T. and Fernandes, C. (1993) *Reading in Recession*. Windsor: NFER-Nelson.

Goswami, U. and Bryant, P.E. (1990) *Phonological Skills and Learning to Read*. Hove, E. Sussex: L. Erlbaum.

Goswami, U. (1992) 'Orthographic analogies and reading development'. The Spearman Medal Address, *The Psychologist*, July 1993, 313–315.

Goswami, U. (1994) 'The role of analogies in reading development', *Support for Learning* **9** (1), pp. 22–26.

Gresham, F.M., Elliott, S.N. and Black, F.L. (1987) 'Teacher-rated social skills of mainstreamed mildly handicapped children', *School Psychology Review* **16**, pp. 78–88.

Gross, J. (1993) *Special Educational Needs in the Primary School*. Milton Keynes: Open University.

Grundin, N. (1981) Cited in A.E. Tansley and J. Pankhurst *Children with Specific Learning Difficulties*. Windsor: NFER.

Gubbay, S.S. (1975) *The Clumsy Child*. London: Saunders.

Hadfield, N. (1989) 'Survey of newly qualified teachers' training experiences and needs in ITT'. Unpublished Project, Maldon, Learning Difficulties Research Project.

Hall, D.M.B. (1988) 'Clumsy children' *British Medical Journal* **296**, p. 375–376.

Hall, N. (Ed) 1989 *Writing with Reason: The Emergence of Authorship in Young Children*. Sevenoaks: Hodder and Stoughton.

Hall, F. and Hall, C. (1988) *Human Relations in Education*. London: Routledge and Kegan Paul.

Hanko, G. (1994) 'Discouraged children: when praise does not help', *British Journal of Special Education* **21** (4), pp. 166–168.

Hanna, P.R., Hanna, J.S., Hodges, R.E. and Rudorf, E.H. (1966) *Phoneme-Grapheme Correspondence as Cues to Spelling Improvement*. Washington DC, US Office of Education.

Hany, E. A. (1997) 'Modelling teachers' judgement of giftedness: a methodological inquiry of biased judgement' *High Ability Studies* **8** (2), pp. 159–178.

Hatcher, P., Hulme, C. and Ellis, N.C. (1993) 'How children best learn to read', *British Psychological Society Conference Proceedings*. Leicester: British Psychol. Soc.

Hargreaves, D. (1984) *Improving Secondary Schools*. London: ILEA.

Henry, M.K. (1995) 'The importance of roots in the English spelling system', *Annual Conference of the Orton Society*. Houston, Texas, 2nd November.

Harris, A. (1996) 'Raising levels of pupils achievement through school improvement', *Support for Learning* **11** (2), pp. 62–67.

Hastings, N. (1995) 'Seats of Learning?' *Support for Learning* **10** (1), pp. 8–11.

Hegarty, S. and Pocklington, K. (1981) *Meeting the Challenge of Special Educational Needs*. Windsor:

NFER.

Heller, K, Hany, E.A., Passow A.H. (eds) (1993) *International Handbook of Research and Development of Giftedness and Talent.* London: Pergamon.

Henderson, P. (1974) *Disability in Childhood and Youth.* London: Oxford University Press.

Henderson, S.E. and Hall, D. (1982) 'Concomitants of clumisness in young school children', *Developmental Medicine and Child Neurology* **24**, pp. 448–460.

Herbert, M. (1985) *Problems of Childhood.* London: Pan reprint.

Hickey, K. (1977) *Dyslexia: A Language Training Course for Teachers and Learners.* Wimbledon, 19 Woodside, SW9.

Hiebert, E.H., Englert, C.S. and Brennan, S. (1983) 'Awareness of text structure in recognition and production of expository discourse', *Journal of Reading Behaviour* **15**, pp. 63–79.

Hinson, M. and Smith, P. (1993) *Phonics and Phonic Resources.* Stafford: NASEN.

HMI (1986) *Lower Attaining Pupils Project.* London: HMSO.

HMI (1990) *The Teaching and Learning of Reading in Primary Schools.* London: HMSO.

HMI (1991) *Mathematics: Key Stages 1 and 3.* London: DES.

HMI (1992) *Making Provision for Highly Able Pupils in Maintained Schools.* London: HMSO.

HMI (1996) *Annual Report of the Senior Chief Inspector for Schools in England.* London: HMSO.

HMI (1997) *Annual Report of the Senior Chief Inspector for Schools in England.* London: HMSO.

Hoffman, L. (1981) *Foundations of Family Therapy.* New York: Basic Books.

Holt, J. (1984) *How Children Fail.* Harmondsworth, Penguin.

Hornsby, B. and Farrar, M. (1990) 'Some effects of a dyslexia-centred teaching programme', pp. 173–196. In P.D. Pumfrey and C.D. Elliott (eds) *Children's Difficulties in Reading, Spelling and Writing.* London: Falmer Press.

Hornsby, B and Shear, F. (1985) *Alpha to Omega; Rev. Edit.* London: Heinemann.

Housby-Smith, N. (1995) 'In sickness as in health' *Special*, Issue 4, No 3, pp.25–27.

Hughes, M. (1985) *Children and Number.* Oxford: Blackwell.

Hulme, C. (1981) *Reading Retardation and Multisensory Teaching.* London: Routledge and Kegan Paul.

Hurry, M. and Silva, K. (1997) 'Summary of research of a longitudinal comparative study of two types of remedial reading intervention'. *The Times Educational Supplement*, December 12th, p. 1.

Inglis, J. and Lewis, R. (1980) *Clear Thinking.* Cambridge: National Extension College.

Jarman, C. (1979) *The Development of Handwriting.* Oxford: Blackwell.

Jenkins, R.L. (1966) 'Psychiatric syndromes in children and their relation to family background', *American Journal of Orthopsychiatry* **36**, pp. 450–457.

Kahney, H. (1986) *Problem Solving: A Cognitive Approach.* Milton Keynes: Open University.

Kanner, L. (1943) 'Autistic disturbances of affective contact' *Nervous Child* **2** pp. 217–250.

Karnes, M.B., and Johnson, L.J. (1991) 'Gifted handicapped'. In N. Colangelo and G.A. Davis (eds) *Handbook of Gifted Education.* Boston: Allyn and Bacon.

Kellmer-Pringle, Mia (1970) *Able Misfits.* London: Longmans.

Kelly, G. A. (1955) *The Psychology of Personal Constructs* Vols 1 and 2, New York: Norton.

Kempe, H.C. and Kempe, R. (1984) *Child Abuse.* London: Open Books.

Kerry, T. and Kerry, C. (1997) 'Teaching the more able: Primary and secondary practice compared' *Education Today* **47** (3), pp. 11–16.

Knight, B.A. (1992) 'The role of the student in mainstreaming', *Support for Learning* **7** (4), pp. 163–165.

Knox, J. (1992) 'Bullying in school: Communicating with the victim', *Support for Learning* **7** (4), pp. 154–162.

Kolb, D. A. (1984) *Experiential Learning; Experiences as a Source of Learning and Development.* New York: Prentice Hall.

Kosc, L. (1974) 'Developmental dyscalculia', *Journal of Learning Disabilities* **7**, pp. 46–59.

Kounin, J.S. (1970) *Discipline and Group Management in Classrooms.* New York: Holt Rinehart and Winston.

Kraupl-Taylor, E. (1966) *Psychopathology.* London: Butterworth.

Lane, C.H. (1990) 'ARROW: Alleviating children's reading and spelling difficulties', pp. 237–254. In

P.D. Pumfrey and C.D. Elliott (eds) *Children's Difficulties in Reading, Spelling and Writing.* London: Falmer Press.

Laszlo, M., Bairstow, P and Bartrip, P. (1988) 'A new approach to perceptuomotor dysfunction: Previously called clumsiness' *Support for Learning* **3**, pp. 35–40.

LDRP (1998) Case Studies and unpublished papers. Maldon, Learning Difficulties Research Project.

Lindgard, A. (1994) 'The acquisition of literacy in secondary education', *British Journal of Special Education* **21** (4), pp. 180–191.

Lipman, M. (1991) *Thinking in Education.* Cambridge: Cambridge University Press.

Lloyd, S (1993) *The Phonics Handbook.* Chigwell: Jolly Learning.

Lunzer, E. and Gardner, K. (1979) *Effective Use of Reading Project.* London: Heinemann.

Luria, A.R. (1973) *The Working Brain.* Harmondsworth, Penguin.

Luton, K., *et al.* (1991) *Positive Strategies for Behavioural Management.* Windsor: NFER-Nelson.

Maidenhead Group of Teachers 1992 *'Motorway Project': 'Townscapes': and 'The Village of Eddington'* (Wisbech, Learning Development Aids).

Makins, V. (1991) 'Five steps to peace in the classroom', *Times Educational Supplement*, Nov 1st, p. 23.

Marton, F. and Saljo, R. (1976) 'On qualitative differences in learning. Outcome as a function of the learner's conception of the task'. *British Journal of Educational Psychology* **46**, pp.115–127.

Marton, F. and Saljo, R. (1984) 'Approaches to learning'. In F. Marton, J. Hownsell and N.J. Entwistle (eds) *The Experience of Learning.* Edinburgh: Scottish Academic Press.

Maxwell, J. (1977) *Reading Progress from 8 to 15.* Windsor: NFER.

McCombs, B.L. (1988) 'Motivational skills training: Combining metacognitive, cognitive and affective learning strategies' Chapter 9, pp. 141–170 in C.E. Weinstein, E.T. Goetz, and P.A. Alexander (eds) *Learning and Study Strategies.* New York: Academic Press.

McLaughlin, G (1963) *The SMOG Readability Index*, cited in Cohen, L. 1979 *Handbook of Educational Measurement.*

Meek, M. and Thomson, B. (1987) *Study Skills in the Secondary School.* London: Routledge.

Mellanby, J., Anderson, R., Campbell, B. and Westwood, E. (1996) 'Cognitive determinants of verbal underachievement at secondary school level', *British Journal of Educational Psychology* **66**, pp. 483–500.

Miles, T.R. (1993) *Dyslexia: The Patterns of Difficulty, 2nd Edition.* London: Whurr.

Merrtens, R. (ed.) (1997) 'Active ingredients' p. 11, *The Times Educational Supplement: Primary and Pre-school Section*, September 26th.

Mittler, P. (1990) Editorial Foreword In D. Montgomery *Children with Learning Difficulties.* London: Cassell.

Molnar, A. and Lindquist, B. (1989) *Changing Problem Behaviour in Schools.* San Francisco: Jossey Bass.

Mongon, D. and Hart, S. (1989) *Improving Classroom Behaviour. New Directions for Teachers and Pupils.* London: Cassell.

Montgomery, D. (1977) 'Teaching pre-reading through training in visual pattern recognition', *The Reading Teacher* **30** (6), pp. 216–225.

Montgomery, D. (1979) *Visual Pattern Recognition Test for Early Reading.* Windsor: NFER.

Montgomery, D. (1981) 'Do dyslexics have difficulty accessing articulatory information?' *Psychological Research* **43**, pp. 235–243.

Montgomery, D. (1981) 'Education comes of age; A modern theory of teaching,' *School Psychology International* **1**, pp. 1–3.

Montgomery D (1982) 'Teaching thinking skills in the school curriculum', *School Psychology International* **3**, pp. 108–112.

Montgomery, D. (1983) *Study Skills and Learning Strategies.* Kingston, Learning Difficulties Project: 2nd edition 1991 Maldon, LDRP.

Montgomery, D. (1984) *The Evaluation and Enhancement of Teaching Performance.* Maldon: Learning Difficulties Research Project.

Montgomery, D. (1985) *The Special Needs of Able Pupils in Ordinary Classrooms.* Maldon: Learning Difficulties Research Project.

Montgomery, D. (1989) *Managing Behaviour Problems.* Sevenoaks: Hodder and Stoughton.

Montgomery, D. (1990) *Children with Learning Difficulties.* London: Cassell.

Montgomery, D (1992) Informal reading Inventory: *MA Special Educational Needs Module 5: Reading and Spelling difficulties.* London: Middlesex University.

Montgomery, D. (1993) 'Fostering learner managed learning in teacher education' pp. 59–70. In N. Graves (ed.) *Learner Managed Learning.* Leeds: Higher Education for Capability/WEF.

Montgomery, D. (1994) 'Spelling difficulties in able dyslexics and their remediation'. pp. 224–236. In K.A. Heller and E.A. Hany (eds) *Competence and Responsibility.* Gottlingen: Hogrese and Huber.

Montgomery, D. (1994) 'Enhancing student learning through the development and use of cognitive process strategies'. In K.A. Heller and E.A. Hany (eds) *Competence and Responsibility* **2**, pp. 317–335. Seattle and Gottlingen: Hogrese and Huber.

Montgomery, D. (1994) 'The role of metacognition and metalearning', Chapter 8 pp. 227–253. In G. Gibbs (ed.) *Improving Student Learning.* Oxford: Oxford Centre for Staff Development.

Montgomery, D. (1995) 'Social abilities in highly able disabled learners and the consequences for remediation', pp. 226–238. In M.W. Katzko and F. J. Monks *Nurturing Talent: Individual Needs and Social Abilities.* Assen, The Netherlands: Van Gorcum.

Montgomery, D. (1996) *Educating the Able.* London: Cassell.

Montgomery, D. (1997a) *Developmental Spelling.* Maldon, Learning Difficulties Research Project.

Montgomery, D. (1997b) *Spelling, Remedial Strategies.* London: Cassell.

Montgomery D. (1998) *Master of Arts Programmes in SEN and SpLD by Distance Learning: 2nd editions.* London: Middlesex University.

Montgomery, D. and Hadfield, N. (1989) *Practical Teacher Appraisal.* London: Kogan Page.

Montgomery, D. and Hadfield, N. (1990) *Appraisal in the Primary Classroom.* Leamington Spa: Scholastic.

Morgan, and Lyon, (1979) cited in S. Wolfendale and K.J. Topping (eds) 1985, *Parental Involvement in Children's Reading.* London: Croom Helm.

Morse, P. (1984) 'Handwriting and handwriting difficulties' pp. 32–68 In L.L. Cowdery, D. Montgomery, P. Morse and M. Prince-Bruce *Teaching Reading Through Spelling (TRTS): Foundations of the Programme.* Kingston: Kingston Polytechnic.

Morse, P. (1986) *Teaching Reading Through Spelling: The Handwriting Copy Book.* Kingston: Kingston Polytechnic.

Morse, P. (1988) *Teaching Reading Through Spelling: The Handwriting Copy Book 2nd Edition.* Clwyd: Frondeg Hall Publishers.

Morse, P. (1991) 'Cursive in Kingston-upon-Thames' *Handwriting Review* **5**, pp. 5–7.

Morse, P. (1992) 'Getting it right from the start: beginner writers', *Handwriting Review* **6**, pp. 24–26.

Morse, P., Low, S., Prince-Bruce, M. and Cowdery, L.L. (1986) *Teaching Reading Through Spelling: The Later Stages Parts 1 and 2.* Kingston Polytechnic, Learning Difficulties Research Project.

Mortimore, P. and Sammon, P., Stoll, L. *et al.* (1988) *School Matters.* London: ILEA. Moseley, D. V. (1994) 'From theory to practice' pp. 459–479. In G.D.A. Brown and N.C. Ellis (eds) *Handbook of Spelling.* Chichester: Wiley.

Myklebust, H.R. (1973) *The Development and Disorders of Written Language, Volume 2.* London: Grune and Stratton.

NACE (1994) National Society for Able Children in Education; Evidence to Sir Ron Dearing on the National Curriculum needs of more able pupils.

Naidoo, S (1972) *Specific Dyslexia: Research Report of the ICAA.* London: Pitman National Autistic Society (NAS) (1993) *Approaches to Autism.* London: National Autistic Society.

National Oracy Project (1992) *TALK: The Journal of the NOP* **5**, Autumn SEN Issue.

National Numeracy Project (1998) *Numeracy Lessons.* London: BEAM Mathematics.

National Writing Project (1989) *Writing and Learning.* Walton on Thames: Nelson.

Neale, M.D. (1958) *The Neale Analysis of Reading.* London: Macmillan.

Nelson, H.E., Warrington, E.K. (1974) 'Developmental spelling retardation and its relation to other cognitive abilities', *British Journal of Psychology* **65** (2), pp. 265–274.

Neville, M. and Pugh, A. (1977) 'Ability to use a book: the effect of teaching', *Reading* **11** (3), pp. 13–18.

Newman, D., Griffin, P and Cole, M. (1989) *The Constructive Zone: Working for Cognitive Change in Schools.* Cambridge: Cambridge University Press.

Newton, M and Thomson, M. (1976) *The Aston Index.* Wisbech: Learning Development Aids.

Nickerson. R.S., Perkins, D.N. and Smith, E.E. (eds) (1985) *The Teaching of Thinking.* Hillsdale, NJ: Erlbaum.

Nisbett, J.F. and Shucksmith, J. (1986) *Learning Strategies.* London: Routledge and Kegan Paul.

Norrie, E. (1917) Cited in the *Edith Norrie Letter Case Manual.* London: Helen Arkell Centre 1982.

Norrie, E. (1982) *The Edith Norrie Letter Case.* London: Word Blind Institute 1946, Reprinted Helen Arkell Centre.

Olson, D.R. (1977) 'From utterance to text: the bias of language in speech and writing'. *Harvard Educational Review* **47** (3), pp. 257–281.

Ornstein, R. (1982) *The Psychology of Consciousness* 2nd Edit. San Francisco: Freeman.

Osborn, A.F. (1963) *Applied Imagination: Principles and Processes of Creative Problem Solving.* New York: Scribners.

Painter, F. (1982) 'Gifted secondary pupils in England', *School Psychology International* **3** (4), pp. 237–244.

Palinscar, A.S. and Brown, A.L. (1984) 'Teaching and practising thinking skills to promote comprehension in the context of group problem solving', *Remedial and Special Education,* **9** (1), pp. 53–59.

Palinscar, A.S. and Brown, A.L. (1986) 'Interactive teaching to promote independent learning from text', *The Reading Teacher* **39**, pp. 771–777.

Pascal, L (1998) Study Skills Training Course Leaflet, Stafford: NASEN.

Passow, A.H. (1990) 'Needed research and development in educating high ability children', *European Journal of High Ability* **1** (4), pp. 15–24.

Patterson, E. (1981) *Information Skills 8 to 18.* Curriculum paper 3. Hull: Hull College of H.E. Professional Centre.

Paul, R. (1990) 'Critical Thinking' In *Critical Thinking Handbook.* Sonoma: Sonoma State University, Centre for Critical Thinking and Moral Critique.

Peck, R.F. and Havighurst, R.J. (1960) *The Psychology of Character Development.* London: John Wiley.

Perry, W. (1959) 'Students' use and misuse of reading skills: a report to a faculty', *Harvard Educational Review* **29** (III).

Peters, M. (1967) *Spelling. Taught or Caught?* London: Routledge and Kegan Paul.

Peters, M. (1985) Revised edition Op. cit.

Peters, M. and Smith, B. (1986) 'The productive process: An approach to literacy for children with difficulties', pp. 161–171. In B. Root (ed.) *Resources for Reading* London: UKRA.

Peters, M. and Smith, B. (1993) *Spelling in Context.* Windsor: NFER-Nelson.

Peterson, P.L., Fennema, E. amd Carpenter, T. (1989) 'Using Knowledge of how students think about mathematics', *Educational Leadership*, January pp. 43–46.

Piaget J. (1954) *The Construction of Reality in the Child.* New York: Basic Books (Translated by Margaret Cook: original French edition 1937).

Pitman, Sir I. (1961) *The Initial Teaching Alphabet.* London: Pitman.

Pollard, A and Tann, S. (1994) *Reflective Teaching in the Primary School 2nd Edit.* London: Cassell.

Prince-Bruce, M. (1978) *Spelling Difficulties.* Kingston: London Borough of Kingston L.E.A.

Prince-Bruce, M. (1986) *Teaching Reading Through Spelling (TRTS); The Later Stages of the Programme Vol 1 and 2.* Kingston: Kingston Polytechnic.

Prince-Bruce, M., Morse, P. and Cowdrey, L.L. (1985) *Teaching Reading Through Spelling: The Programme: The Early Stages.* Kingston, Learning Difficulties Research Project.

Pumfrey, P.D. (1985) *Reading: Tests and Assessment Techniques: 2nd Edition.* London: Hodder and Stoughton/UKRA.

Pumfrey, P.D. and Elliott, C.D. (eds) (1990) *Children's Difficulties in Reading, Spelling and Writing.* London: Falmer Press.

Pumfrey, P. and Reason, R. (1991) *Specific Learning Difficulties (Dyslexia) Challenges and Responses: A National Inquiry.* Windsor: NFER-Nelson.

Purkey, W.W. (1970) *Self Concept and School Achievement.* New York: Prentice Hall.

Pyke, N. (1996) 'Woodhead method linked to failure', *The Times Educational Supplement* 22.6.96, p. 2.

Quirk Report (1972) *Speech Therapy Services: Report by the Committee of Enquiry into Speech Therapy.* London: HMSO.

Race, P. (1991) 'Developing competence'. In *Professorial Inaugural Lectures.* Glamorgan: University of Glamorgan.

Rawlings, A. (1996) *Ways and Means Today: Conflict Resolution, Training and Resources.* Kingston upon Thames: Kingston Friends Workshop Group, 78 Eden Street, Kingston KT1 1DG.

Rennie, E. (1993) Behavioural support teaching: Points to ponder. *Support for Learning* **8** (1), pp. 7–10.

Renzulli, J. S. (1995) 'New directions in the schoolwide enrichment model'. pp. 162–167. In M.W. Katzko and F. J. Monks *Nurturing Talent: Individual Needs and Social Abilities.* Assen, The Netherlands: Van Gorcum.

Resnick, L.B. (1989) 'Introduction', In L.B. Resnick (ed.) *Knowing, Learning and Instruction Essays in Honour of Robert Glaser,* pp. 1–24 Hillsdale NJ: Erlbaum.

Reynolds, R.E. and Shirey, L. L. (1988) 'The role of attention in studying and learning', pp. 77–101. In C. Weinstein, Goetz, and P. Alexander, *Learning and Study Strategies* New York, Academic Press.

Ridehalgh, N. (1998) 'An evaluation of the relative effectiveness of three different remediation programmes'. Unpublished MA SpLD dissertation, London Middlesex University.

Roaf, C. (1998) 'Slow hand: A secondary school survey of handwriting speed and legibility' *Support for Learning,* **13** (1), pp. 39–42.

Robins, L (1966) *Deviant Children Grow Up 1922–1966.* Baltimore: Williams and Williams.

Rogers, C (1980) *A Way of Being.* Boston: Houghton Mifflin.

Rogers, K.S. and Span, P. (1993) 'Ability Grouping with Gifted and Talented Students. Research and Guidelines', pp. 585–592. In K. Heller, F. Monks and A.H. Passow (eds) op.cit.

Rogers, W. (1991) *You Know the Fair Rule.* Harlow: Longman.

Rogers, W. (1994a) 'Teaching positive behaviour to behaviourally disordered students in primary schools' *Support for Learning* **9** (4), pp. 166–170.

Rogers, W. (1994 b) *Behavioural Recovery: A Whole School Approach for Behaviour Disordered Children.* Melbourne: Australian Council for Educational Research.

Ross, S.M. and DiVesta, F.J. (1976) 'Oral summary as a review strategy enhancing recall of textual material', *Journal of Educational Psychology* **68**, pp. 689–695.

Rotter, J.B. (1954) *Social learning and Clinical Psychology.* Englewood Cliffs N.J.: Prentice Hall.

Royce-Adams, W. (1977) *Developing Reading Versatility.* New York: Rinehart and Winston.

Rumelhart, D. (1997) 'Towards a model of reading'. In S. Dorni (ed.) *Attention and Performance VI.* Hillsdale N.J.: Erlbaum.

Rumelhart, D.E. (1980) 'Schemata: The building blocks of cognition'. In R.J. Spiro, B.C. Bruce, and W.F. Brewer (eds) *Thematic Issues in Reading Comprehension.* Hillsdale, N.J.: Erlbaum.

Rutter, M.L. (1975) *Helping Troubled Children.* Harmondsworth, Penguin.

Rutter, M.L., Maughan, M., Mortimore, P. and Ouston, J. (1979) *Fifteen Thousand Hours.* London: Open Books.

Rutter, M.L., Tizard, J., and Whitmore, K. (eds) (1970) *Education, Health and Behaviour.* London: Longman.

Ryan, M.L., Connell, J.P. and Deci, E.L. (1985) 'A motivational analysis of self determination and self regulation in education', Chapter 1 in C. Ames and R. Ames (eds) Vol 2 *Research on Motivation in Education: The Classroom Milieu.* New York: Academic Press.

Sassoon, R. (1989) *Handwriting – How to Teach It.* Cheltenham: Stanley Thorne.

Sassoon, R. (1993) *The Art and Science of Handwriting.* London: Intellect Books.

Saunders, L. (1988) *Report on the Study of Conflict Management in Classrooms.* London: ISTD/Kings College.

Sayer, B. (1979) *An Investigation into the Acquisition of Study Skills by Children.* Unpublished MA thesis, Lancaster/Edge Hill College of H.E.

Schoenfield, A.H. (1985) *Mathematical Problem Solving.* New York, Academic Press.

Schoemaker, M.M. and Calveboer, A.S. (1994) 'Social and affective problems of children who are clumsy: How do they begin? In S.E. Henderson (ed.) *Developmental Co-ordination Disorder: Special Issue of Adapted Physical Activity Quarterly* **11**, pp. 130–141.

Schonell, F.J. and Schonell, E.E. (1946) *Diagnostic and Attainment Testing 4th Edition.* Edinburgh: Oliver and Boyd, reprinted 1985.

Schools Council (1980) *Study Skills in the Secondary School.* London: Schools Council.

Scott MacDonald, W. (1971) *Battle in the Classroom.* Brighton: Intext.

SED (1978) *The Education of Pupils with Learning Difficulties in Primary and Secondary Schools: A Progress Report.* Edinburgh: HMSO.

Selfe, L. (1977) *Nadia, A Case of Extraordinary Drawing Ability in an Autistic Child.* New York: Academic Press.

Shaywitz, S. E. (1995) 'Gender differences in reading disabilities revisited: Results from the Connecticut Longitudinal Study', *Journal of the American Medical Association.*

Shephard, G. (1986) A comparative study of the effects of paired and shared reading in an infant school'. Unpublished Professional studies Project in SEN, Kingston: Kingston Polytechnic.

Shuard, H., Rothery, A. and Holt, M. (1980) *Children Reading Maths: a Working Paper.* London: National Association of Teachers in Further and Higher Education, Mathematics Education Section.

Skilbeck, M. (1989) *School Development and New Approaches to Learning: Trends and Issues in Curriculum Reform.* Paris Organisation for Economic Cooperation and Development.

Skinner, B.F. (1954) *Science and Human Behaviour.* New York: MacMillan.

Smith, F. (1973) *Psycholinguistics and Reading.* London: Holt Rinehart and Winston.

Smith, F. (1985) *Reading.* Cambridge: Cambridge University Press.

Southgate-Booth, V. (1986) 'Teachers of reading: planning the most effective use of their time'. pp. 80–98. In B. Root (ed.) *Resources for Reading: Does Quality Count?* London: UKRA/Macmillan.

Southgate-Booth, V., Arnold, H. and Johnson, S. (1982) *Extending Beginning Reading.* London: Heinemann.

Spalding, R.B. and Spalding W.T. (1967) *The Writing Road to Reading* 2nd edit. New York: Whiteside and Morrow.

Spache, G. (1940) *The Neale Analysis of Reading.* London: Macmillan.

Span, P. (1993) 'Self regulated learning for highly able children.' In J. Freeman, P. Span, and H. Wagner (eds) *Actualising Talent: A Lifelong Challenge.* Gottingen: Hogrese.

Spender, D. (1983) *Invisible Women the Schooling Scandal.* London: Writers and Readers.

Stewart, M. A. (1970) 'Hyperactive children', *Scientific American* **222** (4), pp. 94–99.

Stonier, T. (1983) *The Wealth of Information.* London: Methuen.

Stott, D.H. (1966) *Studies of Troublesome Children.* London: Tavistock.

Stott, D.H. (1981) 'Behaviour disturbance and failure to learn: A study of cause and effect', *Educational Research* **23** (3).

Stott, D.H. and Marston, N.C. (1970) 'Inconsequence as a primary type of behaviour disturbance in children'. *British Journal of Educational Psychology* **40**, pp. 15–18.

Straker, A. (1998) Director of the project: Introducing key points from the National Numeracy and Literacy Project, *Times Educational Supplement,* January 23rd p. 1.

Swann, W. and Mittler, P. (1976) 'Language abilities of ESN(S) pupils', *Special Education: Forward Trends* **3**, pp. 24–27.

Swartz, R.J. and Parks, S. (1994) *Infusing the Teaching of Critical and Creative Thinking into Elementary Instruction.* Pacific Grove CA: Critical Thinking Press and Software.

Tallal, P. (1980) 'Auditory temporal perception, phonics, and reading disabilities in children', *Brain and Language* **9**, pp. 182–198.

Tallal, P. (1994) 'New clue to cause of dyslexia seen in mishearing of fast sounds. An interview with Dr Tallal', by S. Blakeslee, *New York Times* 16th August, p. 24.

Taylor, J. (1994) *Helping your Hyperactive/Attention Deficit Child.* Rocklin, CA: Prima Publishing.

Taylor, K. (ed.) (1993) *Drama Strategies: New Ideas from London Drama.* London: Heinemann.

Teale, W.H.; Hiebert, E.H. and Chittenden, E.A. (1987) 'Assessing young children's literacy development', *The Reading Teacher* **40** (8), pp. 772–777.

THES (1981) *Times Higher Education Supplement.* Cited in Barrass, (1982) op cit. p. 5.

Thomas, D. (1996) 'An evaluation of the PAT programme'. Unpublished case studies, Maldon, Learning Difficulties Research Project.

Thomas, F. (1988) '"Une question de writing" A comparative study', *Support for Learning*, **13**, pp. 43–45.

Thomas, G. (1985) 'Room management in mainstream education'. *Educational Research* **27** (3), pp. 112–117.

Thomas, K. (1985) 'The special curricular needs of autistic children', p. 5. In AHTACA *The Special Curricular Needs of Autistic Children*. London: NAS.

Thomas, L. (1976) 'Learning to learn', *Personnel Management* **37**, pp. 22–24.

Thomas, L., Harri-Augstein, S. and Smith, M. (1984) *Reading to Learn*. London: Methuen.

Thomas, S. (1997) 'Near point gripping in pencil hold as a possible disabling factor in children with SEN', *British journal of special education* **24** (3), pp. 129–132.

Thomson, M. E. and Watkins, E. J. (1993) *Teaching the Dyslexic Child*. London: Whurr.

Thomson, M.E. (1990) 'Evaluating teaching programmes for children with specific learning difficulties', pp. 155–171 In P.D. Pumfrey and C.D. Elliott (eds) *Children's Difficulties in Reading, Spelling and Writing*. London: Falmer Press.

Thorndike, R.L., Hagen, E. and France, N. (1986) *The Cognitive Abilities Tests: Rev Edit*. Windsor: NFER-Nelson.

TIMSS (1997) *Third International Maths and Science Study*. TheTIMSS International Study Centre, Centre for the Study of Testing, Evaluation and Educational Policy, Campion Hall, School of Education, Boston College, Chestnut Hill, MA 02167 USA.

Tizard, J., Schofield, W.N. and Hewison, J. (1982) 'Collaboration between teachers and parents in assisting children's reading', *British Journal of Educational Psychology* **52**, pp. 1–15.

Torgeson, J.K. (1982) 'The learning disabled child as inactive learner: Educational implications', *Topics in Learning Disabilities* **2**, pp. 45–52.

Tufts, E. (1974) *Our Hidden Heritage: Five Centuries of Women Artists*. London: Paddington Press.

Turner, M. (1991) 'Finding out', *Support for Learning* **6** (3), pp. 99–102.

Vellutino, F.R. (1979) *Dyslexia: Theory and Research*. London: M.I.T. Press.

Vellutino, F.R. (1987) 'Dyslexia', *Scientific American* **256** (3), pp. 20–27.

Vygotsky, A.S. (1978) *Mind in Society: The Development of Higher Psychological Processes*. Cambridge Mass.: Harvard University Press.

Wang, M.C. and Lindvall, C.M. (1984) Individual differences and school environments, I.E.W. Gordon (ed.) *Review of Research in Education II*. Washington DC: American Education Research Association.

Warnock, M. (1978) *Special Educational Needs. The Report of the Special Committee*. London: HMSO.

Waterland, E. (1985) *Read with Me*. Stroud: Thimble Press.

Watson, J. (1996) *Reflection Through Instruction*. London: Falmer Press.

Watzlawick, P., Weakland, J. and Fisch, R. (1974) *Change: Principles of Problem Formation and Resolution*. New York: Norton.

Webster, A. and McConnell, E. (1987) *Children with Speech and Language Difficulties*. London: Cassell.

Wedell, K. (1973) *Learning and Perceptuomotor Difficulties in Children*. New York: Wiley.

Weikart, D. (1967) *Preschool Intervention. A preliminary report from the Perry Preschool Project*. Michigan: Ann Arbor.

Weinstein, C.E., Goetz, E.T. and Alexander, P.A. (1988) *Learning and Study Strategies*. New York: Academic Press.

Wendon, (1985) *The Pictogram System*. Barton, Cambs: Pictogram Supplies.

West, D.J. (1982) *Delinquency*. London: Heinemann.

Western, C. (1996) 'Teaching needs of able pupils with Aspergers' Syndrome'. Lecture presented to the European Council International Schools, Swiss Section, Geneva, September.

Weston, P. (1992) A critical review of research on differentiation, Paper One in Peter, M. (ed.) *Differentiation, Ways Forward*. Stafford: NASEN.

Wheldall, K. and Merrett, F. (1984) *BATPACK, Positive Products*. Birmingham: Birmingham University Press.

Wheldall, K. and Merrett, F. (1985) *Positive Teaching. A Behavioural Approach*. London: Unwin.

Wheldall, K and Merrett, F. (1986) 'Looking for a positive route out of poor class behaviour', *Special Children* **2**, pp. 22–27.

Williams, A. (1990) 'Mathematics in transition', *British Journal of Special Education* **17** (2), pp. 57–60.

Wilson, J. (1993) *P.A.T. Phonological Awareness Training: A New Approach to Phonics*. London: Educational Psychology Publishing.

Wilson, J. (1994) 'Phonological awareness training: A new approach to phonics'. *PATOSS Bulletin* November, pp. 5–8.

Wilson, M. and Evans, M. (1980) *Education of Disturbed Children*. London: Schools Council/Methuen.

Wing, L. (1981) *Asperger: A Clinical Account*. Reprint from the *Journal of Psychological Medicine*, London: National Autisitic Society.

Wing, L. (1995) *Autistic Spectrum Disorder; An Aid to Diagnosis. 3rd edition*. London: National Autistic Society.

Winkworth, E. (1977) *User Education in Schools: A Survey of the Literature on Education for Library and Information Use in Schools*. British Library Research and Development Department.

Witty, P. and Kopel, D. (1936) 'Factors associated with the aetiology of reading disability', *Journal of Educational Research* **29**, pp. 449–459.

Wishart, J. (1995) 'Review of research on children with Down's syndrome'. British Psychological Society Conference, *The Psychologist* June pp. 253–254.

Wolfendale, S. (1987) *Primary Schools and Special Needs: Planning and Provision*. London: Cassell (2nd edition 1997).

Woodhead, C. (1996) *The Chief Inspector's Annual Report on English Schools*. London: HMSO.

Woodhead, C. (1997) *The Chief Inspector's Annual Report on English Schools*. London: HMSO.

Wragg, E. (1997) Quoting on Radio 4 from Bennett, S.N., Wragg, E.C., Carre, C.G. and Carter, D.S.G. (1992) 'A longitudinal study of primary teachers perceived competences and concerns about National Curriculum implementation', *Research Papers in Education* **7** (1), pp. 53–78.

Wray, D. (1989) *Teaching Information Skills Through Project Work*. London: Hodder and Stoughton/UKRA.

Wray, D. (1994) Comprehension, monitoring, metacognition and other mysterious processes'. *Support for Learning* **9** (3), pp. 107–113.

Yewchuk, C.R. and Bibby, M.A. (1989) 'The handicapped gifted child: problems of identification and programming', *Canadian Journal of Education* **14** (1), pp. 102–108.

Index